Journey With Me

ENDORSEMENTS

Those of us who have served the Lord cross-culturally have at one time or another stood at a spiritual crossroad in our missionary career. *Journey With Me* is a must read for anyone ministering as a global servant. The ancient pathways of spiritual formation are essential for lasting growth in our faith journey. If you desire to recapture the radiant power of ancient pathways for spiritual formation, accept Herb Lamp's personal invitation to *Journey With Me*. It will be a delight to your soul!

PERRY BRADFORD
executive director, Barnabas International

Herb Lamp's *Journey With Me* overviews the basic spiritual disciplines and concepts that are crucial for healthy ministry in challenging cross-cultural environments. Each chapter builds on the previous and ignites hope that we can thrive and flourish when we are connected and centered in Jesus. Herb does not proscribe more work and activities that we should be doing. But rather he presents the historical pathways of spiritual formation as opportunities for greater vitality and connectedness to the Source of Life. I wish this resource were available thirty years ago when I embarked in cross-cultural ministry. It is an essential read for all global workers endeavoring to advance the gospel in difficult places.

JOHN DALLMANN
CEO/president, Engineering International Ministries Global

This book is one that member care professionals, life coaches, and overseas workers must have in their life care toolbox. I have seen the joyful fruit of Herb Lamp's work with missionaries over the years and know that these are words of truth. The ancient pathway is still the one true way that leads to a life overflowing with the fullness and health of Christ.

BILL DUNHAM
director of Marketplace Ministries, Christian and Missionary Alliance

Journey With Me is an extremely valuable resource for anyone engaged in global ministry. Through deep personal experience and the multitude testimony of others, it is an honest accounting of the significant and spiritual challenges facing those called to cross-cultural work. It also provides a comprehensive and rich menu of biblical and spiritual practices to not only help prevent and cope with the dangers of burnout and discouragement, but to strengthen one's spiritual life. I strongly endorse this book as one of the best books to help guide one's own journey of spiritual formation in the midst of ministry. It is exceptional!

ROBERT A. FRYLING
author of *The Leadership Ellipse: Shaping How You Lead by Who You Are*

As a major fan of all things spiritual practices, I find that Herbert Lamp covers the entirety with story, biblical example, historical connection, and wise explanation. It is exciting to find such a thorough rendition of centuries of spiritual practices. *Journey With Me* truly is a journey not only for global workers, but for all of us seeking a deeper connection with God.

JAYNA L. GALLAGHER, MA
spiritual director, Wheaton College Graduate School

Journey With Me is engaging, perceptive, challenging, and above all prophetic. Veteran cross-cultural worker, Herbert Lamp, understands the stresses and distresses of missionary life, together with the imperative of cultivating pathways that connect with God. The book evinces a profound love of the Lord and his global servants filling in the arid patches of our soul with lush practical insights. I wish I had read this book when I first started ministering decades ago.

REV. ROBERT L. GALLAGHER, PHD
professor emeritus of intercultural studies, School of Mission, Ministry, and Leadership,
Wheaton College Graduate School

Journey With Me is a much-needed resource for ministry workers. We see around us ministry workers who are tired, overly active, and not living a balanced life. Each chapter invites the reader to reflect and consider aspects such as silence, communal discernment, and submission. This should be a required read for anyone preparing for ministry or used as a guide for spiritual retreats around the world.

NYDIA R. GARCIA-SCHMIDT
area director, North America and South America, Wycliffe Global Alliance

With real life stories, biblically grounded theology, and attention to the needs of global servants, the ancient pathways of spiritual formation come alive in the practicality and the effective nurture of the soul. I'm grateful for this important contribution to the spiritual formation movement worldwide and commend Herb's efforts on all of our behalf.

STEPHEN A. MACCHIA, DMIN
founder and president, Leadership Transformations
director, Pierce Center, Gordon-Conwell Theological Seminary
author of 16 books, including *Becoming a Healthy Church* and *crafting a Rule of Life*

Herb's gentle spirit, wisdom, and experience are woven throughout this great book. Packed with thought-provoking insight, practical tips, and questions to ponder, *Journey With Me* is a terrific resource for global servants, sending churches, mission organizations, and those praying about a call to cross-cultural work. Truly a must read for anyone desiring deeper intimacy with Christ.

SCOTT VAIR
president/CEO, World Orphans

Journey With Me

Spiritual Formation for Global Workers

Herbert F. Lamp, Jr.

WILLIAM CAREY PUBLISHING
visit us at missionbooks.org

Journey With Me: Spiritual Formation for Global Workers

© 2021 by Herbert F. Lamp, Jr. All rights reserved.

No part of this book may be reproduced, stored in a retrieval system, or transmitted in any form or by any means—electronic, mechanical, photocopy, recording, or otherwise—without prior written permission from the publisher, except brief quotations used in connection with reviews in magazines or newspapers. For permission, email permissions@wclbooks.com. For corrections, email editor@ wclbooks.com.

Unless otherwise specified, all Scripture quotations are from the Holy Bible, New International Version© copyright © 1973, 1978, 1984 by International Bible Society. Used by permission of Zondervan Publishing House. All rights reserved.

Scripture quotations marked "NLT" are taken from the Holy Bible, New Living Translation, copyright 1996. Used by permission of Tyndale House Publishers, Inc., Wheaton, Illinois 60189. All rights reserved.

Scripture quotations marked "The Message" are taken from *The Message*, copyright © 1993, 2002, 2018 by Eugene H. Peterson. Used by permission of NavPress. All rights reserved. Represented by Tyndale House Publishers, Inc.

Scripture quotations marked "ESV®" are taken from The ESV® Bible (The Holy Bible, English Standard Version®), copyright © 2001 by Crossway, a publishing ministry of Good News Publishers. Used by permission. All rights reserved.

Scripture quotations marked "NASB" are taken from the New American Standard Bible®, Copyright © 1960, 1971, 1977, 1995, 2020 by The Lockman Foundation. Used by permission. All rights reserved. www.lockman.org

Published by William Carey Publishing
10 W. Dry Creek Cir
Littleton, CO 80120 | www.missionbooks.org

William Carey Publishing is a ministry of Frontier Ventures
Pasadena, CA 91104 | www.frontierventures.org

Cover and Interior Designer: Mike Riester
Cover image: Alexander Milo, unsplash.com
Copyeditor: Andy Sloan
Managing Editor: Melissa Hicks

ISBNs: 978-1-64508-395-5 (paperback)
      978-1-64508-397-9 (mobi)
      978-1-64508-398-6 (epub)

Printed Worldwide

29 28 27 26 25 2 3 4 5 6 IN

Library of Congress Control Number: 2021941420

CONTENTS

Introduction	8
Chapter 1: The Theology of Spirituality: The Ancient Pathways of Communion, Community, and Co-Mission	13
Chapter 2: Soul Care: The Ancient Pathway to Wholeness	25
Chapter 3: The Word of God: The Ancient Pathway to God	37
Chapter 4: Our Prayer Life: The Ancient Pathway to Intimacy	45
Chapter 5: Reflection: The Ancient Pathway toward Trust	57
Chapter 6: Rule of Life: The Ancient Pathway toward Intentionality	65
Chapter 7: Sabbath and Retreat: The Ancient Pathways to Rest	73
Chapter 8: Spiritual Warfare: The Ancient Pathway to Victory in Christ	83
Chapter 9: Different Approaches to God: The Ancient Pathways of Worship	91
Chapter 10: Silence and Solitude: The Ancient Pathways toward Emptying and Filling	99
Chapter 11: Lifelong Learning: The Ancient Pathway to Humility	105
Chapter 12: Spiritual Direction: The Ancient Pathway toward Discernment	115
Chapter 13: Hospitality: The Ancient Pathway to Space and Freedom	123
Chapter 14: Submission: The Ancient Pathway of Following	129
Chapter 15: Incarnational Ministry: The Ancient Pathway of Presence	139
Chapter 16: Suffering: The Ancient Pathway to Joy	147
Chapter 17: Communal Discernment: The Ancient Pathway to Wisdom	157
Chapter 18: Temptation and Truth: The Ancient Pathway to Holiness	165
Chapter 19: Comparison and Competition: The Ancient Pathway to Forgiveness	177
Conclusion	184
Acknowledgments	185
Bibliography	187

INTRODUCTION

My wife, Debbie, and I were appointed missionaries to the former Yugoslavia in 1981. We arrived there with our sixteen-month-old son to begin language study in Belgrade, the "White City." We lived isolated from fellow workers because at that time we were behind the Iron Curtain and had to limit contact with our mission.

As we invested in full-time language study, the days were stressful and lonely. Language study is not conducive to spiritual empowerment, and I soon felt spiritually dry and empty. In our second year of language study, our first daughter was born; and Debbie initially stopped her formal language study to take care of our two children. Unforeseen by us, our relationship became distant as I started traveling and teaching while Debbie held down the fort at home. We felt the growing strain, not just relationally but also spiritually. Having no one else to share and pray with in our heart language, our spiritual lives withered even further.

This was well before the days of computers and the Internet. Our personal quiet times in the Word were our only source of spiritual input. With two young children, Debbie found it almost impossible to have any time with God when I was traveling. The earlier she got up to be with the Lord, the earlier the children woke up as well. Finally, she decided to stop attempting when she realized she was getting up at three o'clock in the morning!

All of this was compounded by a growing sense of spiritual opposition, which we were ill-equipped to handle. We were attacked on a myriad of fronts, which, if I am honest, often defeated us. We were simply worn down through the constant stress and pressure. Yet, six years after our arrival on the field, we were asked to move to Vienna, Austria, for a new ministry assignment with our mission. Although this would be a new country and a new language, and Debbie had just given birth to our third child, we complied with this request.

This led us into an active ministry that was rewarding, but also demanding. My hours at work doubled and I rarely had a day off. I had no sense of Sabbath and felt a very heavy ministry load. After a few years of this, it wasn't surprising that I went into severe burnout, which we now know, in hindsight, to be the early stages of clinical depression. Unfortunately and detrimentally to myself, my family, and our ministry, this wasn't properly diagnosed and I didn't receive the healing and help I needed. My spiritual life was as empty as my emotional life. Two years into this new assignment I was unable to cope any further, so I handed off my work responsibilities and returned to the US feeling like a complete failure.

Upon returning, I was given a home office position, which allowed me to grow into and get involved in an embryonic movement toward pastoral missionary care. Over time, and with renewed spiritual focus, I regained my spiritual vitality.

Introduction

Though not totally understanding what I had experienced, I was desperate not to go back to my former ways, so I started to take measures to protect my soul.

In my new role, I began to hear story after story that was very similar to my own. These dear servants of God were routinely facing stress resulting from cultural adaptation, team conflicts, ministry challenges, marital struggles, personal struggles, issues with children, and more. I also found that they oftentimes had a very poor understanding of how their spiritual lives were being impacted in the midst of their life stresses.

Over the years, and especially through my doctoral studies, I began to examine the relationship between ministry and the souls of cross-cultural workers.[1] I started asking core questions about life and ministry. How do we balance a heart for God and hands for service? How can we practice intentional spiritual formation in our busy lives? How can we minister from the overflow of our relationship with God rather than treating ministry as a replacement for intimacy? After years of asking these questions, interacting with missionaries, and experiencing personal growth, Debbie and I developed a five-day spiritual formation retreat. Community learning became a unique aspect of our retreats. Rather than a lot of teaching from the front, the retreats depended on each participant's willingness to engage and lead one another as we learned about different spiritual practices.

None of the spiritual disciplines we practiced in our retreats were new to the church, though sometimes they were new to some of the participants. The prophet Jeremiah actually introduces them to us:

Stand at the crossroads and look;
  ask for the ancient paths,
ask where the good way is, and walk in it,
  and you will find rest for your souls. (6:16)

While the ancient pathways are for everyone, I believe global servants face some unique challenges in walking them. There are certain challenges and obstacles that are specific to the missionary life and so require specific attention. These factors make balancing a heart for God with hands for service a real challenge for the global servant. This is why I have written this book.

Most missionaries are not the spiritual giants some like to think we are. Despite such book titles as Hudson Taylor's *Spiritual Secret*, there really is no secret formula for the spiritual life. We struggle in ordinary ways to connect with God, just like anyone else. Even if you don't minister across geographic, ethnic, linguistic, or cultural boundaries, you can still benefit from these ancient pathways, so I encourage you to continue reading and explore the content and reflections in this book. Whether you are a global servant or a servant in your hometown, God desires for all of us to have a rich relationship with him.

---

1 Herbert F. Lamp, Jr., "Toward a Theology of Submission and Obedience in Missions" (DMin diss., Gordon-Conwell Theological Seminary, 2011).

Who Are Global Servants?

I want to define what is meant when we use the term *missionary*. It is sometimes bluntly proclaimed that all Christians are missionaries. Unfortunately, this can confuse the concept of mission (Missio Dei) and missions. Church historian and missionary, Bishop Stephen Neill, noted, "If everybody is a missionary, nobody is a missionary."[2] So while all are to be witnesses, kingdom servants, and bear responsibility to mission, not all are sent-out missionaries to the nations. William David Taylor puts it this way:

> *We do a disservice to the "missionary" by universalizing its use. While all believers are witnesses and kingdom servants, not all are missionaries. We do not glamorize or exalt the missionary, or ascribe higher honor in life or greater heavenly reward, and neither do we create an artificial office.*
>
> *This focused conclusion comes from a biblical theology of vocations (God has given us diverse vocations and all are holy, but not all the same); a theology of gifts (not all are apostles nor all speak in tongues—1 Cor. 12:29) and therefore not all Christians are missionaries; and a theology of callings (the Triune God sovereignly calls some to this position and task).*[3]

For the purposes of this book, the terms *global servant* and *missionary* refer to: men or women who have been called by God to cross-cultural work; serving within or outside their own national boundaries, but still crossing some kind of cultural, linguistic, or geographic barrier as a called, authorized, and commissioned sent one.[4] The global servant has a conviction and recognition of a call to missionary service, an intense desire to obey and go wherever God leads.

Jesus often spoke of his own call and obedience to the Father. "'My food,' said Jesus, 'is to do the will of him who sent me'" (John 4:34). God has called global servants to go to the nations by sending them to do the will of the Father, by the love of the Son, and in the power of the Holy Spirit. However, for missionaries not only to survive but to continue to thrive, we need to take a deeper look into the hearts of God's messengers. How are the hearts of global servants formed? How is their spirituality displayed in their specific and unique callings? These are important questions for the twenty-first century missionary.

---

[2] Stephen Neill, quoted in William David Taylor, "Missionary," in *Evangelical Dictionary of World Missions*, edited by A. Scott Moreau (Grand Rapids: Baker, 2000), 644.

[3] Taylor, "Missionary," 645.

[4] *Missionary* is the traditional word for a person involved in cross-cultural ministry. However, because of the risks involved in using the term across red zone areas of the world (areas where global workers live in very unstable conditions, such as civil war, unrest, persecution, natural disasters, or crime), we will sometimes in this book use the term *global servant* or *worker* when we mean missionary. This is now becoming the accepted phrase in mission circles.

Introduction

Hearts and Hands

Global servants are often activists by nature. They like to get things done. They are nourished through activity and even struggle and conflict. They are prophets and apostles. They use their hands for the kingdom. This, of course, does not describe every missionary, but it does describe many.

An internal drivenness motivates many of us to strive for success in our ministry, not for God's glory alone but also for our own self-validation. Alas, many a global worker feels a need to justify their ministry before their supporting churches by sharing all their work activities. Churches also sometimes compare the fruit of their various missionaries to see who should get the top dollar. Churches want their missionaries to be busy! So there is pressure, both internally and externally, for missionaries to prove their worth by constantly talking about their work. Reading a series of missionary prayer letters can confirm this fact, as recounting activities often dominates what is reported.

This pressure to perform is not a new phenomenon for God's servants. The Old Testament prophet Elijah experienced a serious case of burnout and fatigue after his great victory over the prophets of Baal at Mount Carmel. It took rest and hearing the still quiet voice of God to restore Elijah to life and ministry. Today's global servants sometimes find themselves in Elijah's condition: fatigued and burned out, fearful and desperate, feeling that they've had enough. But that is because they have forgotten their source of life.

Each of the following chapters describes one pathway of a spiritual discipline that aids our communion with the Triune God. Each pathway can stand alone, so if you are interested in a particular discipline you can go directly to that chapter without disrupting the flow of the book. These practices are all life-giving, or what Jonathan Edwards called "means of grace."[5]

If you are a global servant, I know you live a very busy life. This book addresses the reality of our lives as active servants of the kingdom and how we can resist letting that activity so dominate us that we lose our first love—Christ and his church. As you take the time and energy to read through this book, I hope you will find refreshment, peace, and a richer, deeper connection to our Savior. Lastly, as you read these pages, I pray "that the God of our Lord Jesus Christ, the glorious Father, may give you the Spirit of wisdom and revelation, so that you may know him better" (Eph 1:17).

---

5 Kyle Strobel, *Formed for the Glory of God: Learning from the Spiritual Practices of Jonathan Edwards* (Downers Grove, IL: IVP, 2013), 71.

The starting point *of Christian missions is the New Testament church. The greatest missionary of this era was the apostle Paul. In the words of the great church historian, Kenneth Scott Latourette, Paul has been "at once the prototype, the model, and the inspiration of thousands of successors."[6]*

The most detailed and accurate record of Paul's missionary journeys are found in the book of Acts, which records three missionary trips, plus travel to Jerusalem and later to Rome. Most of the epistles of the New Testament are correspondence between Paul and the churches he founded. We can learn much about missions and missionary work in these primary sources. But Paul's writings, of course, also have the added stamp of being held by the early church and all following generations of global servants as the authoritative Word of God.

When you read Paul's writings and follow his missionary journeys, you get a sense of someone who has faced life and ministry in its truest forms. Paul knew what missionary service costs, including suffering for Jesus. In 2 Corinthians 6, Paul lists over thirty individual stressors that he had encountered, such as troubles, hardships, beatings, imprisonments, riots, hard work, sleepless nights, hunger, and dishonor.

As he does in terms of mission methods and strategies, Paul also sets the example for spiritual strength and perseverance for today's global servant. In fact, Paul writes more about a missionary's need for inner spirituality than he does about missionary tasks, tools, and resources. Clearly this was Paul's secret for his missionary effectiveness—his life was hidden in Christ (Col 1:3).

Paul
Missionary Apostle to the Gentiles

---

6 Kenneth Scott Latourette, *A History of the Expansion of Christianity*, vol. 1, *The First Five Centuries* (Peabody, MA: Hendrickson Publishers, 1970), 80.

The Theology of Spirituality
The Ancient Pathways of Communion, Community, and Co-Mission

Before we look at the ancient pathways of spiritual formation for the global servant, I want to address the theological underpinnings that support and encourage our spiritual growth. This first chapter looks at the theology behind our intimacy with God, the spiritual community we are to live into, and our Spirit-empowered service. Within such a context, we practice our personal spiritual disciplines.

Spiritual Intimacy with God

The simple words of Jesus, "Follow me" (Mark 1:17), may be the earliest and best definition of Christian spirituality. The command reveals the two foundational truths behind all Christian growth: Jesus is the focus, and discipleship is the method. Following Jesus as his disciple is a lifelong process. This process of spiritual formation is the supreme task of the church. Early Christians described spiritual formation this way: To be a Christian is to know, love, and serve Jesus Christ.[7]

The order of knowing, loving, and serving is progressive. As in any relationship, knowledge comes before love. We cannot really love someone we only theoretically know. Love springs from experiencing someone relationally. Then out of our love flows service. The mature Christian, then, is someone who knows Jesus intimately through learning about him in his or her head (knowledge), heart (love), and hands (service).

What is true for the individual disciple is also true for the church as a whole. To be the church is to be a band of disciples who are a "learning community that seeks together in faith to know Jesus, to grow together in love for Jesus and to align our lives, mission, and way of being in the world to the in-breaking of the reign of Christ."[8]

---

[7] For a discussion on these three aspects of Christian discipleship, see Gordon T. Smith, *Called to Be Saints: An Invitation to Christian Maturity* (Downers Grove, IL: IVP, 2014), 38–48.

[8] Smith, 39.

What Is Spiritual Formation?

For the sake of clarity of terminology, "Christian spirituality" represents the believer's relationship with God and life in the Spirit as a member of the church of Jesus Christ—one's identity in Christ. "Spiritual formation" refers more to the process of sanctification, in which the believer grows into the righteousness of Christ through the active working of the Holy Spirit through means such as spiritual disciplines. Though there is congruency between the two terms, spirituality is the broader standing and spiritual formation is more the means.

One's Christian spirituality therefore revolves around the axis of knowing and loving Christ intimately and then serving him with passion. However, missionaries sometimes confuse the order of this process by placing hands (service) before heart (relationship with God). We can move too quickly into ministry, only giving lip service to our relationship with Christ. As I shared in my own story, this simply does not work. Heart always precedes hands in the economy of spiritual formation.

This priority of heart intimacy with God is affirmed by Andrew Brunson, a global servant who, in 2018, was detained, imprisoned, and then released by the Turkish government for proselytizing. He appeals to mission organizations to pay more attention to intimacy with Jesus ahead of ministry objectives for missionaries. He says that his closeness with Jesus was vital in getting him through his imprisonment.[9]

Isaiah 52:10–54:17 is one of the most powerful and visionary passages in the Bible. It reveals the heart of the loving Father for his creation. It speaks of the coming of the Suffering Servant, sent by the Father to redeem and save the world. It is fitting that the Moravians, the first great Protestant missionary movement (launched in 1732), made this passage the basis of their motto: "To win for the Lamb the reward for his suffering." William Carey, the father of the modern missionary movement, also saw Isaiah's words as key to evangelizing the world when, on May 30, 1792, he preached one of the greatest and well-known missionary sermons of the church age. Speaking from Isaiah 54, his sermon had a major ripple effect across the Christian world.

What moved Carey and the early Moravians to follow the call of God just like the first Christians in the New Testament was the belief that God was still at work in the world, personally calling people to himself based upon the suffering of his Son on the cross. In Peter's words, these called people are "chosen by God

---

9 "Andrew and Norine Brunson Q & A at Mission Leaders Conference," YouTube video, 27:36, Missio Nexus, September 21, 2019, https://www.youtube.com/watch?v=9jNYokjiV9c.

and precious to him—you also, like living stones, are being built into a spiritual house to be a holy priesthood, offering spiritual sacrifices acceptable to God through Jesus Christ" (1 Pet 2:4–5). Through intimacy with God, missions is birthed. A. W. Tozer called this relationship the knowledge of the Holy.[10]

Spirituality Prioritized

To fulfill the Great Commission, we must go deeper than good guidelines and best practices. To properly meet the needs of global ministry, we must attend to our own hearts. In his classic book on revival, *The Dynamics of the Spiritual Life*, Richard Lovelace wrote that "virtually all of the problems of the church including bad theology issue from defective spirituality."[11] If so, then it is imperative to passionately promote our relationship with Jesus as of first importance. A personal relationship must exist between the living God and the global servant. Exploring, expressing, and engaging the longing that God has placed in our hearts for himself is the core of the cross-cultural worker. Such longing for God must be an integral part of the spiritual journey for the missionary because it is also a critical factor in shaping the vision of any mission activity.

While this may seem obvious, in my experience this is not always so evident. Christian mission boards spend a great deal of effort and resources in strategizing and promoting their work, but often neglect the hearts of their people. They assume the work of the Holy Spirit has already taken root and has been developed through the global servant's local church. They spend a great deal of time evaluating a new candidate's church involvement, but little on what their church has actually produced in the spirituality of the prospective missionary.

Yet, while organizations ignore spiritual formation in their staff, it is exactly this desire for intimacy with the Father that moved the heart of a global servant to respond to the Great Commission in the first place. A clear view of God enables us to unite around a God-focused center, out of which we can minister from a place of integrity and peace. Spiritual practices that help us welcome God's purposes with a humble and receptive posture do much good in us—but it has to come out of a desire for intimate relationship for these practices to bear real fruit.

God's love for us and ours for him is centered on his Son, Jesus. The medieval writer, Thomas à Kempis, says the believer's chief study is Christ:

"He who follows me, walks not in darkness says, the Lord" (Jn 8:12). By these words of Christ, we are advised to imitate his life and habits, if we wish to be truly enlightened and free from all blindness of heart. Let our chief effort, therefore, be the study of the life of Christ.[12]

The heart of Christian spirituality must be a study of Christ, by patterning after and fully participating in Christ's abundant life. To do this well, we utilize the resources given by the Holy Spirit within a believing community. However,

---

10 A. W. Tozer, *The Knowledge of the Holy* (New York: HarperCollins, 1961).
11 Richard Lovelace, *The Dynamics of the Spiritual Life* (Downers Grove, IL: IVP, 1979), 58.
12 Thomas à Kempis, *The Imitation of Christ* (Peabody, MA: Hendrickson Publishers, 2004), 3.

this must mean more than simple adherence to certain Christian doctrines or the practice of some Christian disciplines for practice's sake. Rather, genuine Christian spirituality is walking in truth and love by the power of the Spirit, in living interaction with Christ and his community for the Father's glory. It is Trinitarian and relational. It is alive. It is individual and yet corporal.

Spiritual life is found in *perichoresis*, a Greek term literally meaning "rotation," which the early church fathers used to describe the Trinitarian dance of the Father, Son, and Holy Spirit. We are invited into this dance to experience true life before the Father, through the Son, and by the power of the Spirit. Whenever we find ourselves outside the dance of this divine life, we have lost touch with true spirituality. Out of the overflow of this connected life with the Father comes abundancy.[13] When we are spiritually empty, we can only take from others; but when we are abundantly full, we have much to give.

Spiritual Formation and Crossing Cultures

Jonathan Edwards, the great eighteenth-century Puritan pastor and theologian, describes spiritual formation practices as a means of grace. To illustrate, he talks about Jesus' miracle of turning the water into wine at the wedding of Cana (John 2:1–11). According to Edwards, our role in the Christian life is to "fill the water pots," and Jesus' role is to turn the water into wine. These means of grace, or spiritual disciplines, are ways to fill us with water; they establish the conditions of receiving from God.[14]

Christian spirituality is played out in different ways because we are uniquely created and gifted by God himself. This diversity is something to be celebrated and not criticized. No single spirituality can adequately reflect and satisfy everyone. As Paul says in Romans 12:4–6, God has endowed members of the body of Christ with different gifts and functions. The effective use of gifts (e.g., leadership, hospitality, preaching, teaching) in various cultures calls for various personalities and spiritual activities appropriate to both the particular culture and biblical truth.

The global servant is called to bring Jesus, not his or her Christian culture, to the mission field. Historically, this has been a struggle for missionaries as they try to determine what is biblical spirituality and what is cultural spirituality. A major issue for missionaries in the Muslim world concerns to what degree Muslim converts to Christ need to leave their Muslim cultures.

No matter how we view the various levels of cultural and religious engagement, one thing is clear: While Muslim-background believers may not identify with Christian culture, they do identify with Christ. "Our aim is that we will follow Isa al-Masih (Jesus the Christ), and we will teach them (new believers) that Isa

---

13 See John 10:10.
14 See Romans 6:13 and 12:1.

al-Masih is the Savior and we will baptize them."[15] This Muslim-background Christ-follower has no desire to take on a new religion. "I will not be a Christian; I just want to follow Jesus," he says.[16] Jesus is at the center of his spirituality. This believer's spirituality is not based upon becoming a cultural Christian, but upon a desire simply to follow Jesus. Jesus is the center of his spirituality.

The point here is not to debate whether or not such believers are genuine Christians. The point is that the centrality of Jesus Christ is necessary for anyone to be a true follower in any culture. My guess is that many who keep their identity in the Muslim culture and yet follow Jesus as Savior are more genuine in their faith than some cultural Christians in the West who attend church but have no relationship with Jesus.

Spiritual Formation in Community

While it is true that each of us bears individual responsibility for our walk with Christ, we were never meant to journey alone. As believers, we have a commitment to relate both to Christ and to his church (1 Cor 12:12–27). God's clear intent is for us to be part of his body, growing together spiritually. Too much discipleship material is written only for individuals. Paul wouldn't approve of isolating spiritual growth apart from Christ's body (Eph 4:15–16). All of his letters (even the one to Philemon) were written to be shared with churches or groups of believers. For the New Testament Christians, learning and growing in their faith was done together, in community.

However, being in Christian community can be a challenge for the global servants who come from a worldview that places an emphasis on individuality over community. Workers who have left long-established communities back home, including close family and friends, can struggle with working on teams whose fellowship can sometimes appear shallow. Many carry burdens privately, afraid to share them with others. But this hiddenness hinders everyone's spiritual formation by denying one of the greatest resources God has given us to mature as Christians—the local Christian community.

As beings created in the image of God, we are relational creatures—created to model and express love within a community of fellow beings. We simply cannot love in isolation; to love we must have others to love. Paul says it this way: "If you have any encouragement from being united with Christ, if any comfort from his love, if any fellowship with the Spirit, if any tenderness and compassion, then make my joy complete by being like-minded, having the same love, being one in spirit and purpose" (Phil 2:1–2). The communal nature of God in which we are to grow spiritually together in love is the basis of Christian community.

---

15 David Garrison, *A Wind in the House of Islam: How God Is Drawing Muslims around the World to Faith in Jesus Christ* (Monument, CO: WIGtake Resources, 2014), 119.

16 Garrison, 118.

The Danger of Isolation

Most global servants would agree that Christian community is essential for spiritual growth. But how do you find spiritual community when you and your family might be the only believers in your local community? It's hard to find fellowship when you are planting a church in an area with few or no believers. Thankfully, the Trinitarian circle where the Father, Son, and Holy Spirit indwell one another and are indwelt by one another is open and we are all invited into their *perichoresis*. What this means is that we are never truly alone. God is always abiding with his children.

J. Hudson Taylor, one of the great missionaries of the nineteenth century and founder of the China Inland Mission, learned this through his own spiritual struggles. He described this "as the profound secret of drawing for every need, temporal or spiritual, upon 'the fathomless wealth of Christ.'"[17] In a letter to his wife, Taylor wrote of this discovery: "Ah, there is rest! I have striven in vain to rest in Him. I'll strive no more. For has He not promised to abide with me—never to leave me, never to fail me? And dearie, He never will."[18]

Though abiding in Christ is always available, we also desire human fellowship. First, we can still spiritually interact with people even if they are not believers. Is it not a joy to practice the fruit of the Spirit with all people? Is it not a joy to practice the "one anothers" of the New Testament with anybody?

I recently talked to a Cambodian believer who works in a large office complex. He told me he practices the "one anothers" with any fellow worker, whether the head of the corporation or the janitor. He is the only Christian he knows of in his office. As I was talking to this gentle older man, I realized why so many of my fellow workers described him as the most humble and kind man they know. He shines Christ's love on every person he meets, believer or nonbeliever.

Second, even with the challenges of geographic distance and lack of team members, we shouldn't allow ourselves to be habitually isolated from other Christians. It is vital to our spiritual health to seek out healthy community. Without it we will be impeded as we face the physical, emotional, and spiritual contests that surround us. It is true that, unlike some other professions where people are more often hired and fired from a larger pool, global servants for the most part must work with those who are assigned to their team. This can put additional stress on community dynamics when people are so very different in personality, gifting, and backgrounds. However, this is a call for us to be even more intentional about working for the unity of our team.[19]

---

17 Howard Taylor and Geraldine Taylor, *Hudson Taylor's Spiritual Secret* (Chicago: Moody Press, 2009), 14.

18 Hudson Taylor, quoted in Taylor and Taylor, *Taylor's Spiritual Secret*, 153.

19 This was a major cause of difficulties among missionaries working with the Waorani tribes in Ecuador in the 1960s and 1970s. Refusing to cooperate together caused controlling and abusive behavior toward the emerging national church. See Kathryn T. Long, *God in the Rain Forest* (New York: Oxford University Press, 2019).

There may be nothing you can do to increase the number of your team, but you can be proactive in seeking additional resources. With the help of technology, you can provide yourself resources such as books, podcasts, sermons, and other spiritual aids. You can also increase your communities through email, online groups, and conference calling, among other things. These are just a few suggestions for shepherding your souls. If your organization doesn't have a member-care department, other ministries, such as mine with Barnabas International, serve the mission community through global pastoring via phone calls, field visits, Zoom and Skype calls, and teaching opportunities.

Our enemy is determined to keep us in darkness and isolation. When we become isolated, we have no one to encourage, console, equip, or challenge us. We can lose perspective and hope. Community can be hard, but it is a prime way that God uses to bring healing and hope to all of us.

Missionary Service

Global servants are called to serve Jesus as his ambassadors. But what exactly does that mean? What is the missionary's task? Perhaps the best definition of our role comes from Jesus himself, when he commissioned the apostle Paul:

> *I have appeared to you to appoint you as a servant and as a witness of what you have seen of me and what I will show you. I will rescue you from your own people and from the Gentiles. I am sending you to them to open their eyes and turn them from darkness to light, and from the power of Satan to God, so that they may receive forgiveness of sins and a place among those sanctified by faith in me.*
>
> —Acts 26:16–18

Jesus' commissioning of Paul echoes the Old Testament accounts of the calling of many of the prophets—notably Isaiah, Ezekiel, and Jeremiah.[20] Each case involves the language of sending. As the prophets were sent to Israel and Judah, so Paul was sent as an apostle to the Gentiles. This sending revolved around two purposes. Paul was sent as a servant and as Jesus' witness to what he had seen (v. 16), in order to open the eyes of the blind and to proclaim the message of the gospel (v. 18). Jesus called Paul to be sent out as a servant-messenger. This mission of service and testimony is described as joyous labor repeatedly in the New Testament.[21] To be sent by Jesus as his servant and his witness is a great responsibility, but it is equally a great joy.

---

20 See Isa 6:8–9; Ezek 2:1–3; 3:4–8; Jer 1:1–17.

21 See Acts 8:8; 13:52; 14:17; 16:34; Rom 15:32; 16:19; 2 Cor 1:24; 7:7; Phil 1:4, 25–26, 29; I Thess 2:20; 2 Tim 1:4; Heb 13:17; 1 John 1:4; 2 John 4, 12; 3 John 3–4.

Service and Jesus

Many global workers have strong wills and personalities, which can aid us in the work we do. While our strength helps us to endure, it can also get in the way—in the way of the cross of Jesus. Just as Jesus took on the very nature of a servant, we too must gain the heart and soul of a servant, following in his footsteps.[22] We learn to be like him by abiding in him and being fully dependent upon his life in us (John 15:5). However, we don't try to slavishly imitate him (an impossible task anyway), but instead we participate in his life and become naturally transformed into his likeness, becoming servants as he was a servant. As Siang-Yang Tan says, "Servanthood, or following Jesus all the way, therefore means that we live in Jesus all the way."[23]

It is imperative to point out that serving like Jesus served does not equal becoming a doormat for everyone's personal demands and desires. Jesus repeatedly upended other people's expectations of him. Even though he identified as a servant (Matt 20:28), he willingly came "to give his life as a ransom for many" (Mark 10:45). Martin Luther famously wrote, "A Christian is a perfectly free lord of all, subject to none. A Christian is a perfectly dutiful servant of all, subject to all."[24]

And herein lies the paradox. We are called to freedom in Christ, yet at the same time we are called to also serve. The connection between freedom and service centers in on our understanding of the difference between servanthood and servitude. Servanthood incorporates the ideas of willingness, choice, and voluntary commitment. Servitude, on the other hand, connotes bondage, slavery, and involuntary labor.[25]

Missionaries can easily fall into the trap of servitude because we fear that we aren't pleasing God if we don't serve everybody at all times. When this happens, we end up taking responsibility for others that God never intended, and we become subject to burnout. The net result can be more harm than good for both the server and the one being served, because we are serving grudgingly and out of guilt rather than love.

We should be able to say no freely at times simply because we understand that God has not called us to personally meet the request or need being asked of us. "In true servanthood, then, we give up control to the Lord our master and not to people."[26] Being God's servant and message-bearer is not based upon our skill and gifting. It is based upon God's overflow of his love through our own service, freely given and received.

---

22 See Phil 2:6–7; Matt 20:28; John 13:14–16.

23 Siang-Yang Tan, *Full Service: Moving from Self-Serve Christianity to Total Servanthood* (Grand Rapids: Baker, 2006), 29.

24 Martin Luther, "Concerning Christian Liberty," in *First Principles of the Reformation*, ed. H. Wace and C. A. Buckheim (London: William Clowes and Sons, 1883), 104.

25 Kenneth C. Haugk, *Christian Caregiving: A Way of Life* (Minneapolis: Augsburg, 1984), 71. Though Paul calls himself a slave (*doulos*) in many of his letters, this word can carry a more nuanced understanding of a servant who willingly chooses to serve. See G. T. D. Angel, "Slave," in *The New International Dictionary of New Testament Theology*, vol. 3, ed. Colin Brown (Grand Rapids: Zondervan, 1978), 592–98.

26 Tan, *Full Service*, 41.

Growing Deep Roots

In terms of theology, the church has viewed spiritual formation as the process of sanctification, which is carried out through the power of the Holy Spirit in the practice of spiritual disciplines. These disciplines are what I am calling the ancient pathways. These pathways are lifelong journeys and the primary work of the church. Dallas Willard calls discipleship the central task, but also the central problem for believers:

> *The central problem facing the contemporary church in the Western world and worldwide, is the problem of how to routinely lead its members through a path of spiritual, moral, and personal transformation that brings them into authentic Christlikeness in every aspect of their lives, enabling them, in the language of the apostle Paul, "to walk in the manner worthy of the calling with which you have been called" (Eph 4:1 NASB).*[27]

If spiritual formation is the central problem facing the church today, it is of utmost importance that we train young missionaries in these pathways before and during their mission service. There must be more to spiritual formation than being active in the Christian community, affirming a certain set of beliefs, and acting with a certain pattern of behavior. Genuine spiritual formation is much deeper than this. It must be intentional, disciplined, and focused on day-to-day choices of obedience—which, however seemingly small in the beginning, continually grow.

Global servants don't journey on each of the ancient pathways at all times, but intentionality is important. Research has indicated that even though the majority of missionaries claim their spiritual lives to be of great importance, only a small minority actively plan spiritual formation into their lives, and even less discuss their spirituality with their mission leadership.[28] This research shows that something isn't lining up between our professed goals and our actual behaviors.

Like channels of a mighty river, spiritual disciplines enable us to be flooded with God's transforming grace. We flow in these streams of Spirit-led growth and are changed from the inside out, with the gospel being at our center. "The gospel is the power of God for the beginning, middle, and end of salvation. It is not merely what we need to proclaim to unbelievers; the gospel also needs to permeate our entire Christian experience."[29]

Mission work should not be driven by speed, show, or solely upon results, but by the concern that planted faith communities are able to have deep roots and survive under the challenges that will inevitably arise. Life transformation takes place when the all-encompassing nature of the gospel is realized, not just in head knowledge but through changes in the hearts of global servants and in those

---

27 Dallas Willard, foreword to *Spiritual Formation as if the Church Mattered*, by James C. Wilhoit (Grand Rapids: Baker Academic, 2008), 9.

28 Jim Fieker, "Top Observations of IMPACT Leader Research Project and the Implications to our Mission Organizations" (unpublished manuscript, 2008), 1.

29 Donald S. Whitney, *Spiritual Disciplines for the Christian Life* (Colorado Springs: NavPress, 1991), 29.

they disciple. If this doesn't take place, then the gospel won't become rooted where it is planted.[30]

Let's now look at these ancient pathways toward spiritual growth—these pathways that anchor our hearts in God and release our hands for service.

Reflection and Points to Ponder

- Global servants often feel rejected, unloved, or unrecognized by others and by God. Unless we replace these feelings with the truth of our identity in Christ, we might flame out in our own spiritual lives, let alone in our capacity to lead others to healthy growth in Christ. What is the source of your identity as a global servant? Are you rooted in Christ or does your identity come exclusively from roles and titles?

- How do you put your biblical knowledge into action, even in the most mundane aspects of your life and ministry? How can you better connect with Jesus as the center of your daily life? Do you feel called to Jesus first and to a place or ministry second, or the other way around? How can you cultivate a greater desire for Jesus—learning from him, loving him, and serving him?

- Biblical community finds its essence and definition within the being of God. How does an understanding of the Trinity foster our belief and practice as the body of Christ? How can we better reflect this loving relationship within our own communities?

- Many global workers are becoming more aware that being a lone ranger has serious negative impact upon kingdom advancement. We can become ineffective when we lose our own sense of identity as a community—the people of God. How might you, in your local context, increase community and decrease individualism? How is the life you are leading reflecting the community nature of the Godhead and the value of belonging to the family of God?

- What criteria do you use when you decide how to allocate your time and talent? What drives your daily schedule and your personal goals? What fills your deepest need for acceptance, meaning, and self-worth? Are you driven to serve God other than for His own glory?

---

30 Eddie Gibbs, *LeadershipNext: Changing Leaders in a Changing Culture* (Downers Grove, IL: IVP, 2005), 41–42.

For Further Reading

Ruth Haley Barton, *Strengthening the Soul of Your Leadership* (Downers Grove, IL: IVP, 2008). A discussion of servant leadership, including spiritual practices to enhance a leader's reliance upon God's Spirit in their leadership role.

Adele Ahlberg Calhoun, *Spiritual Disciplines Handbook: Practices that Transform Us* (Downers Grove, IL: IVP, 2005). Calhoun briefly overviews more than sixty spiritual disciplines, presenting scriptural support and practical reflection questions.

Evan B. Howard, *The Brazos Introduction to Christian Spirituality* (Grand Rapids: Baker, 2008). Textbook style, but very comprehensive, tracing spiritual formation from the early church to today.

Stephen A. Macchia, *Becoming a Healthy Team* (Grand Rapids: Baker, 2005). A look at how to create biblical health in a team structure.

Michael Reeves, *Delighting in the Trinity: An Introduction to the Christian Faith* (Downers Grove, IL: IVP, 2012). An exploration of how our Christian faith must and can be rooted in the doctrine of the Trinity.

Gordon T. Smith, *Called to Be Saints: An Invitation to Christian Maturity* (Downers Grove, IL: IVP, 2014). Going beyond justification and conversion, this book focuses on what it means to be sanctified and transformed by the gospel.

Siang-Yang Tan, *Full Service: Moving from Self-Serve Christianity to Total Servanthood* (Grand Rapids: Baker, 2006). Tan carefully reviews the vast literature on Christian leadership and gives a careful proposal of what the servant leader looks like on a daily basis.

What I am about to share caught me by surprise.

I had prepared much and prayed much for this spiritual formation retreat that I was helping to facilitate. The whole time there, I had a sense of God's presence and guidance. The atmosphere had an amazing fullness to it.

On the second day, I had to share on a topic and prepare those present for the experience of a particular spiritual practice. Afterward, I had some time of silence, so I went out to a bench overlooking a pond and started focusing on God. I love nature, and it fosters a deeper awareness of God for me.

I started out considering Scripture, but God quickly moved me to silence and contemplation. Soon I felt overwhelmed by his loving presence deep within my soul. No words can describe what I felt. Tears started flowing. Time passed quickly, and the growing sense within held a deep affirmation of God's presence with me in a life-giving, energizing way, that could only speak of love—his love. I knew this as a gift, not as a reward or something I merited. The overwhelming nature of moments like this can be overpowering for me. This one endured longer than what I can normally withstand.

God awakened me to time, and I knew he was reminding me of my responsibilities. As I arose, I wiped the tears away, holding a deeper sense of affirmation, calling, and direction. No words of encouragement had crossed my awareness, just a sense that God came close. That day remains engraved in my memory, as do the circumstances. Moments like these etch a rich and indelible realization of God's love in my soul.

Doug
a global servant in Poland

Soul Care
The Ancient Pathway to Wholeness

Years ago, when my wife and I were new to the field, a veteran global worker told me there are only two types of missionaries who survive on the field. The first is the pioneer who has incredible self-will and strength. The second is so dependent upon God's calling that they are able to endure anything that comes their way. I have found this sentiment, over the years, to be somewhat true.

For those of us who relate to the pioneer, our strong personalities help us to endure and cope with what life throws at us. But our personalities can also get in the way, because we rely on them too much. As my own life story illustrates, strength will only get you through so much. My solo efforts only led me into burnout and depression. Surviving and thriving on the mission field requires more than just personal strength.

But although inner commitment to God's guidance is a good start, that doesn't encompass the whole picture either. It is true that knowing God has called you to a ministry and a place is essential, but empowerment to thrive can only come from the power of the Holy Spirit. Just as the pioneers who trust solely on their own strength, those who trust solely on their calling will also, at some point, come to the end of their own limited abilities.

If I was asked how to stay on the field long-term today, I would say that neither outward strength nor inward conviction is the key to longevity. Rather, cultivating God's loving presence is the mark of perseverance and endurance—the key to longevity. "Perseverance must finish its work so that you may be mature and complete, not lacking anything" (James 1:4).

Caring for one's life in Christ, though it is often ignored by many, is essential for any global servant to survive on the mission field. Like Martha in the story recorded in Luke 10:38–42, we too can be so busy in ministry that we forget the Lord. When Jesus entered the village where the two sisters lived, Martha generously invited Jesus into their home—although she soon became preoccupied and distracted with guest preparations. Conversely, Mary sat at Jesus' feet, listening intently to him as he spoke. When Martha saw Mary's apparent inactivity, she became upset and complained to Jesus that Mary was not helping her. In Jesus' famous reply, he acknowledged that Martha was worried about many things, but that Mary had chosen what was better. Ministry, and simply life itself, can draw us away from Jesus. What are some of the circumstances and attitudes that draw global servants away from Jesus?

Life is so busy. Life is especially busy for people living in a foreign culture. Navigating life (especially in the early years) takes a lot of extra energy, and many tasks take much longer to accomplish. One morning during our first month on the field I made a list of ten minor things I needed to do or buy for our home. I told Debbie I wasn't sure how long it would take, but I would probably be back well before noon. I returned home late in the afternoon—with only one thing accomplished! This was a wake-up call for me that even simple tasks were going to take a lot longer than I expected or understood. When our personal and professional lives are so full, our spiritual lives can easily become overlooked and neglected.

Life is so stressful. In addition to busyness, stress is also a major factor in the global servant's health and well-being. Stress is the response of the entire person to various internal and external demands (stressors). Although some stress is needed for us to perform in certain situations, when stress is prolonged or increases beyond our capacity it can easily manifest itself in physical problems, such as insomnia, hypertension, or headaches—as well as in mental and emotional problems, such as irritability, depression, or burnout. Too much stress can affect our spiritual, emotional, and physical lives. Spiritual doubts and apathy are also common signs of too much stress in one's life. Research has shown that simply communicating in a foreign language is one of the greatest stressors in a missionary's career.[31] Under prolonged or intense stress, our spiritual lives often suffer because we try to compensate by working harder, taking away our time to care for ourselves physically, emotionally, and spiritually.

Life is so burdensome. Fairly recently, the term *compassion fatigue* has come into our vocabulary. People who work in caring services, such as ministers and missionaries, play host to a high level of compassion fatigue. Day in and day out, these individuals work in caregiving environments that routinely present heart-wrenching, emotional challenges.[32] This painful reality, coupled with firsthand knowledge of living in a broken world, takes its toll on global servants, especially those in relief and development ministries. In these circumstances, spiritual formation takes a backseat to emotional turmoil and what we need most; comfort and encouragement from the Lord can become the last thing we seek.

Life is geared to prove our worth. We live in a time where consumerism, trendy strategies, and measurable results often drive our mission goals. The slow work of God's Spirit in transforming lives, including our own, is easily preempted by our desire for programmable and numeric success. We become addicted to the "bigger is better" approach, which then drives our personal and professional

---

31 Marge Jones and E. Grant Jones, *Psychology of Missionary Adjustment* (Springfield, MO: Gospel Publishing House, 1995), 42–52.

32 An example of compassion fatigue is the 2020 COVID-19 pandemic which stretched the medical community to the breaking point of physical and emotional exhaustion.

lives. We have a need to justify ourselves by working longer and longer hours doing things for the Lord, but less and less time being with him.

Life is not often restful. I have asked many missionaries what they do for rest and relaxation. Few can give me a good answer. Most simply do not plan for Sabbath. Things they enjoyed back home are no longer available or are too difficult to experience on the field. Some feel guilty over taking any time off at all when there are such pressing needs to address. Many simply ignore this aspect of their lives, to the detriment of their own selves and families. It is not hard to see that by doing so they are at risk of becoming weary in doing good (Gal 6:9).

Life is expensive. Many global servants say they cannot take holidays or fun outings because it is simply too expensive for them to do so. Many missionaries live on a very tight budget, and when it feels like the choice is whether to put food on the table or go away on a vacation, the choice is to meet the daily needs.

Life is confusing. Global servants are not immune to following the newest ministry trend or model of ministry. But we need to ask the Lord if this trend or model is for our ministry. Morris Dirks says, "The culture in which Christian leaders serve is prone to steer them toward the pursuit of career dreams and ministry ideals for the wrong reasons. The at-risk nature of the work begins to bear down on the leader and the outcome takes them to places they never anticipated."[33]

These are just a few of the factors that may draw missionaries away from intimacy with Jesus. Patricia Brown points out the danger of a lack of soul care for the Christian workers who mistakenly believe they don't need shepherding themselves:

> *The failure of leaders to deal with their own souls, their inner life, is deeply troubling not only to themselves but also for other persons in the misery they cause. The destructive consequences from leaders who fail to work out of a deep sense of their inner self are staggering.... Leaders have a particular responsibility to know what is going on inside their souls.*[34]

J. R. Briggs has reported some astounding and sobering research regarding ministerial burnout: thousands of pastors leave the ministry every year due to burnout; large numbers of ministry marriages end in divorce, and families are adversely affected; almost half of the pastors in North America have gone through times when they would leave their ministry if they had another way to make a living; a majority do not have close friends; and many report they have little spiritual life.[35] That last fact is tragic. Global servants and leaders in the church today clearly have a desperate need for soul care.

Healthy Hearts

The key to understanding our individual spiritual state lies in our hearts. Global servants need to continually ask themselves, "Is my heart healthy? Even though I am in ministry, am I healthy inside?" Proverbs 4:23 says this quite clearly:

---

33 Morris Dirks, *Forming the Leader's Soul: An Invitation to Spiritual Direction* (Portland: SoulFormation, 2013), 24.

34 Patricia D. Brown, *Learning to Lead from Your Spiritual Center* (Nashville: Abingdon, 1996), 11.

35 J. R. Briggs, *Fail: Finding Hope and Grace in the Midst of Ministry Failure* (Downers Grove, IL: IVP, 2014), 46–47.

"Above all else, guard your heart, for it is the wellspring of life." David also expresses his longing and praise for God in the Psalms: "My heart is steadfast, O God, my heart is steadfast; I will sing and make music" (57:7).

Both Jesus and Paul affirm this understanding of our hearts. Jesus rebuked the Pharisees who trusted in their knowledge without letting it change their hearts.

> *Woe to you, teachers of the law and Pharisees, you hypocrites! You give a tenth of your spices—mint, dill and cummin. But you have neglected the more important matters of the law—justice, mercy and faithfulness. You should have practiced the latter, without neglecting the former. You blind guides! You strain out a gnat but swallow a camel.*
>
> *Woe to you, teachers of the law and Pharisees, you hypocrites! You clean the outside of the cup and dish, but inside they are full of greed and self-indulgence. Blind Pharisee! First clean the inside of the cup and dish, and then the outside also will be clean.*
>
> *Woe to you, teachers of the law and Pharisees, you hypocrites! You are like whitewashed tombs, which look beautiful on the outside but on the inside are full of dead men's bones and everything unclean. In the same way, on the outside you appear to people as righteous but on the inside you are full of hypocrisy and wickedness. —Matthew 23:23–28*

And Paul talks about how Christ must dwell in our hearts in faith before we can know the fullness of God:

> *I pray that out of his glorious riches he may strengthen you with power through his Spirit in your inner being, so that Christ may dwell in your hearts through faith. And I pray that you, being rooted and established in love, may have power, together with all the saints, to grasp how wide and long and high and deep is the love of Christ, and to know this love that surpasses knowledge—that you may be filled to the measure of all the fullness of God. —Ephesians 3:16–19*

We are able to endure when we are changed from within. To do this we need to have self-understanding. Without self-understanding we are blind to the deep, broken places in our lives. Self-understanding comes about when we see ourselves as God sees us: broken but redeemed souls totally dependent upon him. Jesus said, "Blessed are the pure in heart, for they will see God" (Matt 5:8). This can only come about when we are in close relationship with Jesus and live an open, sincere, and pure life—true to ourselves and true to God.

We must examine the dark side of ourselves to understand where our hearts are being laid astray.

Shadow Sides: True Self and False Self

Thomas à Kempis wrote: "A humble understanding of yourself is a surer way to God than a profound searching after knowledge."[36] This is a great truth. It teaches us to remember that our hearts have both light and darkness inside them. In the apostle Paul's letter to the Romans, he acknowledged how he wrestled with this dilemma:

---

36 Thomas à Kempis, *The Imitation of Christ* (Peabody, MA: Hendrickson Press, 2004), 4.

I do not understand what I do. For what I want to do I do not do, but what I hate I do. . . . As it is, it is no longer I myself who do it, but it is sin living in me. I know that nothing good lives in me, that is, in my sinful nature. For I have the desire to do what is good, but I cannot carry it out. For what I do is not the good I want to do; no, the evil I do not want to do—this I keep on doing. —Romans 7:15, 17–19

Our deep brokenness is a product of our sin nature and lifelong unhealth, which requires more than superficial answers for healing. This process takes longer than we desire, because we first need awareness of the broken places and sin in our lives. Only then can we start to address them.

The gospel invites us into this process. The human heart has been created for unlimited happiness in unlimited truth and love. However, our old nature often gets in the way of what God wants to do in our heart. This causes an impasse. The term for this is called our *false self*. The false self is the mask we have created from early childhood to hide our *true self* in order to avoid the inner pains and hurts we have suffered. Most people are blissfully unaware of their false selves.

I grew up with a perfectionist father who never expressed emotional love to his children. Consequently, I never sensed unconditional love and subconsciously felt the need to earn approval and prove myself worthy, especially of authority figures. I also had a huge need to control events to appear competent. I would often over-prepare for any task I was supposed to do so I could eliminate any careless mistakes on my part. This is how I tried to convince myself I was competent and worthy of approval and love.

Before I went through my depression, if you would have told me I was seeking approval through performance, I wouldn't have believed it. Since my false self had done such a convincing job, I didn't realize my motivations behind my service. I was hiding behind a mask of performance and perfectionism to avoid the pain of possible rejection from the father figures in my life.

Through counseling, God's Spirit was able to help me gently take off my mask and learn this truth about my false self. Sometimes I am still tempted to put my mask back on, but the difference now is that I am much more aware of when I do this and so I can counter it by tending better to my own soul. This soul care restores my balance and transformational relationship with the Lord. My family has commented about this transformation, affirming that now I am the real person they know. The person that was being projected to the world was never the true me, and they knew this, even before I did. By stripping off my false self, I did not lose anything precious but rather gained the real me.

So how do we unmask ourselves? Listen to the first words Jesus spoke as he started his earthly ministry: "From that time on Jesus began to preach: 'Repent, for the kingdom of heaven is near'" (Matt 4:17). Repentance is essential for revealing and dealing with our sin and false selves. Biblical repentance is not about beating yourself up in an effort to achieve self-approval and self-correction. Instead it is turning the misguided direction of our hearts from ourselves back to dependency upon the Lord. Then we can reject the idols of this world and repent of all that interferes—the sins and fears that hide our true selves. "For you died, and your life is now hidden with Christ in God" (Col 3:3). This is not just bandaging the wounds of our heart; this is giving us a completely new heart (Ezek 36:25-28).

When we unmask our false stony hearts, we are remade with a new heart through the regeneration of the Holy Spirit. We are recreated into the person God always intended us to be. Sin holds no more sway over us and we can now live and minister out of our true heart—our true self—as we experience the joy and love of Christ.

But again, this transformation is a process. Unless graciously and supernaturally removed by God in a one-time act, many of our ordinary sinful behaviors, thoughts, attitudes, actions, and feelings are still very much with us. Our false self has manifested and become familiar with every level of our being, and even after salvation becomes difficult to root out. Theologically, this is called "total depravity." And though it doesn't mean that we are as bad as we can be, it does mean that every aspect of our lives is touched with sin's condition. This is the reason we need the ongoing sanctifying work of God's Spirit. By entering the process of lifelong spiritual formation, we can minister out of our true selves and open ourselves up to be true and authentic conduits of God's love.

Robert Mulholland puts it this way:

Everything that God has done, is doing and will ever do in our lives to conform us to the image of Christ (which is the image of our wholeness) is not so that we may someday be set in a display case in heaven as trophies of grace. All of God's work to conform us to the image of Christ has as its sole purpose that we might become what God has created us to be in relationship with God and with others.[37]

As we shed our false selves, we create the ability to minister to others out of the overflow of the Holy Spirit's work in our lives, becoming and living in our new nature. Common missionary frailties such as self-centeredness, compulsive working, and a distorted sense of self-identity can be transformed through the work of God. This brings us the hope that Paul speaks of in Romans when he says, "May the God of hope fill you with all joy and peace as you trust in him, so that you may overflow with hope by the power of the Holy Spirit" (15:13).

Self-Identity

John Calvin famously wrote: "Without knowledge of self, there is no knowledge of God. True, sound wisdom, consists of two parts, knowledge of ourselves and knowledge of God."[38]

Knowledge of ourselves is a key part of spiritual growth for the global servant. But there are two major dangers when it comes to our self-identity.

First, many missionaries arrive on the field with a distorted self-identity. They have already been through so much just to get to the field. There likely have been years of professional study and a major period of support-raising, where they

---

37 M. Robert Mulholland Jr., *Invitation to a Journey: A Road Map to Spiritual Formation* (Downers Grove, IL: IVP, 1993), 40.

38 John T. McNeill, ed., Ford Lewis Battles, trans., *Calvin: Institutes of Christian Religion*, vol. 1 (Philadelphia: Westminster Press, 1960), 35.

have been the center of attention and praised for giving their lives so sacrificially. Then they arrive on the field thinking they have a major advantage in education, skill, and knowledge. They come with money and resources to get things done. In these circumstances it is easy to get a big head, feeling that we are a savior to the people we come to rather than servants and ambassadors of the Lord.

Second, and in contrast to a puffed up self-identity, many global servants can quickly feel undervalued and lose a sense of who they are in their new culture where people around them see them do no identifiable "job." Leaving our home culture, where we held positions of status and accomplishment, and entering a new culture, where we know little if anything, can make us feel powerless and weak. Our self-identity as an accomplished person is lost in the chaos of the transition. It's easy to feel adrift, alone, and misunderstood. It can take months or even years to feel a sense of normalcy again.

Unfortunately, both opposites can exist at the same time in the same person—no one is immune.

There are three ways we can approach our self-identity. The first attitude is *self-centeredness*. Because of insecurity, energy is expended inward for self-fulfillment and security. Focus is always on oneself.

The second attitude is *disguised self-centeredness*. Energy is seemingly expended outward for others, but in reality it is given only for self-reward. The focus again stays on oneself.

The last attitude is *self-love*. Our identity is secure in Christ, with a healthy understanding of self-love and soul care. Focus flows outward from oneself to God to others.

When we come to understand deeply in our hearts that we always are, always will, and always have been loved by God, we can start to believe that there is nothing we can do to make him love us more and there is nothing we can do to make him love us less. We need to remind ourselves that our real identity lies in the fact that God loves us and has adopted us into his family as his dearly beloved children. Without this heart understanding, we remain insecure in our thoughts, activities, and behaviors. We will strive to prove ourselves, but our identity will still be rootless, depending upon the circumstances that surround us. Healing of our wounds and brokenness is not possible, because we are too afraid to address our needs. We forget the words that the apostle John proclaimed: "How great is the love the Father has lavished on us, that we should be called children of God! And that is what we are!" (1 John 3:1).

Wounded Healers

When I returned home from the field burned out and feeling like a failure, God used this to motivate me to help others avoid the experiences I had gone through. God used my brokenness to introduce member care in my mission organization. Paul affirms that when we accept our whole selves, the good and the bad, we can use our experiences and trials to minister to others:

Praise be to the God and Father of our Lord Jesus Christ, the Father of compassion and the God of all comfort, who comforts us in all our troubles, so that we can comfort those in any trouble with the comfort we ourselves have received from God. For just as the sufferings of Christ flow over into our lives, so also through Christ our comfort overflows. If we are distressed, it is for your comfort and salvation; if we are comforted, it is for your comfort, which produces in you patient endurance of the same sufferings we suffer. And our hope for you is firm, because we know that just as you share in our sufferings, so also you share in our comfort. —2 Corinthians 1:3–7

In this short paragraph, Paul strongly connects suffering and comfort. In five verses, verbs and nouns for "comfort" occur ten times, and the concept of suffering is directly and indirectly referred to seventeen times. Paul shows us that we are united in our sufferings and our comfort as brothers and sisters in Christ. The comfort we receive from God through Christ is to be shared in mutual exchange with one another. We are provided comfort not solely for ourselves, but it is also given to us so that we in turn can comfort others. Paradoxically, one of the great "joys" of enduring pain is to find meaning in that pain and being able to share that meaning to comfort others.

In our own woundedness, we can become a source of life for others. In Henri Nouwen's book *The Wounded Healer*, he asks how someone's sufferings can become a source of healing for another. He says, "Making one's own wounds a source of healing, therefore, does not call for a sharing of superficial personal pains but for the constant willingness to see one's own pain and suffering as rising from the depth of the human condition which all men share."[39]

If we ignore our brokenness, we miss the opportunity for God to fully heal us. Though we may try, we can never outrun our pain, nor can we heal ourselves. Though on this side of eternity we continue to live in a world of sin and brokenness, including our own, the freeing power of the gospel brings us healing and comfort. It allows us a fuller knowledge of ourselves, of who we were created to be. Then, through the overflow of this comfort and healing, we can minister from our hearts, not from ulterior motives, but as our true selves—as wounded healers. We must pay attention to our souls, caring for this precious life God has given us in his Son.

Reflection and Points to Ponder

Self-care is a foundational and critical component of longevity and success for the global servant. It takes intentional practice in order to restore, refresh, relax, and regroup. Self-care activities fall into five domains: physical, mental, emotional, relational, and spiritual. These domains overlap, but all of them are important in your self-care. Take a moment and explore each domain with the intention of self-examination.

---

[39] Henri J. Nouwen, *The Wounded Healer* (New York: Doubleday, 1979), 88.

Physical Self-Care: Taking steps on behalf of our bodies
- How does my food intake affect my mental and emotional functioning?
- What physical activities do I engage in to care for my body?
- Do I prioritize sleep and allow my schedule to accommodate the amount of rest my body needs—not just the amount upon which I can survive?
- What activities can I regularly engage in that contribute to relaxing and restoring my body?

Mental Self-Care: Being intentional about what we put into our minds
- What types of TV shows and movies do I choose to watch? How might they contribute or detract from my mental self-care?
- What types of reading material do I choose to read? Do I read only serious works? Do I read only for fun? Would a more balanced reading plan benefit me?
- What role does music play in my thought life?
- How comfortable am I with silence in my home, in my car, in nature, etc.? When I'm in silence, what do I usually find myself thinking about?

Emotional Self-Care: Being authentic and honest about our emotions
- Do I tend to over-connect or under-connect to my feelings?
- How can I better attend to my emotions?
- When I experience feelings of happiness, sadness, anger, or worry, how often do I take time to reflect on the reasons I am feeling that way?
- How do my emotional reactions to my circumstances affect my relationship with God?

Relational Self-Care: Cultivating reciprocal relationships in which we are equally attended to, sought out, cared for, and nurtured

- What makes me uncomfortable in relationships? What makes me shine in relationships?
- How many reciprocal friends do I have?
- Is there something I can change in regard to how I relate to others that might help my relationships to become healthier and more balanced? Are there any relationships I need to let go of so I can pursue better overall health?

Spiritual Self-Care: Staying in a place of humility and grace, awestruck by the privilege of being a servant of the living God

- Do I believe that attending to my soul is selfish?
- Have I grappled with my dark side? Do I know what masks I hide behind? How would I describe both my false self and my true self?
- Meditate on your identity in Christ through these Scriptures: Genesis 1:27; Jeremiah 1:5; John 1:12; Romans 6:6; 15:7; 1 Corinthians 6:17–20; 12:27; Galatians 3:27–28; Colossians 2:9–10; 3:1–3; 1 Peter 2:9; and 1 John 3:1–2.

For Further Reading

David G. Benner, *The Gift of Being Yourself: The Sacred Call to Self-Discovery* (Downers Grove, IL: IVP, 2004). An excellent resource on the exploration of Christian identity.

Adele Ahlberg Calhoun, *Spiritual Disciplines Handbook: Practices that Transform Us* (Downers Grove, IL: IVP, revised edition, 2015). In my opinion, the best modern resource on the spiritual disciplines and how to practice them.

Bill Tell, *Lay It Down: Living in the Freedom of the Gospel* (Colorado Springs: NavPress, 2015). A great book on the overwhelming grace of God. The gospel is about more than just saving us from our sin; it is about making us new creations in Christ.

After spending our first term

in Cambodia, our family returned to the United States for one year. I quickly joined a women's Bible study that met each Wednesday morning. I cherished these times to study the Word with other ladies who spoke my language and could encourage me as a wife and mother. As a verbal processor, it helped me to study the Bible and then discuss it with other ladies.

One day, we were asked to think of the worst possible thing that could happen in our lives. As I struggled to fit back into American culture and raise my three girls, it occurred to me that the worst thing for me would be to lose my husband, Jeff. The study leader asked us to play it out in our minds. So I did. It was awful. I could not imagine how I would manage life without Jeff, much less be filled with joy as I raised my girls on my own.

At the end of the study we were asked if God was good. Would he still be good if the worst imaginable thing happened? Would God still be a God who sees and cares for me even if the most horrific thing occurred? I came to the conclusion that God is God and he would remain the same loving, good Father even if Jeff died. Spending time in the Bible with other ladies helped me solidify a truth about God which, little did I know at the time, would be extremely important in the days to come.

Within a few years of that study, Jeff had a massive seizure and was diagnosed with a malignant brain tumor. What was going to happen to my husband? Would he die? What would that mean for me and my girls? How would life keep moving forward? I was reminded of that Bible study several years before. I knew that no matter what happened, God would still be God. A peace rushed over me. I wasn't sure what the journey held for my family, but I knew I could trust God and that who he was had not changed, even though I was facing tragedy.

I am extremely grateful for the opportunity to study God's Word when things were relatively easy in my life. The truth that I learned before helped me to remain faithful and steady when life got really difficult. By God's grace, the surgeon removed the tumor completely and my husband was healed. The Holy Spirit reminded me of what I had studied from Scripture, so the truth was deep in my heart when I needed it most.

Karyn
global servant in Southeast Asia

The Word of God
The Ancient Pathway to God

A young missionary has just arrived on the field—eager to serve the people God has called him to. He begins language study and connects with a small local body of believers. Every Sunday he goes to church and practices his language skills. He soon notices, however, that he is receiving very little spiritual nourishment. Most of his time during the preaching is spent looking up words in his dictionary and trying, but failing, to make sense out of the sermon.

He decides to start reading the Bible in his new language during his devotional times. But the translation is old and difficult to understand. Once again, most of his time is spent in the dictionary rather than the Bible. Soon he is asked to preach and teach the Scriptures. As a result, the need to research and study the Word becomes his go-to mode. Reading Scripture for spiritual edification is replaced with intensive study, because the young missionary feels tremendous pressure to get things right for his new friends. But all along he senses a spiritual dryness and a lack of power in his soul. The Word had become a tool for ministry, but not the source of energy and life.

I know this story all too well because it is *my* story. By losing scriptural connectedness, I lost my spiritual vitality. It is understandable that a new missionary going through language study will struggle to read the Bible in his second language. However, the problem intensifies when language study is substituted for Bible reading. This is compounded when we begin ministry and start to use the Bible simply as a tool, as a means of ministry, rather than also being a personal connection to God's truth and love.

Biblically Based Spirituality

Eugene Peterson tells an amusing story about his seven-year-old grandson, Hans, who pretended to be studying a New Testament even though he couldn't read. He draws the analogy of many of us who open our Bible but really don't know how to read it. He says there must be a problem, a "difficulty that we all share in common when we pick up our Bibles and open them. . . . Why isn't it easy?"[40] Peterson believes there is something wrong, as he goes on to state:

---

40 Eugene H. Peterson, *Eat This Book: A Conversation in the Art of Spiritual Reading* (Grand Rapids: Eerdmans, 2006), xi.

> *The challenge—never negligible—regarding the reading of Christian Scriptures is getting them read, but read on their own terms, as God's revelation. . . . Not that Christians don't own and read their Bibles. And not that Christians don't believe that their Bibles are the word of God. What is neglected is reading the Scriptures formatively, reading in order to live. . . . In order to read the scriptures adequately and accurately, it is necessary at the same time to live them. . . . It means letting Another have a say in everything we are saying and doing. It is as easy as that. And as hard.*[41]

So the problem isn't that we don't read the Bible, but that we don't let the Bible read us. Just before his arrest, Jesus prayed these words for his disciples: "Sanctify them by the truth; your word is truth" (John 17:17). If the Bible is the source of truth and godliness in our lives, it must be the center of our spiritual disciplines.

One of my mentors, Dr. David Currie, from Gordon-Conwell Theological Seminary, asserts that the Bible is the basis for all of our spirituality. "Spiritual formation is based upon the Bible as God's reliable and authoritative revelation. The Bible, our primary source of truth, guides and informs the use of spiritual disciplines and models of spirituality as they have emerged worldwide and through time."[42]

We benefit from being open to the various ways we can hear from the Word. Reading, hearing, studying, memorizing, singing Scripture, and hearing sermons are just a few examples. But when we rely on only one method, such as listening to sermons, for example, we miss out on other formational means to grow in the Word. Many global servants struggle on the field because the method of receiving God's Word they were used to is no longer available to them in the same way. Receiving God's Word through multiple means is a mark of a wise follower of Jesus.

For the remainder of this chapter we will explore two basic approaches to Scripture that most of us use: the study method, which can be labeled an informational approach; and the reading method, which can be called a transformational approach.[43] Both methods allow the Bible to come alive to us, permeating our hearts and minds.

The Study Method as a Spiritual Discipline

In Joshua 1:8 and Psalm 119:11–15, we are told to keep the Word on our lips. Perhaps this means we are to read or quote Scripture out loud. In an oral society with a low literacy rate, which was the case in Israel at the time, oral reading reinforced the Word for people. We are also told in Psalms 19:14 and 119:11–15 to keep the Word in our hearts, perhaps through memorization. Memorizing Scripture helps root it deep in our souls.

---

41 Peterson, xi–xii.

42 David Currie, Gordon-Conwell Theological Seminary, class notes, 2007.

43 I am simplifying here, as I do understand that Bible study is also transformative and that Bible reading informs as well as transforms.

God wants us to experience many ways to study the Bible, so as to use our own individuality and gifting to enjoy his Word. If you have a hard time studying because of your unique personality or time constraints, be creative: explore different methods which might work for you.

Today we have many available and accessible resources, in both physical and digital forms, to help in understanding, studying, memorizing, and meditating on Scripture. Every global servant will benefit from making sure they have access to a variety of these helps for their personal study. In today's mission world, there really is no reason why this cannot be accomplished.

However you do it, Bible study is essential for spiritual growth. The work of David Garrison, a missiologist who studies the religion of Islam, encompasses Muslims on a global scale—discovering sixty-nine movements toward Christ since 2000, which involve seventy different locations in twenty-nine countries.[44] Garrison's research found that many Muslims are coming to Christ because they have been given a Bible, which they have read, particularly in the Gospels.

> *Another path to faith in Christ for Muslims has been the discovery for themselves that Muslims believe Christ is who he claims to be. Unlike the Qur'an, which can only be truly represented in the Arabic language, the Bible begins with a translation into the local language. More than one Muslim-background believer commented: "I do not understand Arabic or the Qur'an. But I understand the Bible."*[45]

A new Muslim-background believer said that whenever he didn't understand the Injil (New Testament), he could always go to a fellow believer and, through study, obtain answers. "Nasr gave me an Injil, and I began to read it. Things I didn't understand, I would take back to him, and he'd explain. That was the beginning."[46]

The point here is that only when the Holy Scriptures are studied and understood can life-change be possible. A Muslim-background believer may have memorized the Qur'an, but it seems meaningless to them if they don't understand it. It's the same for us. We may know Scripture, but if we don't study and learn so we can understand what it means, we won't grow.

Of course, we don't want to rely too much on study alone for our Bible intake. This was my problem when I first went to the field. I assumed that if I was studying the Word for preaching and teaching purposes, I would somehow hear from God through his Word for myself. Good teachers and preachers certainly do apply Scripture to themselves first, but we can easily be tempted to study primarily for others and not for ourselves. When we do so, we stop sitting personally under God's Word. To stay committed to a life disciplined by Scripture, we must look at how the Bible transforms us.

---

44 David Garrison, *A Wind in the House of Islam: How God Is Drawing Muslims Around the World to Faith in Jesus Christ* (Monument, CO: WigTake Resources, 2014), 5.

45 Garrison, 174.

46 Garrison, 219.

The Reading Method as a Spiritual Discipline

Bible reading is the pathway to moral integrity and life transformation. How does reading God's Word differ from studying God's Word? The chart below gives a helpful comparison of the differences.

In the *study* method, you . . .	In the *reading* method, you . . .
Dissect the text	Savor the text and enter into it
Ask questions about the text	Let the text ask questions of you
Read, compare, and seek new ways of applying facts	Read to let God speak to you (considering facts already absorbed)

With the study method, we are looking at information for our minds to comprehend in our heads. With the reading method, we are seeking transformation in our hearts to change our lives. While we need both methods, the traditional approach to the Bible in the West has been geared much more toward head information than heart transformation. We need to keep a balance between head and heart in our Bible intake.

Lectio Divina

So how do we read the Bible for ourselves? For over fifteen hundred years, people have followed the practice of *Lectio Divina* (or *Lectio* for short). *Lectio Divina*, which literally means "sacred readings" in Latin, refers to the holy reading of the Scriptures. It requires prayerful reflection of the text, leading to communication with God in prayer. In fact, most Christian spiritual writers define Lectio as more of a prayer discipline than a reading discipline. Simply put, Lectio is reading a short passage of Scripture and then reflecting upon a word or short passage which the Spirit of God has brought to our mind in our reading.

In the last twenty years or so, Lectio has been regaining popularity within both Catholic and Protestant circles. Lectio Divina's roots go back to a text called "The Rule of St. Benedict" (*Regula Benedicti* or RB) in the first part of the sixth century. Chapter 48 of RB begins with general instruction against laziness. "Idleness is the enemy of the soul. Therefore, the brothers should have specified periods of manual labor, as well as for prayerful reading [Lectio Divina]."[47] Richard Peace explains how Lectio was first practiced in the monasteries of Western Europe.

> *The early monks approached the Bible by means of Lectio Divina. It worked for them like this: During the time set aside for personal reading, prayer, and reflection, a monk would go to a private place and begin to read aloud a passage from scripture. Often this would be taken from the Psalms or Gospels. The monk spoke out loud until he was struck by a particular word or phrase. Then he would stop and ponder this word or phrase, understanding*

---

[47] Saint Benedict, *Saint Benedict's Rule for Monasteries*, trans. Leonard J. Doyle (Collegeville, MN: Liturgical Press, 2001), 48:1, 8.

it to be a word from God for him. This meditation (which is what he was doing) led naturally into prayer as the monk offered back to God what he heard. As he moved deeper and deeper into prayer he would come to a place where he rested in the presence of God. Such a state of contemplation was actively sought.[48]

The assumption behind Lectio is that human beings are equipped with the ability to hear God. This refers not only to special saints, but to everyday folks, like you and me. God's voice is most often heard through his Word. "Faith comes from hearing the message, and the message is heard through the word of Christ" (Rom 10:17). Lectio is a practice that helps us connect directly to the Lord through Scripture. If nothing else, Lectio teaches us to listen with our hearts to our Father's words.

Lectio Divina eventually developed into a fourfold process, which Christians still use today. These are the four phases to the rhythm of Lectio: reading (*lectio*), meditation (*meditatio*), prayer (*oratio*), and contemplation (*contemplatio*). In her book *Sacred Rhythms*, Ruth Haley Barton outlines it well. The following is my paraphrasing of her material.

1. The first movement is to read (*lectio*). In this step we read the passage out loud, listening for a particular word or phrase that the Spirit brings to our attention. "This word somehow stands out from all the rest, causes a visceral reaction or attraction."[49] After the reading, there is a brief period of silence in which we remain before God, without necessarily trying to figure out what that word means. The we read the passage again.

2. The second movement is to reflect (*meditatio*). Here we linger over those words or images, paying attention to where and how we are engaging with them: Are they awakening memories, or whispering to current situations in our lives and ministries? Are they pressing upon us with the urgency of a sin we need to deal with? Is God shining his light on something we didn't know was in our hearts—e.g., a hope or a desire? We meditate on the passage with the conviction that it is the same Spirit who inspired its writing that is now at work applying it to us, and so we listen with care. Then we read the passage again.

3. The third movement is to respond (*oratio*). This time we attend to our feelings and silently offer them back to God as a prayer of our heart. Is there an invitation or a challenge we need to respond to? Then we pray back that word or phrase we have responded to as we offer it up to God. Then we read the passage for a final time.

---

48 Richard Peace, *Contemplative Bible Reading: Experiencing God through Scripture* (Colorado Springs: NavPress, 1998), 11.

49 Ruth Haley Barton, *Sacred Rhythms: Arranging Our Lives for Spiritual Transformation* (Downers Grove, IL: IVP, 2006), 57.

4. The fourth and final movement is to rest in God (*contemplatio*). Here we rest in God's loving presence with what he has revealed to us, realizing that God is the one who will reveal what he has shown us. Our resolve is simply to carry it with us, and throughout the rest of the day to live out his Word. We are to stay open and listen to God during the day. Often for me, the Word I received in the morning makes even better sense at the end of the day than it did at the beginning.[50]

Lectio Divina is so powerful because it combines a balance of silence and Word. When engaged in reading, please don't stress out about following a strict pattern. Living the habit of Lectio is really quite simple and is best learned through practice rather than explanation. Lectio is all about a relationship with God, and over time it aids in his transformational power in our lives.

Two Dangers in Study and Reading

One word of caution concerning our interaction with Scripture. There are two dangerous detours we need to be aware of as we read and study Scripture. The first detour happens when our Bible study becomes too objective. The words of James apply here:

> *Do not merely listen to the word, and so deceive yourselves. Do what it says. Anyone who listens to the word but does not do what it says is like a man who looks at his face in a mirror and, after looking at himself, goes away and immediately forgets what he looks like. But the man who looks intently into the perfect law that gives freedom, and continues to do this, not forgetting what he has heard, but doing it—he will be blessed in what he does. —James 1:22–25*

The second detour is when our Bible reading becomes too subjective and we read into a text our own interpretation of what we want to believe or think we should hear from it. This has the potential to let us stray far from the original meaning, as well as allow us to ignore parts of the Bible we don't want to read or consider. We must always hold loosely what we think we are hearing from the Lord and seek to confirm it through the honored means of community input, as well as test it with other passages of Scripture. When we read the Bible and only listen to our own voice, we defeat the purpose for reading God's Word in the first place.

The choice, however, doesn't need to be between choosing dry scholasticism or irresponsible subjectivism. We need to approach Scripture with both objective study and submissive listening. That is why I make time for both Lectio and study in my personal devotions every day. We need analysis and application. We need knowledge and insight. We need to understand, but also to live the Word in the context of our daily lives, and not just in the context of our ministry tasks.

Jesus has some challenging words for us about understanding and applying Scripture. "On one occasion an expert in the law stood up to test Jesus. 'Teacher,' he asked, 'what must I do to inherit eternal life?' 'What is written in the Law?' he [Jesus] replied. 'How do you read it?'" (Luke 10:25–26).

---

50 Barton, 56–58.

This passage wonderfully illustrates Jesus' capacity for turning an abstract theological discussion into a conversation about real-life issues. Jesus first calls the lawyer to reflect upon Scripture—asking for scriptural support for his position. But then later in the passage, after the expert answers, Jesus calls him even further, leading the man to ask, "Who is my neighbor?" (v. 29). Jesus then provides a concrete example in the story of the Good Samaritan.

Eugene Peterson comments on this story: "There was nothing wrong with the scholar's knowledge of Scripture. But there was something terribly wrong in the way he read it, the *how* of his reading. . . . It poses Jesus's question to us: 'How do you read?'"[51]

No spiritual discipline is more important than the intake of God's Word. We know the person of Jesus Christ through the Bible. We come to this knowledge through reading and study, and by applying the Word to both our heads and our hearts. We further cultivate the Word by giving it fruitful soil to germinate and produce growth in our lives (Matt 13:8, 23). When we follow the ancient pathway to the Father through the Word, we will always find him there—guiding our perception, understanding, and application, and providing spiritual awakening.

Reflection and Points to Ponder

- In this chapter we have explored the differences between Bible study and Bible reading. Can you describe the differences between the two methods, and especially how you can apply both approaches to your own use of the Bible?
- How has God spoken to you through the study of his Word? How has Bible study affected your life?
- When the Word of God appears dry to you, what do you imagine is causing the dryness? The passage? Your busy life? Something else? Can you change anything to make the Bible come more alive in your study or reading?
- How has your spiritual reading of the Bible been influenced by the head/heart dynamic?
- Reflect upon times when simply reading the Word has been helpful in hearing God's voice. How have the Scriptures brought you into the presence of Christ?

For Further Reading

Thelma Hall, *Too Deep for Words: Rediscovering Lectio Divina* (Mahwah, NJ: Paulist Press, 1988). A basic introduction to contemplative reading and listening to the Word of God, including five hundred Scripture passages for prayer.

Eugene H. Peterson, *Eat This Book: A Conversation in the Art of Spiritual Reading* (Grand Rapids: Eerdmans, 2006). A book on how to read the Bible not only for information but also for transformation.

---

51 Peterson, 83–84.

While in colleges, my ministry leaders encouraged us to fast during the day or from one meal to help remind us to pray. I joined in these times of fasting, rejoicing in the experience that when I felt hungry I just prayed, and God relieved my hunger. Over the years I have tried other fasts in addition to food fasts, though they were all occasional and inconsistent.

My family and I have been overseas now for five years, and there are several aspects of our work here where we desperately need to see God's movement. Recently, as I was thinking about these areas, I remembered the encouragement to fast and pray. I decided to fast until the evening meal with my family for the next day. As the day progressed, I realized how much I was used to satisfying myself with food. I saw how easily I would distract myself with a snack or thoughts about what to make for lunch. And I realized that I could not desperately wait for God to move if I could so easily satisfy my longings. It was a physical reminder of a spiritual matter. If I can easily be satisfied by what is around me, I will not cry out to the only One who can fill every part and provide for my every need. If I forget that I am needy because my belly is full, I forget to cry out in dependence.

A few days after this experience, I heard God ask me to fast for seven days for the salvation of my children and parents. I thought, "Yes, okay, I will do this. I am desperate for God to move because only he can change their hearts." Then I counted the days out on my fingers and I thought, "Lord, this is several days. I'm not sure that I like this. But I'm willing to do things that don't make logical sense if it brings me to the place where I am depending entirely on you, waiting for you, trusting you."

The first day I was joyful about pressing into prayer over these matters so dear to me. I spent extra time in prayer and in reading the Bible. I was reminded to pray as I went about my usual daily tasks. Some of the days were not so joyful and reflective, but my natural drive to keep my belly full and my appetite satisfied meant that I continued to cry out to God during the day, asking for him to move.

When the seven days were fulfilled, part of me was very glad to enjoy breakfast again. Another part of me didn't want to give up what I felt during that time. I am thankful for the opportunity to engage in the spiritual disciplines of fasting and prayer to remind myself not to be so easily satisfied, not to give up and get distracted until I see God move. Though I don't completely understand how it works, I believe there is also something in fasting that impacts the power of our prayers. The practice of refusing the pleasures of this world for a time to ask for something more, something greater, something eternal, is a discipline worth learning so that we do not grow numb and lazy."

Sarah
global servant in North Africa

Our Prayer Life
The Ancient Pathway to Intimacy

Throughout the history of the church, the top question spiritual mentors ask others is: How is your life of prayer?

Our prayer life, more than anything else, reveals the quality of our relationship with God. How do we understand prayer? How do we practice prayer? How does prayer shape our lives and our hearts for God? Is it just a duty, or an act of love? Do we pray continually, or just periodically? These are the questions we will explore in this chapter.

Global servants often find prayer to be one of the most difficult of the spiritual practices. Early in my missionary career my prayers were mainly focused on ministry—asking God for help and interceding for others. While both are good prayer practices, I had yet to learn that prayer is so much more. I often found my devotional life empty. I was giving out so much for others, but I felt that I was receiving so little back from God. Most of the time my heart was dry and barren.

When I shared my concerns with a colleague, he shared how empty his prayer life had become also. We didn't have any real answers to this problem, but we weren't content to let things stay the way they were. We decided that we would do something no matter what, even though we didn't really know what to do.

We eventually decided to get together once a week. We didn't meet to talk strategy or even to discuss accountability issues, as many men do. We got together to worship. We simply spent one hour each week singing and praising God together. Believe me, these weren't pretty times, as neither of us had strong or pleasant voices, but we did it anyway. Sometimes it felt like we were just going through the motions. But we persisted, and discovered that God honored our intentions.

I decided to write out some of my prayers, and I also started to keep a prayer journal, which I had never done before. This prayer journaling eventually morphed into a lifelong habit. It took me several years to discover other ways of praying, but it all began when my missionary colleague and I just started singing together.

What Is Prayer?

Even though I think prayer is one of the most difficult spiritual practices, it is also one we might practice more than we realize. Saint Augustine, who lived about four hundred years after Jesus, expressed this idea when he said, "True, whole prayer is nothing but love."[52] What Augustine meant is that in whatever manner we pray, true prayer centers upon a love relationship between us and our Father. When we love God, we are praying. When we pray, we are loving God. The Trinity is always in constant love, and therefore is in constant prayer. As I noted earlier, this is *perichoresis*—the dance of the Godhead. The remarkable thing about all of this is that we too, as God's children, are invited into the dance. How do we do this? Through our prayer life.

One of the desert fathers, Evagrius the Solitary (346–399), wrote one of the earliest treatises about prayer, entitled *On Prayer*. Evagrius defined prayer as "communing with God in the depths of our hearts."[53] This means prayer is the place of deepest and most honest connection between us and the Father.

Richard Foster says that to be effective pray-ers, we need to be effective lovers. "Overwhelming love invites a response. Loving is the syntax of prayer."[54] Prayer is not only about asking God to enhance our ministry. It is about entering into a full and deeply profound love that involves giving and receiving, in mutual dialogue. This is what I didn't understand as a young missionary. I saw prayer more as a devotional act than an act of devotion.

Andrew Murray tells us that prayer is foundational to our growth. Waiting in prayer lets us experience the fullness of our salvation, being more about receiving and listening than about speaking.

> *If salvation truly comes from God and is entirely His work, just as our creation was, it follows that our first and highest duty is to wait on Him and to do that work which pleases Him. Waiting then becomes the only way to experience full salvation—the only way to truly know God as the God of our salvation. All the difficulties which are brought forward, as keeping us back from full salvation, have their cause in this one thing: the defective knowledge and practice of waiting upon God.*[55]

Psalm 62:1 says: "My soul finds rest in God alone; my salvation comes from him." The first phrase of this verse is hard to translate from the Hebrew. Literally, it reads: "Only unto God silence my soul." This explains the wide variation in translations among English versions of the Bible. However, I find the translation from the New English Bible one of the finest. It reads, "Truly my heart waits silently for God." This implies a loving trust between the person praying and God. The faithful wait for God to speak, because in their established relationship with the Lord, there is trust.

---

52 Richard J. Foster, *Prayer: Finding the Heart's True Home* (San Francisco: Harper, 1992), 1.

53 *Evagrius Ponticus' Chapters on Prayer*, trans. Sr. Pascale-Dominique Nau (self-pub., lulu.com, 2012), 1.

54 Foster, 3.

55 Andrew Murray, *Waiting on God* (New Kensington, PA: Whitaker House, 1981), 11.

Prayer is about love, trust, and finding a place of stillness and silence before him. It is a kind of motionless waiting—holy inactivity—in anticipation that God alone will act. Psalm 62:8 tells us to "pour out your hearts to him." The verb "pour out" describes completely emptying a vessel of all liquid, holding nothing back. We can enter the still confidence of God's presence when we hold nothing back— our heart fully exposed with all its sin, brokenness, fear, weakness, anxiety, and grief. In this vulnerability, we can wait and trust in our Father for his deliverance. This is Murray's idea of how prayer impacts our salvation.

Various Forms of Prayer

Let's look at prayer in two simple forms: heart prayers and hand prayers. Heart prayers focus on our intimacy with the Father, such as praise, worship, confession, and thanksgiving. Hand prayers focus on what we do in service, such as supplication and intercession.

Heart Prayers

First, heart prayer is as varied as the ways we relate to God. We pray to a living God—one with whom we are in constant relationship. Therefore, like our other relationships in life, we communicate with the Father, Son, and Holy Spirit in a variety of ways, dependent upon where we are in our relationship at that moment. For example, there are times when I am traveling and the only way I can communicate with my family is through email or telephone. However, when I am at home, we talk face-to-face. This analogy is not perfect, of course, but it conveys the understanding that if my prayer life truly reflects my heart before God, then at any given moment that reflection is also true to my current state of being. So if I have sinned, I pray confessional prayers. If I am full of gratitude, I pray with thanksgiving and praise. If I have a need, I pray in supplication. If I am burdened for another, I intercede.

Second, as we have discussed, prayer can be nonverbal. We will explore this more when we discuss contemplative prayer, but for now let me say that such prayer is challenging but essential to a maturing prayer life. Heart prayer means deep, centered prayer in which God often takes the initiative.[56] Paul says in Romans 8:26 that there are times when "We do not know what we ought to pray for, but the Spirit himself intercedes for us with groans words cannot express." God's Holy Spirit moves within us as we pray. This is why silence is a significant component of mature prayer. We wait and listen for him—to hear him speak. An example of this is when we feel an extra-heavy burden to pray for someone, although we don't know exactly what to pray for, and so we just commit that person to the Lord.

Nevertheless, sometimes our heart prayers seem dry and empty. This is a common experience for many global workers because, like my own story, many missionaries are so work-driven that their prayer lives have dried up and they have lost the sense of the presence of God. Now while it is possible that some

---

[56] David Teague, *Godly Servants: Discipleship and Spiritual Formation for Missionaries* (n.p.: Mission Imprints, 2012), 38.

of the reasons for this could be the loss of a sense of God's redeeming work, habitual sin, a lack of faith in God's Word and promises, or narcissistic self-willed prayers, many times it isn't wrong attitudes or behaviors which cause us to feel that God is absent. Rather, God is doing something else for us.

Richard Foster correctly identifies what our posture ought to be before God when this happens. Not surprisingly, it involves waiting.

> *I would like to offer one more counsel to those who find themselves devoid of the presence of God. It is this: wait on God. Wait, silent and still. Wait attentive and responsive. Learn that trust proceeds faith. . . . Trust is confidence in the character of God. Firmly and deliberately you say, "I do not understand what God is doing or even where God is, but I know that He is out to do me good." This is trust. This is how to wait.*[57]

If we are stuck and cannot go forward in our prayers, let's not go backward by blaming God or jumping to action too soon. Let's stay in neutral if we must, grounded in the assurance that God is for us and not against us—that he is working. Let's wait expectantly before him in an attitude of heart prayer, convinced his will is good and perfect for us and for our times.

Hand Prayers

Prayers traditionally understood as either praying for one's own needs (supplication) or praying for others' needs (intercession) are what I call hand prayers. Keep in mind, hand prayers should never be disconnected from heart prayers. Just as with heart prayers, the key prerequisite for hand prayers is an intimate relationship with Jesus. Without heartfelt closeness to Jesus, we can never understand his purposes and therefore pray effectively for ourselves or others.

As global servants, our prayer lives are part of our work. Patrick Johnstone, the author of *Operation World*, says, "We do not just pray for the work; prayer is the work!"[58] A missionary who does not intercede is guilty of spiritual laziness. James says, "Anyone, then, who knows the good he ought to do and doesn't do it, sins" (James 4:17).

Devotional writer Ole Hallesby states, "A child of God can grieve Jesus in no worse way than to neglect prayer. . . . Many neglect prayer to such an extent that their spiritual life gradually dies out."[59] Being careless about hand prayers affects our heart prayers as well, because when we don't pray we aren't making ourselves available to God.

> *Intercessory prayer is like an ellipse, which rotates about two definite points: Christ and our need. The work of the Spirit in connection with prayer is to show us both, not merely theoretically, but practically, making them vital to us from day to day. Comfort yourself in the thought that it is the Spirit who is working these things in your heart every day.*[60]

---

57 Foster, 24.

58 Patrick Johnstone, *Operation World: The Day-to-Day Guide for Praying for the World*, 6th ed. (Grand Rapids: Zondervan, 1993), 11.

59 O. Hallesby, *Prayer* (Minneapolis: Augsburg, 1975), 229.

60 Hallesby, 163.

Prayer ministry depends upon daily experience. If we neglect hand prayers, we may find that a time will come when we desperately need to intercede for someone but have lost the discernment and the will to do so. We grow in prayer by praying. The more we connect with God, the more we gain understanding of how to pray for others.

We are seeing one of the greatest harvests for Jesus in the Muslim world. Scholar David Garrison has researched faith movements in the Muslim world. During the first fourteen hundred years of Islam, there were a total of thirteen movements to faith in Jesus. But in the first twelve years of the twenty-first century, sixty-nine movements to Christ in the Muslim world occurred.[61] How has such a dramatic change taken place?

> Garrison's answer is that "prayer has been the first and primary strategy for virtually every new initiative into the Muslim world."[62] He quotes a Muslim-background follower of Jesus: "I believe that the prayers of the people all over the world have been raising up to heaven for many years. In the heavens these prayers have accumulated like the great clouds during the monsoon season. And now they are raining down upon my people the miracles and blessings of salvation that God has stored up for them."[63]
>
> Prayer draws us near to God, and when we move toward God, we also join him in his love for the nations.
>
> It is a mystery how God uses our prayers to affect eternity. But he chooses to do so, and as he does we become even more aligned with his kingdom vision and purposes and live kingdom lives. It is amazing to me how I sometimes become apologetic to my donor base about spending great amounts of time in prayer. I feel I must defend myself because I'm not out there witnessing and doing, but only praying. I have such weak faith sometimes. Hand prayers are a mighty force in the global servant's life.

Confession and Repentance

In confessional prayer, we simply acknowledge and repudiate the sin in our lives without excuse or abridgment. Repentance and confession are two often-neglected areas in the spiritual formation of global servants, yet they are both essential to for a Spirit-filled life. Jesus tells us in the Sermon on the Mount that the poor in spirit are blessed (Matt 5:3). When we are prideful, we cannot fully know God's grace. But when we are poor in spirit, we are willing to open ourselves up to receive the grace of God in full measure. This allows us to experience the reality that God's "truth will set you free" (John 8:32). When we come to God in true confession, with no agenda, he pronounces his forgiveness in Christ and graces us with his blessing.

By honestly admitting our sinful propensities, we open ourselves up to experiencing the fullness of God's healing love. Saint Ignatius of Loyola is attributed

---

61 David Garrison, *A Wind in the House of Islam* (Monument, CO: WIGTake, 2014), 18.
62 Garrison, 18.
63 Garrison, 241.

as saying, "Sin is unwillingness to trust that what God wants for me is only my deepest happiness." We can relate to David's experience of feeling God's heavy hand upon his guilt, as well as the relief brought about by confession and forgiveness. "For day and night your hand was heavy upon me; my strength was sapped as in the heat of summer. Then I acknowledged my sin to you and did not cover up my iniquity. I said, 'I will confess my transgressions to the Lord'—and you forgave the guilt of my sin" (Psalm 32:4–5).

Confession insists there is no unpardonable sin except the refusal to repent. When we refuse to repent, we blaspheme the Holy Spirit's call to mercy (Mark 3:29). Fortunately, there is never a time that God will not grant his grace to those who are truly repentant.

While sin is specific, or personal, it can also be general, or communal. Even if we personally have not been involved in the past sins of the missionary movement, we must acknowledge that at times and in places through the years, missionaries have been guilty of great communal sins such as imperialism, patronization, racism, and pride. I know very few mission agencies who corporately practice the discipline of confession. This healthy self-examination is something I believe will empower agencies and lead to an even greater witness for Christ, if done honestly and regularly. There is great healing power in corporately acknowledging sin, when appropriate, and repenting before both God and his people.[64]

When do we need to involve others in our confessional prayers? By confessing our sin before others, we are forced to speak our sin out loud. Vocalizing our confession moves us into a deeper sense of being loved and reveals our humility before fellow brothers and sisters. It is quite a freeing event. On many occasions I have met with missionaries struggling with guilt over a past sin. As an exercise in true repentance, it was important to have another person confirm their forgiveness in Christ. The experience of joy and freedom in confessing before both God and man is a powerful and cementing benchmark for us in letting go and moving on.

One word of caution when we confess before others. It is important to privately confess sins which should be kept private for the sake of others. We should only confess this sin in confidence and in one-to-one times, not corporately lest we embarrass innocent people. Only confess publicly, in front of a group, those sins which have affected the whole group. I once was part of a group of missionaries praying when a man stood up and confessed his lustful thoughts for a woman in the group. This was totally inappropriate and wrong. He should never have done this in public, and we had to deal with the fallout afterward.

Confession is not only good for the soul; it is also good for the body! When we repent and confess, we might get relief from physical and mental stress and experience a profound peace. Recent neuroscience research has confirmed that confession changes our brain capacities.[65] Through confession, our tendency to ignore emotions, inattentiveness to memory, behavior, the erosion and confusion

---

64 I was pleased to see in 2020 some mission agencies confess and repudiate the missionary movement's historical contribution to racism.

65 Phileena Heuertz, *Mindful Silence: The Heart of Christian Contemplation* (Downers Grove, IL: IVP, 2018), 7.

which sin brings to our minds, are transformed. As psychiatrist and author Curt Thompson observes,

> *In the discipline of confession, you honestly reflect on your narrative with a well-trusted friend, counselor, or spiritual director. This enables you to be sensitive to the elements of implicit and explicit memory, along with physical and mental manifestations of emotional slights that, if unchecked, can easily lead you down the low road of behavior.*[66]

Beyond just the actions we commit, sin lies deep within us. Confession frees us from the hold that sin has over our total being.

Take note, however, that we must *choose* to confess and repent. This is why we call confession a discipline. Yes, it is grace-filled, because to truly repent we need the work of the Holy Spirit's power. But it is a discipline because we must also choose to do something. True confession moves us from saying "I am sorry if I hurt you" to "I am sorry that I hurt you." There is no blaming, no victimizing, only honest truth: "I sinned—forgive me, Father."

These factors remind us that confession is personal (between me and God); interpersonal (between others and myself); and corporate (within a worshipping community). Dallas Willard says, "Confession is one of the most powerful of the disciplines for the spiritual life. But it can easily be abused, and for its effective use it requires considerate experience and maturity, both for the individual concerned and the leadership of the group."[67] Confession steers us toward a greater awareness of ourselves. It leads us through repentance and sorrow to the joy, hope, freedom, and righteousness that Christ gave us when he died on the cross for us.

Contemplative Prayer and Ignatian Spirituality

A central topic of Christian prayer is contemplation.[68] Contemplative prayer is abiding prayer. It is an attitude of listening carefully to God as we live "hidden in Christ" (Col 3:3). Contemplative prayer is dependent upon the state of our heart. We wait before God, committing our heart to his workings. "Be strong, and let your heart take courage, all you who wait for the Lord!" (Ps 31:24 ESV).

Ignatian spirituality helps us in this matter.[69] The heart of Ignatian spirituality is a total surrender to God's will and plan for our lives. This leads to trusting in God's loving presence discerned through the interior movements of the heart. Ignatius termed these movements "consolation" and "desolation." In consolation, one is drawn to the will of God; and in desolation, one is drawn away.[70]

---

66 Curt Thompson, *The Anatomy of the Soul* (Carrollton, TX: SaltRiver, 2010), 197.

67 Dallas Willard, *Spirit of the Disciplines* (San Francisco: Harper & Row, 1988), 189.

68 John H. Cole and Kyle C. Strobel, eds., *Embracing Contemplation: Reclaiming a Christian Spiritual Practice* (Downers Grove, IL: IVP, 2019), 2.

69 Born in the Basque province in northwest Spain, Íñigo López de Loyola (c. 1491–1556) was the founder of the Society of Jesus (Jesuits) and author of The Spiritual Exercises of St. Ignatius.

70 Ignatius of Loyola, *The Spiritual Exercises of St. Ignatius*, trans. Louis J. Puhl (New York: Vintage Books, 2000), 175–76.

Through this process one can learn to recognize and follow God's voice amid the many conflicting voices of the flesh, the world, and the devil. It is lifelong equipping for spiritual discernment whereby we become more self-aware, better understand our motives, increase our prayer abilities, and make wise decisions. We do this by learning to detach ourselves from our worldly desires by holding them very loosely. In Ignatian vocabulary this is called "holy indifference."[71] The by-product is greater humility, which comes from increased freedom to be and do God's will for us.

A key part in Ignatius' book, *The Spiritual Exercises,* is the daily prayer of Examen.[72] The Examen invites us to reflect on our day's activities and discern where we saw or felt God's presence. It involves reflecting and reviewing one's day by asking God "to bring to mind attitudes, actions, and moments when you fell short of exhibiting the character of Christ or the fruit of the Spirit."[73] We ask God for spiritual insight by listening deeply to where God has been present to us during the day and where he has been absent. It fosters good judgment—learning from our mistakes (our desolations) and seeing where we have been conformed to the image of Christ (our consolations). Reviewing our daily life and recognizing God at work brings great joy.

Examen is not complicated. It involves several simple questions to explore the day's events and the experiences of your heart. Here are some examples:

- Today, what have I been most grateful for? Today, what have I been least grateful for?
- When did I give and receive the most love today? When did I give and receive the least love today?
- When did I feel most alive today? When did I most feel life draining out of me?
- When today did I have the greatest sense of belonging to myself, others, God, and the universe? When did I have the least sense of belonging to myself, others, God, and the universe?
- When was I the happiest today? When was I the saddest?
- What was today's high point? What was today's low point?
- When did I most sense God's presence? When did I most sense his absence?[74]

Of course, we need to be careful not to be exclusively dependent upon our feelings. But feelings do matter, and this is the purpose of Examen—to explore and discern if and where God has been working, and not just take life at face value, so we may process our consolations and desolations rightly by bringing them to the Lord.

---

71 Ignatius, 179.

72 Ignatius, 77.

73 Ruth Haley Barton, *Sacred Rhythms: Arranging Our Lives for Spiritual Transformation* (Downers Grove, IL: IVP, 2006), 101.

74 The simplest and perhaps best explanation I have found for the Prayer of Examen is the children's book *Sleeping with Bread: Holding What Gives You Life* (Mahwah, NJ: Paulist Press, 1995). Most of these questions come from this book.

When global servants pray the daily Examen, they begin to develop some extraordinary wisdom. Examen produces greater flexibility, breadth, and depth, because it addresses our fundamental relationship with God. It encourages and stimulates close personal attachment to the person of Jesus and provides the means for each global servant to learn and to find God in all things, while cultivating a humble and submissive spirit. This is the seed of holiness.

Fixed-Hour Prayer

One afternoon I was visiting a mission headquarters when I heard a long gong-like sound echo through the hallways. The mission leader I was with paused and said, "It is three o'clock and we need to pause for a few minutes to reflect upon the Lord." She proceeded to take us to a quiet room where we spent fifteen minutes in silent prayer. What I just experienced with this young and progressive organization was the ancient discipline called fixed-hour prayer, or fixed hours.

As early as Hippolytus of Rome (c. 170–235), the daytime office hours were practiced by the early church in recalling the hours of the crucifixion (Terce, Sext, None). However, the office hours were fully developed as a major part of communal prayer in monasteries during the early and middle medieval period (c. 400-900). Saint Benedict (c. 480–547), who is considered the father of the monastic movement, is the most well-known figure behind the office hours.[75] Divine Hours came out of the Benedictine understanding that work and prayer are to coexist together. Benedict said, "To pray is to work and to work is to pray."[76]

Divine Hours are part of the liturgy of the Western church. Liturgy includes the church's ordinances, such as the Lord's Supper and baptism; fixed hours; special events, such as funerals and weddings; and the liturgical calendar, which includes Advent, Christmas, Lent, and Easter. Saint Benedict taught an integrated custom of praying at daily set intervals which consisted of up to eight sessions of psalmody during each twenty-four-hour period. The actual hours consist of the following:

- Night prayer—Vigils
- Waking-up prayers—Lauds
- Prayers for beginning work—Prime
- Prayers of thanksgiving in mid-morning—Terce
- Noon-day prayer of commitment—Sext
- Mid-afternoon prayer—None
- Evening prayer of stillness—Vespers
- Going-to-sleep prayer of trust—Compline[77]

---

75 For a look at Benedictine spirituality from a Protestant perspective, I recommend Dennis Okholm, *Monk Habits for Everyday People: Benedictine Spirituality for Protestants* (Grand Rapids: Brazos Press, 2007).

76 George Lane, *Christian Spirituality: A Historical Sketch* (Chicago: Loyola Press, 2005), 20.

77 Kevin W. Irwin, "Liturgy," in *The New Dictionary of Catholic Spirituality*, ed. Michael Downey (Collegeville, MN: Liturgical Press, 1993), 609.

Thinking of praying at all these times can be overwhelming, but each period is brief, and we don't need to do this legalistically. If you aren't able to make a prayer time, give yourself plenty of grace (especially in the night!). In the Roman Catholic tradition, there is a specific set of elements which take place during the hours. For our usage, however, it might be best at first to pray the Psalms, interposed with silence and worship.[78]

Why practice fixed hours? What benefit does it have for the global servant? Let me put it this way: In our natural setting, global servants, especially those of us from North America, tend to be disproportionately formed by and conformed by our cultural surroundings. So without proper reflection, we can easily become consumer-driven, efficiency-minded, results-oriented, and time-dominated. Instead of offering our time to God, we do just the opposite. Fixed-hour prayers works against this tendency by redeeming each period of each day by giving it back to the Father.

By turning our hearts and minds to God at specific hours of the day, we integrate our being and doing natures, which allows us then to better discern where God is leading. There are various ways that you can remind yourself to stop and pray—from the gonging of the bell at the mission headquarters to setting an alarm on your watch or phone. However you remind yourself to keep fixed hours, the key is to keep practicing. Consistency is vital, and the habit of doing it trains our heart.

The whole purpose of this kind of praying is to train us by the rhythms of seasons and days, by keeping us honest before our Lord, and by allowing us to reconsider our first love—Jesus. Scripture consistently calls us to remember the Lord and his mighty works.[79] Life is both progressive—moving toward a goal—and cyclical—the turning of the years and seasons. As we grow in grace, each season and each year bring additional and distinct learning experiences. Praying helps us to stay better connected to God, ourselves, and our community in all seasons of life.

---

78 Some evangelicals struggle with fixed-hour prayer because they do not believe it is found in Scripture (though they make exception for the book of Daniel (cf. Dan 6:10). However, the book of Acts does point to the apostles going to the Temple at set times to pray (Acts 2:42,46, 3:1). If you find yourself uncomfortable practicing fixed-hour prayer, please do not force it. After all, what is of most importance is that you prayer itself, not the specific times you do it.

79 See Ex 13:3; 16:12; Num 15:39; Ps 42:4–6; 77:11; 105:5; Eccl 12:1; Isa 46:8; Mark 14:9; John 14:26; 2 Tim 2:8; 2 Pet 1:12.

Reflection and Points to Ponder

- In this chapter we have explored various prayer practices. Do you find yourself drawn to one practice over the others? How can you become more intentional in its use?
- How do you react to the word *contemplation*? What sorts of things could you contemplate? How can you document your thoughts and prayers so you can further meditate on them?
- How might you practice the daily Examen? Would evening or morning (and therefore reflecting back on the previous day) work better for you? What might help you to better name your consolations and desolations?
- What do your intercessory requests before God reveal about your desires, motives, priorities, and goals? How might centering your heart on God, rather than your objectives, influence your supplications and intercessions?
- How do you feel about memorizing prayers or reading the prayers of others? Would you benefit from a book of prayer, such as following the Book of Common Prayer, for seasonal prayers?
- Reflect upon whether there would be any benefit to you in setting up a schedule of fixed-hour prayer. What would constitute your prayers during the workday? How can you remind yourself of God's continual presence and activity in your life, if fixed hours are not a solution for you?

For Further Reading

Richard J. Foster, *Prayer: Finding the Heart's True Home* (San Francisco: HarperCollins, 1992). A look at over twenty different types of prayer.

J. Gary Millar, *Calling on the Name of the Lord: A Biblical Theology of Prayer* (Downers Grove, IL: IVP Academic, 2016). A thorough look, through Scripture on how prayer is shaped and formed around the fulfillment of the gospel.

In seminary, a professor introduced me to a form of spiritual journaling which involved writing out the words of Scripture by hand and then writing my own commentary on the text. This was not a time to do exegesis, but rather a time to hear from God. It was the habit of writing out what I felt God was saying to me in these devotional notebooks which helped foster the desire to commit my reflections to writing. As I did so, I also found myself writing out what God was doing in my life. It was during a time of this reflective personal Bible study that God made clear his call in our lives to serve him in Iceland.

While I was reflecting on the story of David and Goliath and imagined the Philistine giant taunting the armies of Israel to send someone over to fight him, I had a vision of a giant standing on Iceland. It was as if that giant were saying, "I dare you to send someone over here!" At that moment, I knew I had a choice. Would I trust God and his power to meet the challenge of missionary service in that outpost? In my journal I recorded my "yes" response, and that began my adventure of cross-cultural ministry.

Some seventeen years ago, I started recording my thoughts and prayers while I was studying the Bible. At that time my daughter, who is an artist, presented me with a lovely-decorated journal and encouraged me to write daily. In that first journal's flyleaf she quoted Cecil Day Lewis, who said, "We write not to be understood, but to understand."

This has been my theme over the years. I've started almost every day now by reflecting on the previous day in my journals. Often I am rejoicing in what God is showing me, repenting for past sins, recording my hurts and wounds, or rehearsing my longings and deep desires before the Lord. I simply cannot imagine a day that doesn't begin with a cup of coffee, my Bible, and my journal. Once a year I look back over my journal entries and note themes. God has used this practice to help me clarify goals and identify aspirations.

Over the years of our missionary career, I have found the habit of journaling to be a secret and sacred place of "re-collection" and "re-creation" for me. When I am confused, harried, frustrated, or hurting, I find that writing my thoughts provides an outlet for me to come face to face with God and with myself. Through the mirror of my journal, though at times like in a glass darkly, I find that reflective space that helps me authentically follow Jesus.

Greg
global servant in Iceland

Reflection
The Ancient Pathway toward Trust

Otto Adolf Eichmann was a prominent member of the Nazi government and was responsible for the deaths of millions of Jews during World War II.[80] Eichmann was captured and tried for war crimes in 1960. He was described as a man obsessed with a dangerous and insatiable urge to kill. Yet, in her reflections of the trial, journalist Hannah Arendt made some remarkable observations. Among other things, she concluded that the horrendous evil for which Eichmann was responsible was the product of his inability to engage in critical thinking. The key was Eichmann's mindlessness, or as Arendt put it, "sheer thoughtlessness . . . extraordinary shallowness . . . authentic inability to think."[81]

Arendt asks a critical question: "Could the activity of thinking as such, the habit of examining and reflecting upon whatever happens to come to pass, regardless of the specific content and quite independent of results, could this activity be of such a nature that it conditions men against evil-doing?"[82]

If Arendt is correct, and our minds are shaped to keep evil at bay through the gift of reflection, then we need to pay attention to paying attention!

Without reflection, we lose the ability to see God at work in our lives. Without reflection, we lose perspective in regard to our lives and ministries. Without reflection, we lose the awareness that God is with us and not against us. Without reflection, we lose the sense of joyful delight that each day should bring.

"These things I remember as I pour out my soul: how I used to go to the house of God under the protection of the Mighty One with shouts of joy and praise among the festive throng" (Ps 42:4).

Reflection and Honest Self-Examination

One of the criticisms against reflection is that self-reflection easily becomes too self-indulgent. In other words, reflection causes us to be too self-focused rather than other-focused. Critics often site Jeremiah 17:1–9, which states that the heart is deceitful, and therefore incapable of telling us the truth about ourselves.

---

80 Story as told by John Swinton, *Raging with Compassion: Pastoral Responses to the Problem of Evil* (Grand Rapids: Eerdmans, 2007), 181–83.
81 Hannah Arendt, *Eichmann in Jerusalem: A Report on the Banality of Evil* (New York: Penguin, 1994), 4.
82 Arendt, 4.

There is, of course, truth in the warning of Jeremiah. But the context of the whole chapter shows that the prophet is not condemning reflection per se.

> *"Blessed is the man who trusts in the Lord, whose confidence is in him. He will be like a tree planted by the water that sends out its roots by the stream. It does not fear when heat comes; its leaves are always green. It has no worries in a year of drought and never fails to bear fruit."*
>
> *The heart is deceitful above all things and beyond cure. Who can understand it? "I the Lord search the heart and examine the mind, to reward a man according to his conduct, according to what his deeds deserve." —Jeremiah 17:7–10*

Jeremiah calls us to be people who trust in the Lord, even in hard times. Yes, the heart is deceitful; but since God searches the heart, we can rely upon his examination. The problem therefore is not self-examination, but rather self-examination apart from the Lord. Psalm 139 confirms this by declaring that God knows the human self and understands what makes us tick at our deepest levels. Paul also teaches that life in the Spirit brings greater clarity and assurance because the Spirit helps us understand ourselves (Rom 8:26–27).

The parable of the prodigal son (Luke 15:11–32) illustrates the danger of reflection apart from God. The eldest son in the story represents the nominal Christian who has an inflated sense of self. He justifies himself by his own measurements, and hence neglects God's examination (vv. 31–32). However, the youngest son also characterizes a wrong approach to self-examination. He represents the fearful or nervous person who has a deflated sense of self. He is full of self-contempt and criticism (v. 21). The older son is embittered, but he shouldn't be because God will give him his due. The younger son believes he is rejected, yet God still proclaims his sonship. This parable tells us that whether we evaluate ourselves too highly or too lowly, what matters is God's perspective of who we are.

Jesus and Reflection

Jesus was a supremely reflective person.[83] He trusted the Father and often reflected upon where he saw God working. He affirmed God's presence and plans for his life (John 5:17).

Jesus' justification for everything he did was based upon his close relationship with the Father. He was a reflective person, but he was anything but passive. When he pulled away to a solitary place, he pulled away to pray. When he spoke to the moment, he did so out of his own heart reflections. When he prayed the Psalms, he showed he had deeply ingested them. Jesus shows us that true reflection leads to some form of action.

I recently had a conversation with a missionary who was overwhelmed in his work. He used the word *burdened* to describe how he was feeling. *Burdened*

---

83 See examples in Matt 4:1–11; 6:25–26; 9:4–5; 12:38–45; 13:31–32; 16:13–28; Mark 1:29–34; 3:1–7; 4:1–20; 6:4–6; 9:9–13; Luke 4:1–13, 42; 7:36–50; 10:25–42; 15:1–32; 18:40–41; 19:29–44: John 1:38; 5:6; 6:22–56; 8:1–11; 10:1–30; 13:1–17; 38; 18:34; 21:15–18.

Reflection

is the perfect word to describe what happens when we are so busy with our ministries that we end up ignoring, or at least not reflecting on, our union with God. Without periodic reflection, our work can become burdensome because we lose the perspective that God is with us and upholding us in our ministry.

Throughout the history of the church there have been many spiritual teachers who have emphasized the need for finding God in the middle of everyday life. Brother Lawrence, in his seventeenth-century book, *The Practice of the Presence of God*, wrote, "The most holy and necessary practice in our spiritual life is the presence of God."[84] Jean-Pierre de Caussade, a French Jesuit priest, emphasized the "sacrament of the present moment."[85] Thomas Kelly, an American Quaker, wrote about the "continual awareness of God in the soul."[86] Frank Laubach, a well-known Wycliffe missionary in the Philippines, wrote in 1930,

> *I feel simply carried along each hour, doing my part in a plan which is far beyond myself. This sense of cooperation with God in little things is what so astonishes me, for I never have felt it this way before. I need something, and turn around and find it waiting for me. I must work, to be sure, but there is God working along with me.*[87]

Staying in tune with Christ requires daily reflective attentiveness. If we are to become active reflectors, it is helpful to remember the saying: "Attend and intend." *Attend* considers the reflective side of things, and *intend* considers the action and purpose side of things. We act, but only after listening to God and attending to where and when he wants us to.

The Puritans called this process "preview and review."[88] They began their day by previewing in the Bible, journaling, and examining their calendar, while they focused on the day ahead and inviting and surrendering to Jesus for what was to come. Reviewing happened when they spent an equal amount of time at the end of the day, noting highlights and disappointments. Then they prayed over situations and relationships that might require further follow-up and action.[89]

Ways to Reflect:
The Lord's Table, Gratitude, and Journaling

Three spiritual practices especially help us to remember and reflect upon God's workings in our lives: celebrating the Eucharist, the practice of gratitude, and active journaling.

---

84 Brother Lawrence, *The Practice of the Presence of God* (New Kensington, PA: Whitaker House, 1982), 59.

85 Jean-Pierre de Caussade, *Abandonment to Divine Providence*, trans. John Beevers (New York: Doubleday, 1975), 16.

86 Thomas R. Kelly, *A Testament of Devotion* (New York: Harper Collins, 1941).

87 Frank Laubach, *Practicing His Presence* (Goleta, CA: Christian Books, 1976), 5.

88 Michael J. Sheeran, *Beyond Majority Rule: Voteless Decisions in the Religious Society of Friends* (Philadelphia: Philadelphia Meeting of Religious Society of Friends, 1983), 91–92.

89 Sheeran, 91–21.

The Lord's Table

The most important reflection we can do is to reflect upon the grace of our Lord. In instituting the Lord's Supper, Jesus calls us to "do this in remembrance of me" (Luke 22:19). Taking communion is a holy communal discipline.

This can be challenging for global servants who work in pioneering fields where there is often no one else to share the Lord's Table with. I still recommend that these pioneers practice communion, even if it is only with their family. When we partake of the Lord's Table, we are called to reflect on our past, present, and future life before God:

Past: Who we were without Christ: Sinners, lost and in need of a Savior.

Present: Who we are in Christ: Redeemed, by the gift of grace through faith and our confession of sin.

Future: Who we will be because of Christ: We proclaim Jesus' coming again and our reigning with him in glory.

By remembering at the Lord's Table all that Christ has done for us, we restore and strengthen our lives before the Father and prepare our hearts for service to come.

Gratitude

A second way we can become more reflective is through gratitude. One of the key graces in life is to have a thankful heart. Paul tells us to pray "with thanksgiving" (Phil 4:6) and to "give thanks in all circumstances" (1 Thess 5:18). Giving thanks is a means of cultivating a healthy heart, one that is close to God. We grow and train our hearts when we foster a lifestyle of gratitude for all that has been given to us.

Henri Nouwen wrote that there are really only two ways to keep the heart from becoming bitter through the betrayals of life. One is to embrace whatever is beautiful in the pain, and the other is to cultivate a heart of gratitude.

> *Gratitude in its deepest sense means to live life as a gift to be received thankfully. And true gratitude embraces all of life: the good and the bad, the joyful and the painful, the holy and the not-so-holy. We do this because we become aware of God's life, God's presence in the middle of all that happens.*[90]

Whether God's presence moves us toward gratitude or gratitude moves us toward seeing God, gratitude gives us a holy perspective in handling all that life brings. But living gratefully doesn't always come naturally or easily. It requires practice. When we practice gratitude, we know that even in hard times we can celebrate, because the pruning that is happening is not punishment but preparation (John 15:1–5). "Everything is grace."[91]

One way to do this is to keep a gratitude journey, and at the end of every day record events, people, moments, thoughts which you can thank God for.

---

[90] Henri Nouwen, *Turn My Mourning into Dancing: Finding Hope in Hard Times* (Nashville: W Publishing Group, 2001), 17.

[91] Nouwen, 19.

It is amazing how quickly such a journal fills up when we seriously look for things for which to give thanks. When we are deeply rooted in Jesus Christ, we overflow with gratefulness. We are drawn into a deeper understanding of all that God has done for us in Christ, and we rejoice with gratefulness for the goodness of God.

Remember, remember, remember . . . Don't forget to remember . . . and to give thanks!

Journaling

Recording our experiences with God helps us to remember. As global servants, our lives are full and busy. We seem to go from event to event in our daily lives. It is hard for us to keep track of everything we do, see, and hear. How many of us have had the experience of visiting one of our supporting churches only to forget names of people who not only know us well but have been faithfully praying for us while we have been gone?

While very embarrassing, forgetting is normal. Journaling helps us remember not just the things we do and the people we meet, but also how we feel about our experiences. It helps us remember where and how God was speaking into our busy lives.

Many well-known Christians—Susan Wesley, George Fox, and David Brainerd, to name just a few—journaled in their diaries. As we enter into this reflective space by writing down our thoughts, experiences, and questions, God uses our words to remind us of something he did or something he is saying, which in turn speaks to us in our present moment. Without this record of God's faithfulness, we often forget exactly how God has led us in the past, and so easily miss how God is leading us now. Simply rereading in our journals God's faithful promise-keeping, reminds us that He is able to help us in our needs now as well.

If journaling just isn't something you find comfortable or easy to do, there are other ways to accomplish the same purpose. Consider blogging by keeping a running commentary on your life (remember, though, that anything posted on the Internet is public for anyone to see). Maybe photographing key moments, people, or experiences might work for you. Some find making crafts that symbolize key markers between them and God to be helpful. I know a global servant in Asia who makes beaded bracelets and necklaces occasionally with each bead representing a God-moment in her life. Collaging is also a wonderful way of using different areas of your brain to recall events and emotions. Whatever you find useful, be proactive and adventurous. You can have fun doing this. Just remember that whatever you do should be private and honest, done repeatedly within your ordinary and daily routine.

Through the safeguards of Scripture and our prayers, we can confidently reflect upon the way God is working in our lives. Action without reflection is meaningless action. If we go through our days without sensing the need to reflect on what we've observed, experienced, felt, or heard we miss the rich connection we can have with the Lord. The discipline of reflection exposes all of this in a healthy, life-giving way.

Through the ancient pathway of reflection, we learn the significance of God's workings in our lives and we begin to see with greater clarity how his grace, power, presence, and blessing are woven throughout each new day. We become people who understand the times and can minister out of the understanding of God's leading.[92] God is at work in every relationship and every experience. As we keep our eyes and ears open to his handiwork in our midst, we can't help but celebrate his divine intervention.

Reflection and Points to Ponder

- If you live a very full and busy life, with very little time for pausing, when and how do you intentionally reflect on what is happening in your life and ministry? How can you begin to practice intentional reflection and better incorporate it into your life?

- For whom or what can you pause and give thanks for today? In what ways do you sense God's invitation to become more attentive to remembering and giving thanks for his many blessings?

- Practice reflecting on and remembering your life by mapping out the lifespan of your walk with God. How did each year or decade of life bring you closer to God? What events or experiences affected or continue to affect your choices and decisions? Where did you most see God at work?

- Do a personal study of Scripture passages that address the value of reflection. Perhaps list verses that speak of remembering. What principles and applications can you draw for the discipline of reflection?

---

92 See 1 Chronicles 12:32.

For Further Reading

Keith R. Anderson, *A Spirituality of Listening: Living What We Hear* (Downers Grove, IL: IVP, 2016). A guide to developing your listening skills before God and in the world.

Leighton Ford, *The Attentive Life* (Downers Grove, IL: IVP, 2008). Using the framework of daily fixed-hour prayers, Ford draws us into a conversation about paying attention to life around us.

Adam S. McHugh, *The Listening Life: Embracing Attentiveness in a World of Distraction* (Downers Grove, IL: IVP, 2015). A call to become better listeners.

Henri J. Nouwen, *The Way of the Heart* (New York: Ballantine Books, 1981). Nouwen's meditations on silence, solitude, and prayer.

Parker J. Palmer, *Let Your Life Speak: Listening to the Voice of Vocation* (San Francisco: Jossey-Bass, 2000). A Quaker educator shares how to better listen to your vocational calling in order to grow in your trust in God.

I first heard the term "Rule of Life" from a friend.

At this time in my spiritual life that sounded like the least helpful solution to my ministry doldrums. My wife and I were planting a growing church, raising two young children, and trying to keep up with supporters a continent away. I was prayerless, even though I believed in prayer in the technical sense. I was reading the Scriptures only to prepare for the next teaching assignment or to find out how certain accounts were worded grammatically in the language I was learning.

I wanted to disciple and teach the men and women God was bringing to faith, but I didn't seem to be growing myself. I wanted to be a servant of Christ who had given my life's "attention to prayer and the ministry of the word" (Acts 6:4—my life verse), but I felt like I was drowning in a sea of busy activity for Christ. "How, I asked myself, could such an ancient Rule help me and be an aid to my parched spirit?"

I told my friend that I would look into what he told me about, but I didn't tell him that I was really planning to just look at it a little and then cast it aside. But I was in for a surprise; before the month was out I had my very own Rule, which has now guided me through the more than twenty years since that moment.

Looking back, I realize that I had a Rule of Life that was really no Rule at all. I was, in essence, trying to coast without the cost of trying to form my life's practices to be what I aspired to be, that which I truly believe I wanted to be. Many will have their own version of a Rule as well, even if we're not often proud of what that is. From one who has walked this path and seen the transforming power that living intentionally by a Rule can have, let us prayerfully consider how the discussion that follows can help us shape our lives toward what God has called us to be.

David
global servant in France

Rule of Life
The Ancient Pathway toward Intentionality

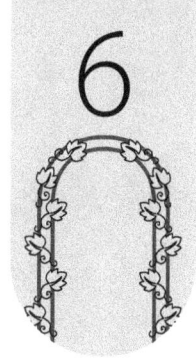

One day many years ago, when we were living in Belgrade, I met with my visiting field supervisor to discuss some ministry plans. We decided we needed to meet again at some future point to follow up on our discussion. He took out his Day-Timer (this was well before the days of digital devices) and said, "Well, I'm not sure when I can make it back here. I'm all booked up." I mentioned a time well into the future, and he replied, "Well, you misunderstand, I'm all booked up for the next year!" I looked over at his Day-Timer and saw that not only was he completely full for the next year, but that he had committed to something virtually every hour for the next 365 days!

Some might feel this showed how important he was. But in reality, I think it revealed bad time management, because he had no allowance for God's interruptions. Instead of controlling his schedule, he was controlled *by it*. We probably all know someone who is like this. Most mission cultures tend to think that being busy is good. However, without understanding the importance of intentionality and creating space in our lives, we reduce our ability to reflect God's glory and purposes in everything we are and do. A Rule of Life is an ancient pathway we can use to recapture time, space, and intentionality.

What Is a Rule of Life?

A Rule of Life is a commitment to live your life in an intentional and certain way. It moves us toward better congruence between our intentions, thoughts, words, and behaviors. It is intended to help us attain and maintain structure to facilitate our whole lives: physical, relational, emotional, psychological, and spiritual. As we develop our Rule, we bring all these aspects of our life into a unified and balanced center before God.

The word *rule* comes from the Latin *regula,* from which we get the word *regulation*, and *regula* comes from the Greek word for trellis. A trellis is a framed structure designed to enable grapevines to get off the ground and grow upwards to be more fruitful. What a good analogy to help us understand what a Rule of Life is. A Rule of Life is a structure which helps us become even more fruitful in all we are and do.

However, these rules are not meant to be a form of legalism. We follow them as long as they are beneficial. We have full liberty to make changes or abandon them entirely when we believe they have failed in their purposes or when we have outgrown their usefulness. We don't need to see a Rule in a negative light. A Rule of Life brings focus and builds positively toward a lifelong habit of personal development.

And even though our Rule is personal, it is not private, because we live in a network of human relationships such as spouse, parent, extended family member, neighbor, coworker, church member, and friend. Even if intended solely for oneself, they do flow outwardly and impact everyone with whom we come into relationship. Therefore, all practices included in our Rule are based upon being active members in all our communities.

Saint Benedict

Benedict of Nursia (AD 480–547) founded the world-famous monastery at Monte Cassino in Italy, which was destroyed during World War II. He wrote what we now call *The Rule of Saint Benedict* (RB) for the purpose of helping the monks under his authority to live in godly community.[93] Benedictine spirituality grew out of these writings. This spiritual core has served as an inspiration to Christians for fifteen centuries and is the seedbed for developing a Rule of Life.

Saint Benedict developed Monte Cassino community's Rule of Life around AD 540, which he called "Little Rule for Beginners."[94] His opening words were "Listen carefully, my children, to the master's instructions and attend to them with the ear of your heart."[95] How interesting that Saint Benedict opened his Rule with the word *listen* and that he connects listening to the heart and not to the ear. He believed God's voice can be heard when both our minds and our ears are open to listening to how God speaks to ourselves, others, and our world. God speaks to the ear of the heart.

This is exactly what Jesus was saying when he shared the meaning of the parable of the sower. Jesus said, "Listen then to what the parable of the sower means: When anyone hears the message about the kingdom and does not understand it, the evil one comes and snatches away what was sown in his heart" (Matt 13:18–19). Jesus is connecting listening with the heart and is concerned about our applying what we see and hear from the Word of God into our lives. This kind of listening is the key to Saint Benedict's whole spiritual teaching. Above all else a Christian is to be a listener, inclining the ear to the heart.

The words we listen to in Saint Benedict's Rule are sensible, sturdy, and simple, yet they are sometimes difficult to hear. They are a plan for living with others in an intentional way. They teach us how to remain tender in a tough world. Here are some of the areas Saint Benedict's Rule explores: listening, prayer, work, stability,

---

93 *The Rule of Saint Benedict,* ed. Timothy Fry (New York: Random House Vintage Press reprint, 1998).
94 Benedict, xxix.
95 Benedict, Prologue: 1.

chastity, hospitality, humility, service, learning, reverence, possessions, responsibility, balance, conflict, friendship, leadership, community, perseverance, celebration, joy, authenticity, Lectio Divina, spiritual discipline, obedience, spoken words, pleasure, and time.

Saint Benedict's Rule is a time-tested pattern for living well with others. His teachings became a standard text and served as the foundational document for community life in monasteries for the next fifteen hundred years. Men flocked to monasteries and women to convents, inspired by the ordered lifestyles the Rule gave to them in their chaotic worlds. These men and women were real people, just like you and me, practicing what Saint Benedict taught, "The first step of humility, then, is that we keep the fear of God always before our eyes and never forget it."[96]

How to Create a Rule of Life

Even though we don't often articulate it, our lives are already full of rules: habits and patterns we keep and maintain. From "brush your teeth after every meal" to Sunday morning worship attendance, we all follow some Rules of Life every day, week, month, and year. So at a foundational level, the question we ask ourselves is not whether we should keep a Rule, but rather what Rule do we keep? How do we go about deciding to craft a Rule of Life for oneself?

Stephen Macchia, author of *Crafting a Rule of Life*, defines a personal Rule of Life this way: "Your personal rule of life is a holistic description of the Spirit-empowered rhythms and relationships that create, redeem, sustain, and transform the life God invites you to humbly fulfill for Christ's glory."[97]

Macchia lists several key ingredients which should make up one's Rule. We explore these areas to determine how we want to engage with and live them out through the Spirit's empowerment. He catalogues them into a threefold process of framing, forming, and fulfilling your Rule:

Framing your Rule of Life
- Roles: What are my primary relationships?
- Gifts: What are my God-given gifts, talents, and temperament?
- Desires: What are my deepest longings and core values?
- Vision: What is the intentional passion God has planted in me?
- Mission: What am I currently doing to pursue my vision?

Forming your Rule of Life
- Time: Spiritual priorities
- Trust: Relational priorities
- Temple: Physical priorities
- Treasure: Financial priorities
- Talent: Missional priorities

---
96 Benedict, 7:10.
97 Stephen A. Macchia, *Crafting a Rule of Life* (Downers Grove, IL: IVP, 2012), 14.

Fulfilling your Rule of Life
- Commitment to the body of Christ
- Context of a spiritual community[98]

In each area we mindfully consider how God made us and what he has called us to do. Based upon these reflections we can then create boundaries in order to maintain our priorities. These boundaries become our Rule of Life and protect our responsibilities of family, work, and personal needs. Remember, this is meant to be a living document which must be tailored to our current life and not held legalistically. It is subject to change as time and situations change. To figure out what your Rule of Life might be, begin by listening and reflecting on what is life-giving and life-draining for you and then work outward into daily patterns and habits. It is important to make sure your life goals are both attainable and realistic for you right now.

Simple examples of a Rule may be as follows: I will pray with my spouse daily. I will Sabbath weekly. I will turn off my smart phone for an hour a day. I will take a vacation every year. I will study my Greek NT for five minutes each day. And so on. Or you may find it more life-giving to follow a more general Rule such as the one I eventually adapted and aspire to: Seek the Lord. Be joyful. Stay humble. Live courageously. Be compassionate. Give thanks. Demonstrate integrity. Be kindhearted. Pray constantly. Have patience. Slow down. Smile often. Love well. Be authentic. Praise God.

It may be helpful to take the time to write out your Rule. Craft your statements in ways that bring out joy in worship, love, and service. Don't be afraid to consult others whom you trust to help guide and develop your Rule. Write it prayerfully, seeking God's direction. And remember, this is *your* Rule; it is not for anyone else. Make it fit your specific values and needs.

Dangers in Creating a Rule of Life

One mistake many of us make when first developing our Rule of Life is to make it too complex. I was guilty of this when I worked on my first attempt at a Rule. I had wanted to thoroughly examine my whole life and include everything I could think of. Therefore, when I had finished writing out my draft I had six main areas to work on with 138 rules to follow! A little too ambitious for my twenty-four-hour day.

Once I was working with a missionary who was all about production and maximizing everything he did. I wondered about his drive to succeed, especially when he came to me because he was dry and had stopped hearing God's voice. We talked a lot about slowing down and letting go, but he had no idea how to do so.

---

[98] Macchia, 7.

As a start, I suggested we develop a Rule of Life that would help him to be structured and intentional but also able to let go, guilt-free. He spent about a month writing out his Rule and then sent me a copy. It was beautiful and very well written, but after I reviewed it more closely and before I talked to him, I wrote on it, "I am tired just reading this!" There was very little life-giving activity in his Rule; it had become a list of dos and shoulds. After talking together my friend expressed relief that he could actually simply his Rule without condemnation fom me!

As you write your own Rule, use these two previous examples as strategies not to repeat. Start small if need be. Work on only one or two areas of your life at a time. Pace yourself. Write out your desires for your life right now and how you think you can move just one step closer to their realization, and then move ahead with small steps. Trying to do too much too soon defeats the purpose of a life-giving Rule and will tire us out and cause us to quit. Remember, we are all in process, so we don't need to do everything all at once and right away.

For global servants, a Rule of Life also addresses one of the most difficult adjustments needed when we arrive on the field—time management. Usually new missionaries have left behind a very busy and active life. When we arrive on the field, unless we are in a formal language-study program, all of a sudden no one is telling us what to do and when and how to do it, nor do we know for sure what to do and when and how to do it. We are basically on our own.

This might sound nice, but it is not so cool. It's easy to sleep in every day, since we hardly slept all night because of the heat and noise of our new environment. It's also easy to stay home and do paperwork rather than to get out into our new and unfamiliar neighborhood. A Rule of Life helps both new and seasoned missionaries alike to balance our tasks and our time with God, so that we are truly rooting ourselves in what we have prioritized. A Rule of Life allows us to lean more fully into all that God wants for us.

Reflection and Points to Ponder

- How do you feel about rules? Do you see them as hindrances to what you want to accomplish in life? How might you reframe your thoughts so that you can see a Rule of Life as something which can be life-giving?

- Reflect upon Jesus' words in John 10:10: "I have come that they may have life, and have it to the full." How might a Rule of Life help you to have an abundant life? How can regular and repeated rhythms help you keep unnecessary distractions away and protect your time with God and others?

- What unspoken rules govern your life right now? How do you determine what you will and won't do? Is there anything you do now that you want to continue? Is there anything that you want to discontinue?

- Regularly examine your life and activities to discern if any changes need to be made to your Rule. Ask yourself where God is drawing you to discover new freedoms and how you can incorporate them more fully into your heart and actions.

For Further Reading

Justin Whitmel Early, *The Common Rule: Habits of Purpose in an Age of Distraction* (Downers Grove, IL: IVP, 2019). Early offers four daily and four weekly habits designed to help us navigate the busy and frazzled days of our work and life.

Timothy Fry, ed. *The Rule of St. Benedict* (New York: Vintage Books, 1998). There are many versions of St. Benedict's Rule; this one is the standard modern version.

Stephen A. Maachia, *Crafting a Rule of Life* (Downers Grove, IL: IVP, 2012). A twelve-step approach to helping you develop your own Rule of Life. This is a great book to explore specific examples of various Rules.

Dennis Okholm, *Monk Habits for Everyday People: Benedictine Spirituality for Protestants* (Grand Rapids: Brazos, 2007). A look at how Benedictine spirituality can enrich the lives and prayer practices of Protestants.

Trish Harrison Warren, *Liturgy of the Ordinary* (Downers Grove, IL: IVP, 2016). How we can learn to practice the presence of God in the overlooked moments and routines of everyday life.

Eight months after our family had abruptly left Africa, I was invited to attend an extended retreat held in the Tennessee countryside. Besides dealing with a serious family health issue and the intensive attention it required, many questions loomed about why—only nine months into our originally planned three-to-five-year field assignment—we had to suddenly leave the field under such difficult circumstances. Had we misheard God? Were we truly called to be missionaries? Why did a calling to serve the global poor, one that was years in developing, come to an end so prematurely?

Arriving at the retreat tired and discouraged, I was confused and struggling to understand how my going to Africa as a missionary hadn't solved my chronic vocational dissatisfaction. I had believed, or at least hoped, that applying my professional skills in service of the international poor in Christ's name would transform more than twenty years of occupational restlessness. It hadn't. Beneath the surface and out of plain view, I was angry at God. "Hadn't we left everything, and literally sold everything we owned, to live for you, God?"

While the opening night of the retreat made it clear to me that God had purposefully invited me to come away with him to the rolling hills of Tennessee, it would take two or three days to truly unplug, quiet my soul, and ready myself to receive what God wanted to say to me.

"Dan, you are my beloved son."

"Let's just be together. Don't worry so much about what you are doing for me. Be with me."

"I'm healing your wounds. I'm gentle."

Over the course of the six-day retreat, my Father allowed me to intimately experience his abundant love. For years I had believed, on the overwhelming evidence of Scripture, that God loved me. But during the multi-day retreat I experienced his deep and abiding love in ways I never had before. Through my participation in a guided rhythm of rest, ancient spiritual practices, and interactions with a small group of fellow retreatants, my weary soul was being renewed and refreshed.

With the companionship of a spiritual director, God reframed my perspective of the events and decisions that had led me to Africa. He graciously showed me how inner wounds, inflicted nearly seven years earlier, had led me to a relentless striving to live my life for God, instead of life with him as he had designed.

Simply stated, the extended retreat created space. Space for God to reveal deeply transformational truths I was unable, even unwilling, to hear due to the hectic, fast-paced, ministry-driven lifestyle I was convinced was necessary to serve him. And it created space for me to truly and fully experience my Father's love for a beloved son.

Dan
global servant in Africa

Sabbath and Retreat
The Ancient Pathways to Rest

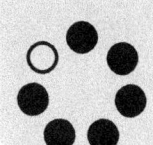

Dr. Thomas Hale, a medical missionary to Nepal, writes, "There is an extra stress involved in constant cross-cultural living, and people need periodic relief from that stress. It's normal and often unconscious stress, but it can build up if we are not careful to pace ourselves, to provide for an outlet, a change, a rest."[99]

Many missionaries react negatively to the idea of rest. We don't go to the field to rest. A mission leader once told me that he would rather have a missionary burn out than rust out. According to this perspective, we are to run ourselves into the ground for the sake of the gospel. Unfortunately, we often find ourselves doing exactly this. We work and we work, without any break, until we burn out, sometimes leaving the field and our ministry prematurely and in a broken condition.

But this isn't what God intends for global servants. God knows we aren't infinite beings. In fact, he has ordained our need for physical and spiritual refreshment. We need time and space to rest. Two spiritual practices which foster this rest are "Sabbath" and "retreat." Each of these practices, while different in their focus, provide rest for our bodies, our minds, and our souls.

God's Word reveals a significant perspective about life, a perspective that centers on the importance of time over the material (space). "The meaning of the Sabbath is to celebrate time rather than space. Six days a week we live under the tyranny of space; on the Sabbath we try to become attuned to the holiness of time."[100] For most global servants, our holy days are often anything but restful, sanctifying, or holy. They are workdays—full of ministry and activity, of people, of coming and going.

Sabbath: Slowing Down or Laziness?

In North American culture, slowing down has a bad connotation. Look at some of the words and phrases Webster's online dictionary uses to define the adjective *slow*: mentally dull; stupid; lacking in readiness, promptness, or willingness; lacking in life, animation, or gaiety. We live in a hyped-up, faster-is-better, turbocharged world. Speed and busyness measure our level of importance. It's easy to feel the pressure to always be active and doing things. Because of this, it's also easy to equate slowing down with laziness. But is this really the case?

---

99 Thomas Hale, *On Being a Missionary* (Pasadena, CA: William Carey Library, 1995), 147.
100 Abraham Joshua Heschel, *The Sabbath: It's Meaning for Modern Man* (New York: Farrar, Straus and Giroux, 1951), 10.

Our soul, by its very nature, is generally slow. We need to slow down in order to connect with ourselves and with God. No matter how hard we may try, we cannot accelerate spiritual growth. The psalmist says, "Be still, and know that I am God" (Ps 46:10). Life requires a pause now and then—a Sabbath moment—to assess where we are going, when we will get there, and, most importantly, why we want to be there. But slowing and Sabbath do not mean we stop living, only that we are being called to live more deeply and in tune with our creator. Laziness happens when we stop pursuing our spiritual growth, not when we slow down to rest and renew with our soul.

So how do we slow down to practice Sabbath in ways that draw us into a deeper life? Marva Dawn, in her excellent book *Keeping the Sabbath Wholly*, mentions four practices which describe how we are to keep the Sabbath: ceasing, resting, embracing, and feasting.[101]

Sabbath: Ceasing

Sabbath originally came from the Hebrew verb *shabbat*, which primarily means "to cease or desist." Genesis 2:2 literally says that God "ceased" on the seventh day. If Sabbath at its core means to cease, that begs the question: What are we to cease from? We cease from the need to accomplish and to be productive. We cease from the worry and tension that our need for efficiency brings. We cease from our efforts to be in control of our world as if we were God. We cease from the possessiveness and materialism that tempts us to acquire more and better things. But primarily we cease from our ministry, our work, and all the things we come to rely on through them.[102]

The Lord, through Moses, commanded his people, "There are six days when you may work, but the seventh day is a Sabbath of rest, a day of sacred assembly. You are not to do any work; wherever you live, it is a Sabbath to the LORD" (Lev 23:3).[103] Notice that the text says "wherever you live." Busy missionaries on foreign fields have no excuses to ignore Sabbath because they feel the situation is different for them. Wherever we are, we need to observe the Sabbath.

A second observation from this verse is that the day is a Sabbath "to the Lord." We cease from work in order to honor our Lord, especially as we gather together in our churches. We assemble to honor God together as a community. God desires that we set apart a whole day to honor him in a sacred assembly by ceasing to work and by worshipping his name and what He has done. For many global servants, due to the nature of our work, it is not always possible to practice the Sabbath during our day of worship. This is OK, and another day may be needed. Rather than the specific day that we remember the Sabbath, what is most important is creating a weekly rhythm of ceasing from work.

Sabbath might be more meaningful when it is practiced as the ancient Hebrews did, by starting it not on the morning of the Sabbath day, but on the

---

101 The following is adapted from Marva J. Dawn, *Keeping the Sabbath Wholly* (Grand Rapids: Eerdmans, 1989).

102 Dawn, 5–16.

103 There is a disagreement in the Church as to the extent of the OT law for Christians. But Jesus affirms Sabbath-keeping, even if he disagrees with the Pharisee's interpretation of the Sabbath in the OT law. (See Matt 12:1-8).

evening before. Running Sabbath from evening to evening has several benefits. First, it enables us to put aside activities of the week and relax the evening before the Sabbath. Most people can't just rush into rest; they need preparation. By starting Sabbath in the evening, we give our hearts time to prepare. Second, it enables us to go to bed with joyful celebration and anticipation. And a night of restful sleep goes a long way toward restoring the soul.

As our children grew older, we decided to celebrate Sabbath on Saturday evenings. We would light two candles to represent the two traditional purposes of Sabbath: "remember" and "observe" (since the Exodus account of the Sabbath commandment says *remember* and the Deuteronomic says *observe*). While lighting the candles I would pray the traditional greeting of the Kiddush: "Blessed art Thou, O Lord our God, King of the Universe, who has sanctified us by your commandments and commanded us to kindle the Sabbath lights."[104] This gave us a marked and decisive time to stop and enter into Sabbath. Then we had our family pizza and movie night. Debbie made the pizza and the kids would choose a movie we all could watch together.

The next day was spent at church in the morning and naps, play, and family and friends in the afternoon. When Sunday evening came, we would close Sabbath with the Havdalah or farewell prayer which included thanking God for the gift of the time spent with Him, ending the prayer with the words: "Blessed are you, O Lord our God, King of the Universe, that you have commanded us to observe the Sabbath day and to keep it holy."[105] These bookend prayers provided a sense of purpose for our time together.

Sabbath: Resting

In addition to ceasing from work on the Sabbath, we are also commanded to rest. Faith missionaries, supported financially by others, may fear that supporters might stop supporting them if they aren't busy all the time. *"What would my supporters think if they knew I was resting and not working? Would they cut off my funding?"* Sound familiar? These unspoken but real fears can make us reluctant to take time off.

For some, a further complication is the struggle of knowing *how* to rest. For so many global servants, their lives seem to compete against the very idea of rest. Coming from a North American context where rest is equated with leisure undertakings (sports, movies, and hiking, for example), some workers may not have similar outlets on the field—or if they do, their limited funds might make it impossible to enjoy such activities. And those who work among the poor might feel guilty enjoying something that the people they minister to cannot do.

---

[104] Cyrus Adler and Lewis N. Dembitz, "Kiddush," in the *Jewish Encyclopedia*, 1906 edition, http://www.jewishencyclopedia.com/articles/9307-kiddush.

[105] Traditional Havdalah, or farewell prayer.

External rhythms like Sabbath, vacations, and holidays are spaces bestowed to us for rest. But when we are unrestful in our hearts, it's difficult to find peace even when we make time to do so. Relaxing can also feel like a waste of God's time, because everything seems to ride on our shoulders. When we take time off, the work doesn't; and when we come back it is waiting, compounded by the time away. This pressure and the tendency to draw our identities from our ministries means we might never rest. But this is problematic, because ignoring rest has both a physical and a spiritual cost.

Sabbath figures prominently in John Calvin's theology.[106] For Calvin, Sabbath rest means soul rest by contemplating God's mighty works of nature. He challenges us to simply lift our eyes up to the night stars and image the majesty of God. Not much of contemporary life is spent looking up. Ashley Cocksworth reminds us that when we look up,

> *We inhabit a different posture. Much of life is spent looking down; not so much at the "devices and desires of our own hearts," as the Book of Common Prayer has it, as the devices in our hands; at smartphones and tablets. Setting aside time at Sabbath ... means resting not only from "total work" but also from the devices that distract our eyes from the sky.*[107]

Sabbath rest is all-inclusive. It touches every area of our lives: spiritual, physical, emotional, intellectual, and social. We rest not only for our bodies but for our souls as well, by resting utterly in the grace of God. Taking Sabbath rest every week teaches us that God is for us and that he is what we need. Martin Luther wrote, "The spiritual rest which God especially intends in this commandment is that we not only cease from our labor and trade but much more—that we let God alone work in us and that in all our powers we do nothing of our own."[108]

What habits help us rest more completely in God's grace? This is a very subjective question, but activities such as being in nature; enjoying beauty, such as artwork; taking in the smell and taste of a wonderful meal; a long, hot bath; hugging loved ones; napping; fasting from electronics; playing music; or getting fun exercise are all great examples of ways to rest. The options are endless. The idea is to slow down and let time be your friend. Enjoy the people around you without an agenda, without a need to compete or accomplish anything. Try to cultivate joy in all things and let go of things that stress you out. Just be.

---

106 John Calvin, *Institutes of the Christian Religion*, ed. John T. McNeill, trans. Ford Lewis Battles, Library of Christian Classics (Philadelphia: Westminster, 1960), 394–401.

107 Ashley Cocksworth, "Sabbatical Contemplation?" in *Embracing Contemplation: Reclaiming a Christian Spiritual Practice,* ed. John H. Cole and Kyle C. Strobel (Downers Grove, IL: IVP, 2019), 90.

108 Martin Luther, "Treatise on Good Works," in *The Christians in Society I*, trans. W. A. Lambert, rev. James Atkinson, vol. 44 of *Luther's Works*, gen. ed. Helmut T. Lehmann (Philadelphia: Fortress, 1966), 72.

Sabbath: Embracing

The third area that Dawn mentions regarding honoring the Sabbath is embracing life.[109] When I grew up, Sabbath (Sunday) generally included *not* doing things like swimming, playing games, or participating in sports. But true Sabbath-keeping embraces life. As Dawn states,

The important point in all our imitation of God is its deliberate intentionality. We don't just think God's values are good. We embrace them wholly.... To embrace is to accept with gusto, to live to the hilt, to choose with extra intentionality and tenacity.[110]

Global servants often host people in their homes, especially on Sundays. For me, one of the great joys in life is having people into our home for a wonderful meal. My wife and I love to invite people over for coffee or brunch, so we have time to enjoy conversation with others. On those occasions I love to go and buy fresh croissants, pastries, or whatever fruit is in season. I love to give people a huge choice of food to simply enjoy. Debbie sometimes argues with me that this might be a waste, which she is absolutely correct about, as only a fraction of the food is eaten. But I like to think of it as a lavish feast presented in honor of those who bless us with their presence in our home. We experience shalom (peace) together, a peace that is all-encompassing, peace with ourselves and with others: health, wealth, fulfillment, satisfaction, contentment, tranquility—in effect, a healthy wholeness of all things.

When we embrace Sabbath shalom, we also embrace our community. There is no doubt that we are better able to give to our community when we minister out of wholeness. Dawn says, "Sabbath keeping is often disparaged as not useful, but we certainly do serve the world better out of wholeness, order, revived spirits, empowered emotions, healthy bodies, renewed minds, authentic relationships, and nurtured senses of ourselves that Sabbath keeping creates."[111]

In Sabbath, we embrace the world around us by not trying to fix it. By getting the rest we need and receiving shalom, we become better able to see what the world needs from us the other six days of the week.

Sabbath: Celebrating and Feasting

Ruth Haley Barton says the only way to truly begin to celebrate Sabbath is to fall in love with it so that "you long for it as you would a lover."[112] Like in our other love relationships, Sabbath brings great joy and happiness. To feast and celebrate Sabbath we first feast on the Word of God. God provides the manna of his Word. When Jesus' disciples urged him to eat something, he said, "I have food to eat that you know nothing about.... My food is to do the will of him who sent me

---

109 Dawn, 98.

110 Dawn, 100.

111 Dawn, 146.

112 Ruth Haley Barton, *Sacred Rhythms: Arranging Our Lives for Spiritual Transformation* (Downers Grove, IL: IVP, 2006), 138.

and to finish his work" (John 4:31–34). We cannot know or do God's will without knowing his Word. Sabbath requires some form of Bible intake.

Second, feasting and celebrating are fun. Am I saying that we can have fun on the Sabbath? Absolutely. Sabbath keeping is not a duty or an oppressive obligation, but a delight—because we delight in God. We can feast with music, beauty, food, parties, games, hospitality, affection, and anticipating Jesus' eventual return.

I find, however, that even in celebrating I still need to honor the day as a day of rest. I am careful to not plan too full a schedule of activities, otherwise this can defeat the whole purpose of Sabbath. Gather some general ideas of what fun and celebration looks like to you, and enjoy celebrating with God without pressure to perform or generate a false sense of joy. If something becomes too much or too burdensome, simply stop. The goal is not to fight through and accomplish. The goal is to enjoy and be free.

I am an amateur painter—with emphasis on *amateur*. I'm not very good, so sometimes painting becomes a chore and hard work. If I'm painting on a Sunday afternoon and I'm bogged down by the effort, I'm defeating the purpose of my Sabbath activity. So when this happens, I stop. In Sabbath feasting, it's better to stop and put things aside for a time than to keep working and fighting through it.

As a busy global servant, taking Sabbath might seem like one thing you can't do. But I believe it is one thing you must do. The weekly practice of Sabbath teaches us that God sustains the world and we are not indispensable. Sabbath keeps us humble and dependent on Jesus, as he calls us to come with him to a quiet place and get some rest (Mark 6:31). Come and Sabbath with Jesus.

Spiritual Retreats: God-Given Fruit

Retreats are opportunities to make space for God by listening and delighting in him for a longer period than just a Sabbath. This is especially important for global servants, because we are on the frontline in the battle for souls. Like warriors who break down when in constant combat, missionaries also need to withdraw to recharge and rest. Fourth-century desert father John Cassian wrote, "If we really desire to enter into spiritual combat . . . human effort will never be able to win here . . . it cannot obtain victory by its own effort unless it is shored up by the help and protection of the Lord."[113] This is what a retreat does for us by periodically letting us retreat from the battle to spend time with God.

Sometimes people think of retreats as a time to gain new skills or knowledge, but this is not what I am referring to here. The early spiritual teachers taught that times of retreat brought God's saints perspective and nourishment which enabled them to reenter the fray with renewed vigor. Adele Ahlberg Calhoun says,

---

113 As quoted in Paul Thigpen, *Saints Who Battled Satan: Seventeen Holy Warriors Who Can Teach You How to Fight the Good Fight and Vanquish Your Ancient Enemy* (Charlotte, NC: TAN Books, 2015), 218.

Rather than going on retreats that slow us down to listen and focus on God alone, we go on "retreats" filled with lectures, late nights, constant activity and interaction with all kinds of people. This sort of retreating is not a bad thing. It is simply not a retreat from the busyness and distractions of life. It is not a time set apart with God alone.[114]

As a new mission leader, my first mentor was a longtime missionary in France. One of the things he urged me to do was to go away periodically by myself, taking nothing with me but my Bible. "Herb," he said, "at first the time is incredibly difficult. You wonder why you are here, and as you wait upon God you hear nothing. But if you persevere God does show up; and while he may or may not answer any of your specific questions, he will always give you what you need at the time." Ever since, I have tried to adapt my mentor's wisdom to my specific circumstances and needs.

Writer Carolyn Weber describes a time as a young mother and university professor when she was so stretched in her life and work that she felt she was facing a nervous breakdown. She confided in an older woman how close she was to giving up. She shares her friend's reaction:

She doesn't laugh, but she doesn't admonish either. Instead, she just leans in closer (a tendency I've come to admire in those of deep faith who interact with others who need to tap into that reservoir). She takes my hands in her beautiful older ones and says my name softly, "O, Caro," like a prayer. I feel the pressure of her wedding band against mine. Then she speaks seven words that have stayed with me ever since. "Even Jesus went out in a boat."[115]

Even Jesus went out in a boat; even he retreated. When Jesus had just fed the five thousand, Mark uses one of his favorite words in his Gospel, "*Immediately* Jesus made his disciples get into the boat and go on ahead of him" (Mark 6:45). In effect, Jesus made his disciples get away from the needs of ministry and retreat for a while. And then Mark says, "After leaving them, [Jesus] went up on a mountainside to pray" (Mark 6:46). Jesus also invites us to retreat with him when he says to his disciples, "Come with me by yourselves to a quiet place and get some rest" (Mark 6:31).

Most of us are not very good at retreating. To pull away from meaningful activities and retreat might sound wonderful for a moment as we contemplate the joy of quiet and rest, but then we start to think, "But what will I do? How can I fill up twenty-four hours, let alone a whole weekend or maybe a week?"

How do we just "be" without "doing"? How do you shape a retreat to make it work for you? Where is the best place to retreat? Answers differ, but most people find that if possible, they prefer to retreat in nature. It is good for our souls to be able to have places to walk or sit, surrounded by quiet and beauty.

I understand this ability to get away into nature is not always available for global servants. Some of us work in urban settings and have little money for travel or lodging. While this may be the case, there are many retreat centers

---

[114] Adele Ahlberg Calhoun, *Spiritual Disciplines Handbook: Practices that Transform Us* (Downers Grove, IL: IVP, 2005), 67.

[115] Carolyn Weber, *Holy Is the Day: Living in the Gift of the Present* (Downers Grove, IL: IVP, 2013), 87.

around the world, and it's possible to find one just about anywhere and for just about any economic situation. But if that isn't possible, clear your calendar and go to another home—maybe of a friend or colleague (you could even house swap)—or stay home, but unplug and hide. The point is to find a way to retreat.

So what do we do when we are alone on retreat? You might find yourself tempted to pack your time with a lot of spiritual activities like reading, journaling, and ministry planning and preparation—or even some recreational fun. Yes, you want to make the most of your time; but if you fill your time up with so much activity, you will lose the purpose of retreat in the first place—to be alone and quiet in the welcoming presence of Jesus. So be careful not to schedule too much. Unscheduled time helps to calm our inner anxieties and slow down our drivenness.

It is also good to have quality time to pray. I find it interesting that many of us missionaries seem to be some of the most rushed pray-ers around. Our prayers are full of words and seem so busy. We seldom just relax and converse with our Father, either with a few words or simple silence. There are many kinds of prayer, but a quiet and resting presence before God is an important element during retreats. If you don't know what to pray for, simply spend time quietly in thanksgiving, or even in silence, as God already knows your heart.

If you find yourself distracted during your time of prayer by worries, or even positive things such as future opportunities, try to let them go. But if they don't go, don't condemn yourself. Simply deal with them the best you can, perhaps by writing down your thoughts so you can address them later; and then try to put them aside for the time being. Sometimes distractions can also be the means of God speaking to you. If this is the case, take a moment to pause and ask God why that particular thing is bothering you and why are you struggling to put it aside. Pause and listen to what God may say to you about it.

One final question: How often should we retreat? This somewhat depends upon our schedule and means. It might also depend upon how long we like to retreat. I prefer quarterly retreats of one to two days each. But others I know plan an extended time of at least one week every year for both heart renewal and for annual planning for the year ahead.

It is possible that when you return from your retreat you may feel that nothing particularly happened. This is normal. I experience this quite regularly. But I often find that the benefits of my time with God become clear once I engage in the battle again. As I resume normal ministry and life, only then can I sense that God has actually done something wonderful, even if I have not noticed it before.

Reflection and Points to Ponder

- If you were to set apart one whole day per week to rest and worship God, what activities would you cease from? Rest from? Embrace? Feast on? What benefits would you expect to gain spiritually, physically, emotionally, relationally, and in regard to your work?
- When you feel empty or restless, how do you fill your heart? What does this tell you about yourself?
- How difficult would it be for you to make space to be alone with God in a retreat setting? What might you do in a personal spiritual retreat?

For Further Reading

Marva J. Dawn, *Keeping the Sabbath Wholly: Ceasing, Resting, Embracing, Feasting* (Grand Rapids: Eerdmans, 1989). A theological and practical guide to celebrating the Sabbath. It brings together both biblical and traditional Jewish practices.

Abraham Joshua Heschel, *The Sabbath: Its Meaning for Modern Man* (New York: Farrer, Straus and Giroux, 1951). A classic work by a great scholar and rabbi. Heschel has written a scholarly yet beautiful series of meditations on the nature of Sabbath and the sanctification of time.

Scot McKnight, *Fasting* (Nashville: Thomas Nelson, 2009). Though not discussed in this chapter, fasting is often practiced alongside Sabbath keeping and retreating. In my opinion, the best book on the subject is McKnight's. He looks at the occasions and purpose of fasting in the Bible; explains how to fast effectively, including different methods of fasting; and speaks to the dangers and problems that can arise when we fast.

James L. Wakefield, *Sacred Listening: Discovering the Spiritual Exercises of Ignatius Loyola* (Grand Rapids: Baker, 2006). A guide through the four one-week retreats of Ignatius' *Spiritual Exercises* from a Protestant perspective.

I feel the heaviness every week when I enter their home. What is that heaviness that makes my heart sad and even my head sleepy? It's a spirit that suppresses truth. But every week these Iraqi women welcome me into their home with kisses and kindness. We work on projects like learning and studying English, and they feed me too much wonderful food.

Last week I was at their house, showing the women pictures from my brother-in-law's recent wedding, and when they found out I sang in the wedding ceremony they wanted me to sing for them. So I sang the song "In Christ Alone." It was wonderful to declare the glory of Christ in that house. As I explained the meaning of the words, it was like a fog went over my friends' eyes, and I could see there was a wall between them and the words about the life Christ offers us. But they are not entirely closed. Before I left, they asked me to pray. I am praying that the veil over their minds would be removed and they would have eyes to see and ears to hear who Christ is.

Ashley
global servant in the Middle East

Spiritual Warfare
The Ancient Pathway to Victory in Christ

8

I well remember my field orientation when I first arrived in Europe as a missionary. My field director said to me, "Herb, you aren't just entering a spiritual battle, you are parachuting behind enemy lines."

Global servants are often surprised at how tangible spiritual forces are on the field. Missiologist Timothy Warner recalls this story:

> *His eyes were glassy, his clothes ragged, his hair matted, and he was desperate. "I'm going to kill this animal," he repeated three times. I thought he was talking about me. The lady of the house gave us all some strong coffee, but he didn't want it. Suddenly he fell on the floor, knocking the dishes off the table. As we dragged him out of the house, he looked up at me and said, "Have mercy on me." Then I recognized his problem. He was demon-possessed. These spells began after he stopped attending an evangelical church and turned to spiritualism.*
>
> *I remember the words of Jesus. "Behold, I give you [authority] over the power of the enemy, and nothing by any means shall hurt you." I felt I should rebuke the demon in the name of Jesus, but what if nothing happened? All the people gathered would ridicule me . . .*
>
> *There I was—a defeated missionary in the interior of Brazil, ready to pack up and go home. When face to face with the enemy, I was afraid.*[116]

The Desert Fathers and Mothers

In the early history of Christianity, some believers went into the quiet, deathly stillness of the desert because they hungered to go deeper with God. Many great teachings came from these desert saints, including their wisdom regarding spiritual warfare.[117]

These desert monks fasted and prayed, and many of them lived in solitary stillness. In their quiet, they faced their deep and dark secrets and reflected on the sinful nature of man and our battle with spiritual forces. They believed spiritual warfare was actually for our own benefit, helping us see God's grace grow within us as we vanquish our prevailing sins and defeat Satan bit by bit.

---

116 Timothy M. Warner, *Spiritual Warfare: Victory over the Powers of This Dark World* (Wheaton, IL: Crossway, 1991), 10.

117 These desert saints, who flourished in the fourth and fifth centuries in Egypt, Syria, and Palestine, were an eccentric and eclectic group. Some of the most influential of these are Anthony of Egypt (c. 250–356), Athanasius (c. 293–373), Evagrius Ponticus (c. 345–99), Basil of Caesarea (c. 330–74), and Benedict of Nursia (c. 480–543).

But this victory of God's grace within us (theosis) over Satan is also more than simply sanctification. As Donald Fairbairn writes, "Theosis . . . was believers' sharing in the warm fellowship that has existed from all eternity between the persons of the Trinity."[118] By sharing in the Son's relationship with the Father and in the love between the persons of the Trinity, we find the greatest weapon in spiritual warfare: a healthy spiritual life grounded in the love of the Trinity.

As the desert saints entered and grew into a deeper love relationship with the Godhead, they realized that their inner struggles became stilled and dissipated. Their lives began to exhibit a deep quietness and peace. The Eastern Orthodox Church named this peace *hesychia,* a kind of inner prayer in which we hear the voice of our Lord through deep trust and inward quiet. Through this process we grow in discernment and increase our ability to distinguish between the voice of Satan, the voice of our sinful self, and the sure presence of God.

Spiritual Conflict

Spiritual warfare addresses our spiritual enemies: the flesh, the world, and the devil. Each one is mentioned in James 4:1–8:

> *What causes fights and quarrels among you? Don't they come from your desires that battle within you? You want something but don't get it. You kill and covet, but you cannot have what you want. You quarrel and fight. You do not have, because you do not ask God. When you ask, you do not receive, because you ask with wrong motives, that you may spend what you get on your pleasures.*
>
> *You adulterous people, don't you know that friendship with the world is hatred toward God? Anyone who chooses to be a friend of the world becomes an enemy of God. Or do you think Scripture says without reason that the spirit he caused to live in us envies intensely? But he gives us more grace. That is why Scripture says:*
>
> *"God opposes the proud but gives grace to the humble."*
>
> *Submit yourselves, then, to God. Resist the devil, and he will flee from you. Come near to God and he will come near to you.*

The Flesh

First, James tells us we battle the evil desires within us. These desires, formed out of our past brokenness and our self image developed to cope with the emotional trauma of early childhood, cause us to sin in thought, word, and deed. This is the deep, dark evil that James calls murder, covetousness, quarreling, and fighting. We could, of course, add many more behaviors, attitudes, and sins to this list.[119]

At the most basic and fundamental level of spiritual warfare, we can't blame anyone but ourselves. We must acknowledge and take responsibility for our sinful choices and actions.

---

118 Donald Fairbairn, *Life in the Trinity: An Introduction to Theology with the Help of the Church Fathers* (Downers Grove, IL: IVP, 2009), 10–11.

119 For example, Gal 5:19–21; 1 Cor 6:9–10; Eph 5:5; Rev 22:15.

Perhaps the best teaching on how to do this comes from Colossians 3, where Paul develops a fourfold approach toward freedom in Christ. First, we are to recognize our identity in Christ (vv. 1–4), which sets us to live in the freedom and truth of who we are. Second, we need to "put to death, therefore, whatever belongs to [our] earthly nature." Paul then lists a multitude of thoughts and behaviors that spring from our sinful nature (vv. 5–9). Third, because we "have put on the new self," we think and behave "as God's chosen people" (vv. 10–14). Finally, we exercise our authority in Christ over our sin and renounce evil (vv. 15–17). We know our lives are "hidden with Christ in God" (v. 3) by experiencing God's peace, Christ's word, the Spirit's worship, and the deep gratitude which resides in our hearts (vv. 15–17).

We are still in transformation and therefore we will still struggle with our flesh until the day of our death or final restoration when Jesus comes again. But thanks be to God, through Jesus we can have victory over our sin!

The World

There is systemic evil in the world. This evil is found in the systems which abuse power—the cultural, political, economic, and even religious systems that make up our society. These abusive systems and the people caught up in them are the manifestations that the apostle John calls "the world"—the things that oppose God and his ordered kingdom:

> *Do not love the world or anything in the world. If anyone loves the world, the love of the Father is not in him. For everything in the world—the cravings of sinful man, the lust of his eyes and the boasting of what he has and does—comes not from the Father but from the world. The world and its desires pass away, but the man who does the will of God lives forever. —1 John 2:15–17*

It is true that all three components of our spiritual battle—the flesh, the world, and the devil—are closely related. Most situations a global servant faces will likely involve some of each element. Timothy Warner explains it this way:

> *The flesh is the earthly qualities about us which enable us to respond to temptation. The world is the milieu in which we live and which is under the control of "the ruler of the kingdom of the air." Satan and his demons know what fleshly parts of us are especially vulnerable, and they use the stimuli of the world around us to arouse sinful thoughts in us. The Devil would be a fool not to try to take advantage of the world and the flesh in his aim to destroy us. One does not have to stretch the Scriptures to see him at work in all these relationships.*[120]

The lure of the world is subtle, and at times we fall under the influence of and value what the world values above God's will. For example, we might find ourselves being drawn to financial success or social status. Now happiness, comfort, wealth, or status are not necessarily wrong in themselves, but they can be major distractions and destructive if pursued above God (Matt 6:24). How easy it is to become occupied by these things and not realize the grip they slowly can take on our lives.

---

120 Warner, 60.

We also may find ourselves being shaped by the world when we complain about what we have given up to serve the Lord. I have known some missionaries who really struggle with the fact they have little materially to show for their life of service. We struggle for years with support raising. We have gone without and now find we are not able to meet escalating costs on and off the mission field. We feel no one knows us well back home, and the honor we receive in our churches is simply two-minute update slots on Sunday mornings. We have fallen into the world's trap of needing significance, fame, and fortune. It's easy at times for these kinds of feelings to take bitter root in our lives. It can happen sometimes before we even realize it.

These feelings might seem natural, but they are a lie from the devil. Jesus understands our struggle: "Foxes have holes and birds of the air have nests, but the Son of Man has no place to lay his head" (Matt 8:20). But Jesus also promises us that "no one who has left home or brothers or sisters or mother or father or children or fields for me and the gospel will fail to receive a hundred times as much in this present age (homes, brothers, sisters, mothers, children and fields—and with them persecutions) and in the age to come, eternal life" (Mark 10:29–30).

As global servants, we need to vigilantly guard our vulnerable hearts from the love of the world. The more our hearts are filled with the love of God, the less attractive the desires of the world become. The Bible reminds us that this world is passing away and only love will remain.[121]

The Devil

Many global servants would readily agree that they have experienced greater demonic intensity on the field than they did in their home culture. C. S. Lewis puts the danger of ignoring or overexposing spiritual forces this way: "There are two equal and opposite errors into which our race can fall about devils. One is to disbelieve in their existence. The other is to believe, and to feel an excessive and unhealthy interest in them."[122]

We must never forget that the struggle against the spiritual powers of darkness is intense and absolutely real, but in Christ we have the victory. It is important to devote ourselves to our spiritual growth because our continued intimacy with the Lord gives us strength and confidence in overcoming our enemy.

There has been much discussion in missionary circles about whether our battles are truth encounters or power encounters.[123] I believe that we do battle in both arenas. We do battle in the arena of truth because the devil is constantly trying to deceive people through lies and falsehoods.[124] Yet the devil also disguises himself through "counterfeit miracles, signs and wonders" (2 Thess 2:9). Power encounters seem to be more prevalent for missionaries on the field. When missionaries (especially those in pioneering work, it seems) lead people from the

---

121 1 John 2:17; 1 Cor 13:13.

122 C. S. Lewis, *The Screwtape Letters* (New York: Signet, 1988 reprint), xix.

123 In truth encounters, we face the demonic through the power of God's truth in the Holy Scriptures. In power encounters, we face the demonic through the power of the Holy Spirit in signs and wonders. See Tormod Engelsviken, *Spiritual Conflict in Today's Mission*, edited by A. Scott Moreau, Lausanne Occasional Paper No. 29 (Monrovia, CA: MARC Pubications, 2002), 59.

124 Luke 4:5–7; 1 Tim 4:1; Rev 12:9.

kingdom of darkness into the kingdom of light they should expect Satan to be present, trying to hinder and disrupt the ministry (Acts 26:18).

We must be prepared to minister in confidence when we face such encounters. Genuine movements of people coming to Christ have started by seeing a person set free from evil forces. Spiritual practitioners from other religions or animism may challenge missionaries to demonstrate their own power. If and when these things happen, global servants need to be able to respond appropriately and not in fear. We must face satanic forces in confidence and strength, and a heart focused on God's love is our greatest and most important weapon as we confront the darkness of Satan.

When we enter into spiritual warfare with demonic forces, we should remind ourselves of two biblical truths. Hebrews 2:14–15 speaks of the first truth: "Since the children have flesh and blood, he too shared in their humanity so that by his death he might destroy him who holds the power of death—that is, the devil—and free those who all their lives were held in slavery by their fear of death." Through Christ's identification with humanity in his incarnation, his crucifixion, and most importantly his resurrection, he has liberated us. This is both an accomplished fact and a continuing process.[125] Unfortunately this means that Satan is still able, for now, to have limited power to do battle. But the good news is that when we claim Christ's victory, even now, he must flee.[126]

The second truth we can claim from Scripture is the fact that spiritual warfare is an activity of the whole church, not just of isolated individuals. In Ephesians 6:10–18—which we refer to as the "whole armor of God" passage—the Greek pronouns translated *you* in our English Bibles are in the plural form. Paul is not addressing the lone warrior, but the whole community of the church. I am so encouraged by the fact that we don't go to battle alone. God's people are meant to work together to defeat the powers of darkness in the world by the preparation of truth and righteousness (v. 14), through feet fitted and ready from the gospel of peace (v. 15), by exercising faith (v. 16), by taking up the helmet of salvation and the sword of God's Word (v. 17), and through fervent prayer (v. 18). This is how God's church stands in strength against demonic forces.

We stand in strength against the enemy when we recognize that he is real and that we will face spiritual opposition. We stand in strength when we learn to appropriate God's protection as we grow in righteousness. We engage in the battle through the victory we have in Christ and as a community of believers. And we will find victory when we utilize God's means of deliverance through truth, faith, and prayer.

Spiritual warfare is not a one-time event or a technique to command spiritual forces. As we continue to grow in Christ, we will see others freed and rescued from "the dominion of darkness" into "the inheritance of the saints in the kingdom of light . . . into the kingdom of the Son he loves" (Col 1:12–13).

---

125 Rom 12:1–3; Eph 4:13–15.
126 1 Pet 5:8–9; Jas 4:7.

Reflection and Points to Ponder

- When have you sensed that you were in spiritual battle? When you hear the term "spiritual warfare," what immediately comes to mind? What is your tendency in an occasion of a "power encounter"—to fight or to flee? How does this tendency affect your appropriation of God's power?

- In which areas of your life do you suspect you may have bought into Satan's lies about your life in general and your ministry in particular?

- Where do you see satanic influence in the "world" in which you live? How can you prepare and stand against widespread and systemic influences?

- Do you assign too much or too little credit to Satan and his demons? What steps can you take to more effectively put on the full armor of God and claim your position in Christ?

- Are there any current openings for the demonic to enter and defeat you in living a holy and fruitful life? What might you do to reclaim your victory in Christ?

For Further Reading

Tormod Engelsviken, "Spiritual Conflict in Today's Mission," *Lausanne Occasional Paper 29*, 2001, ed. A. Scott Moreau, https://www.lausanne.org/content/spiritual-conflict-todays-mission-lop-29. Though a little dated, a still useful overview of spiritual conflict as reflected in church history and our world.

Keith Ferdinando, *The Message of Spiritual Warfare—The Bible Speaks Today* (Downers Grove, IL: IVP, 2016). A comprehensive biblical look at spiritual warfare.

Chip Ingram, *The Invisible War: What Every Believer Needs to Know About Satan, Demons, and Spiritual Warfare* (Grand Rapids: Baker, 2006). A balanced look at the three areas of our spiritual battle: the flesh, the world, and the devil.

As God called us *into missionary service, we were sent to a central African country, where we served for sixteen years. The African people in our country tend to be naturally expressive in all aspects of their lives, and the national believers so simply, yet clearly, brought their culture into their worship with joyous, festive celebrations. Clapping, dancing, and exuberant festivities were very much the norm. Their joy in worship carried over into their daily walk with God, expressing their relationship with him very openly and very clearly.*

Then God moved us to a European-Middle Eastern context, where we served for the next eighteen years. We quickly discovered that the expression of faith in this part of the world was so, so different from what we'd known in Africa. In Western Europe the bent was toward the philosophical, with a more reflective, reserved nature; Eastern Europe was still learning how to worship, but tended toward a stoic, guarded bent; and the Middle East was a melting pot of styles and expressions.

At first the differences in styles were striking, but we slowly came to learn and appreciate that spirituality is not to be judged by one style of worship. Cultures, as well as personal inclinations, have a strong influence on how a person relates to God—whether that be in public worship or in private times with the Father. The way we worship him and relate with him is of no import, however—as long as we recognize him for who he is and adore him in a way that brings him both joy and glory.

John
global servant in Africa, Middle East, and Europe

Different Approaches to God
The Ancient Pathways of Worship

We are distinct and unique individuals, having different personalities, experiences, and ministry giftings. Our walk before God is deeply rich and personal. Since we reflect the creativeness of our Father, it should not be surprising that our different personalities and backgrounds will cause us to gravitate toward different approaches and practices when it comes to spirituality. These tendencies, over time, lead us to band together with other likeminded believers to form spiritualities and rituals that speak profoundly to our own heritage.

Richard Foster uses the metaphor of streams to define our different spiritualities, with Jesus Christ being the wellspring of each.[127] Whatever church tradition we swim in, the headwaters of Jesus are the source which each one of us must come back to, to bathe deeply and refresh ourselves in. As we take the time to see each individual stream as flowing out of Jesus, we also will see how these streams flow together. By swimming in other pools, we might find that a different spirituality touches our own heart and enriches our own spirituality.

We need balance and wholeness in our spiritual life. To pursue spiritual maturity, we need to move out of our comfort zone and explore spiritualities that are opposites of our personal preferences. This might feel strange at first, but it can be a sign of positive change and growth. When we are open to the Spirit's direction, we find a balance and holistic approach that matures us into full Christlikeness.

An extremely helpful guide along this pathway can be found in the writings of Richard Foster.[128] Rather than focus on the three main Christian faith traditions—Roman Catholic, Orthodox, and Protestant—Foster identifies six spiritualities of worship: *the contemplative tradition, the holiness tradition, the charismatic tradition, the social justice tradition, the evangelical tradition, and the incarnational tradition.*

Though we all feel much more comfortable with and identity with one or two streams, we gain more balance when we incorporate at least some aspect of each spirituality into our own religious life.[129] Jesus is the supreme example of

---

127 Richard J. Foster, *Steams of Living Water: Celebrating the Great Traditions of Christian Faith* (San Francisco: Harper, 1998), xv–xvi. Much of the material in this chapter is dependent upon Foster's book.

128 Richard J. Foster. *Streams of Living Water: Celebrating the Great Traditions of the Christian Faith* (San Francisco: Harper, 1998).

129 Foster, 22.

the balanced Christian life, because he exhibited each of these traditions in his own earthly life.[130] Let's take a closer look at these six spiritualities and consider their major strengths and weaknesses.

Contemplative Spirituality[131]

Contemplative spirituality can be defined as a life of faith characterized by interior submission to God through prayer practices guided by the Holy Spirit. Evangelicals sometimes criticize contemplative practices because they believe it dismisses the authority of the Word of God. While some contemplatives are guilty of such abuse, there is nothing in contemplative spirituality itself which requires us to reject the Bible's authority. Jesus practiced contemplative spirituality when he withdrew from the crowds to pray by himself (Mark 1:35).

Contemplative spirituality revolves around a love relationship with God and focuses on prayer and meditation. If you find yourself being drawn more and more into silence and solitude in your prayer life, you are probably more inclined to a contemplative spirituality. If you identify more with Mary than Martha (Luke 10:38–42), you might be a contemplative.

What I love about contemplative spirituality is its priority on seeking God ahead of all things. Phileena Heuertz, former codirector of a mission agency focused on serving the poor in third-world countries, wrote this about her growing experiences of contemplative prayer:

> *I was awakening to a new dimension of faith—where my beliefs in God were no longer simply intellectual ideals, but rather a lived reality. . . . In time by withdrawing a few times a day for contemplative prayer, I realized that solitude was not a distraction from the rest of the world but instead a necessary recalibration for more meaningful connection with the world.*[132]

While contemplative spirituality has found a place among missionaries, we do need to be aware that there is a danger of moving too far into extreme ascetic and isolating practices which devalue community and daily realities. If you find you are isolating yourself more and more from others, and focusing only on your own experience with God, it's possible you may be overly reliant upon contemplation for spiritual nourishment.

Many of the disciplines I am describing in this book come out of this tradition. Silence and solitude, spiritual direction, journaling, retreating, and certain forms of prayer all speak to the contemplative. One of its strengths is its focus on our need to be alone solely with God. Contemplative practices can be of enormous help for the global servant, because they balance our busy lives with the quietness of the moment, allowing us to experience God more directly.

---

130 Foster, 4, 6, 11, 12, 15, 18–19. See John 14:10 (Contemplative); Matt 4:1–11 (Holiness); John 14:16–18 (Charismatic); Luke 4:18–19 (Social Justice); Matt 4:23 (Evangelical); Phil. 2:5–11 (Incarnational).

131 Foster, 22–58.

132 Phileena Heuertz, *Mindful Silence: The Heart Of Christian Contemplation* (Downers Grove, IL: IVP, 2018), 33–34.

Holiness Spirituality[133]

Holiness spirituality focuses on the inward re-formation of the heart through devotion to regular habits such as Bible study, prayer, and church attendance. Some call this spirituality "the virtuous life."[134] The holiness stream has always been part of church history, but its modern form chiefly developed in nineteenth-century Methodism and to a lesser degree in traditions such as Quakerism and Anabaptism. While standing on personal conversion and the inspiration and authority of the Bible, there is typically an emphasis on a second work of grace, leading to Christian perfection.

People who are drawn to a holiness spirituality want to develop good habits of godliness and virtue. If you are attracted to living the virtuous life—living what is good, beautiful, and true—you swim in the holiness stream of Christian spirituality. You don't want so much to get to heaven as to get heaven in you.[135]

I think the great strength of this spirituality is the strong desire to walk the talk, and the congruence between one's heart's desires and God's goodness. You grapple with the down-to-earth realities of sin and the need to train yourself to combat your carnal nature. We can experience confident vivacity when we live out the holiness spirituality.

Probably more than any other spirituality, however, the holiness stream is the spirituality that most missionaries struggle with, because we find it hard to deal with our sins. We can therefore minimize God's grace and embrace legalism, judging ourselves and others too harshly. We put unrealistic standards of conduct upon those we are trying to convert. Legalistic practices can never transform hearts. Scripture tells us it is only through the power of the Holy Spirit that we are transformed (John 3:5–8). A lot of damage has been done in missionary contexts when we have emphasized legalism over the gospel.[136] Yes, each of us is called to be holy (1 Pet 1:15–16) and participate in God's perfecting of our souls (2 Pet 1:4), but this is accomplished only through God's grace, not by our works (Eph 2:8–9).

Charismatic Spirituality[137]

The New Testament Greek word for the gifts of the Holy Spirit, as described in 1 Corinthians 12:7–11 and elsewhere, is *charismata*. If holiness spirituality centers on the power to be, charismatic spirituality centers upon the power to do. Charismatic Christianity is usually identified with Pentecostalism, which composes about a quarter of all global Christians today.[138] If you have a strong

---

133 Foster, 59–96.

134 Foster, 6.

135 Foster, 85.

136 For an example of this see Kathryn T. Long's work on the conversion of the Waorani Indians of Ecuador in her book *God in the Rainforest* (New York: Oxford University Press, 2019).

137 Foster, 97–133.

138 Pew Research Center, "Regional Distribution of Christians," December 19, 2011, https://www.pewforum.org/2011/12/19/global-christianity-regions/.

desire to minister in the power and gifting of the Spirit, you are demonstrating the spirituality of a charismatic.

Jesus lived and moved in the power of the Holy Spirit: through his wisdom teachings (Matt 4:23; 7:29); his ability to see into the very dynamics of good and evil in a person's heart (Matt 5:8; 9:36; 12:25; Luke 9:43; Acts 1:24); and his miraculous healings and miracles (Matt 8:1–4; Mark 1:34; Luke 7:1–10; John 2:1–11). A strength of charismatic spirituality is the way it reminds us that everyone has a *charism* and responsibility to contribute to the mission of the church.

Charismatic spirituality, however, sometimes trivializes our faith because it can focus too intently on the signs and wonders of the Spirit, losing sight of God's overall purposes. In other words, the gifts of the Spirit are not an end in themselves, but only a means for kingdom building. This appears to have been one of the major issues with the church at Corinth an overemphasis on spiritual gifts to the detriment of loving relationships and unity (1 Cor 12–14).

In missions, charismatics often deal with power encounters on the field.[139] This is something that many North American missionaries are ill prepared for both theologically and practically. Both charismatics and non-charismatics need better training in this area. However, I want to encourage charismatic global servants to balance the power aspects of the gifting of the Spirit (outward workings of the Spirit) with the character development of the fruit of the Spirit (inward workings of the Spirit). We need both the power and the fruit of the Spirit to be effective witnesses.

Social Justice Spirituality[140]

Social justice spirituality follows Jesus' example and teachings on human life (Matt 6:1–4; 23:14; 25:31–46; Luke 6:30; 12:33). Every person is created in God's image and loved by him. God cares for his creation, as well as people's physical, emotional, and spiritual concerns. He sent his prophet Amos to declare this with the words: "Let justice roll on like a river, righteousness like a never-failing stream" (Amos 5:24).[141]

This spirituality focuses upon justice and shalom in all human relationships and social structures. People who gravitate to this form of spirituality tend to be compassionate and live for equality and magnanimity among all peoples. Many mission organizations exhibit a strong social justice spirituality. If you are drawn to causes without regard to nationality, race, social class, or gender, but see every believer in Christ (Gal 3:28; Eph 2:11–22), you resonate with this tradition. Ministries that work in the area of relief, development, and social justice are led by members with this spirituality. Its strength is its holistic focus on every aspect of life and the care it gives to God's creation.

---

139 Power encounters are spiritual confrontations between the forces of the kingdom of God and the kingdom of Satan. See, for example, 1 Kgs 18:18–45 and Eph 6:12.

140 Foster, 135–83.

141 See also Isa 11:6; 58:7; Jer 6:14; and especially Mic 6:8, for just a few other prophetic examples.

However, a weakness is the tendency for social justice to become an end in itself. Poverty and justice become all-consuming to the detriment of helping people know the provision and liberating truth of the cross of Christ. We must never forget that true help reaches out beyond the temporal to the eternal. Nevertheless, social justice spirituality has always been part of the mission of the church, and I am grateful that it is front and center in many evangelical agencies today.

Evangelical Spirituality[142]

Evangelical spirituality is characterized by a concern for the essential core of the Christian message, which proclaims the good news of salvation through the person and work of Jesus Christ. Evangelicals believe that each person needs to accept Jesus as their personal Savior, and they have a high commitment to the inspiration and authority of the Bible as the infallible guide for the Christian in life and faith. The heart of evangelicalism in missions is evangelism, church planting, and discipling. It is a Word-centered life. The strength of evangelicalism is its activism in proclaiming the gospel of Jesus both home and abroad (Matt 28:18–19). This spirituality knows God's Word, proclaims it, and evangelizes in both word and deed.

A weakness of evangelicals is our tendency to assert control and to stress that God only works within certain means (primarily through the preaching and teaching of his Word). Such dogmatic assertions have led to many disagreements because evangelicals easily become too passionate and set in their ways, often over minor issues. People in the evangelical tradition will benefit from getting out of their comfort zones by experiencing other avenues of spirituality and expanding their understanding on what are and what are not the essentials of our faith.

Incarnational Spirituality[143]

Incarnational spirituality is rooted in the physical reality of everyday life by believing that all of life is sacramental (also a name for this spirituality). Incarnational spirituality focuses on understanding how the Spirit works in and through the ordinary, by affirming the goodness of creation, and by presenting invisible grace through visible signs. A person who has an incarnational bent loves ritual, symbol, and art because such elements help us see how God is truly among us everywhere. Of course, incarnation is at the heart of the story of Jesus, who humbled himself in taking the form of humanity and obediently dying on the cross for our sake (Phil 2:7–8).

If you enjoy liturgical services, you might be more incarnationally inclined. If you like to connect the spirit with the body, you are more incarnationally inclined. Incarnational spirituality points out the truth that "It is only in our bodies that we experience God at all; without them, we cease to exist."[144] When we separate the physical from the spiritual there is a false dichotomy,

---

[142] Foster, 185–233.

[143] Foster, 235–72.

[144] Tara Owens, *Embracing the Body: Finding God in Our Flesh and Bone* (Downers Grove, IL: IVP, 2015), 59.

because they are intertwined. Author Tara Owens says, "We live our bodily lives—eating, sleeping, touching, weeping—with a whispering sense that we are experiencing sacred in these mundane moments."[145]

The great strength of this spirituality is taking the physical world we live in seriously, which underscores the fact that God is Immanuel. He is with us. The old adage that some are so heavenly minded that they are no earthly good would not be said of someone who is by nature drawn to incarnational spirituality. I love the fact that global servants who live incarnationally really get to know their new homes and neighborhoods. They live among their people. The incarnational life gives us God with skin on.[146] It makes present and tangible what can seem distant and unknown.

If there is any aspect of the church that is incarnational by definition, it has to be missions. The very nature of going across cultural, linguistic, and geographic barriers is to live into an incarnational calling. But such a lifestyle is still difficult for many of us because we focus on doing rather than experiencing. Incarnational spirituality challenges us to be more in touch with nature, relationships, beauty, truth, and goodness—the many aspects of how God reveals himself in our daily lives.

The great peril of incarnational spirituality is the pitfall of idolatry. Recognizing God is in creation can move us toward mistakenly identifying God with creation. We never worship creation, but the God of creation (see Col 1:15-18). This can also crop up when we fail to distinguish between a sacred "thing" (such as image, object—even the the Bible, or act) and the spiritual reality it signifies. The Bible is clear in denouncing the making of any graven image of God (Ex 20:4, 32:8, 34:17; Isa 40:19).

Evaluating Our Own Spirituality

Is there a predominant form of spirituality you relate to and identify with? How would you begin to cultivate that tradition in more meaningful and intentional ways? Should you also regard other streams of spirituality as having something important to teach you?

By understanding each of these streams and spiritualities we accomplish two things. First, we discover where we might have some spiritual blindness in our own life. And second, as we learn about other spiritualities we can grow to appreciate different streams of worshipping God and hopefully learn to accept more and more of our brothers and sisters around the world who might differ from us. The posture of a global servant should always be that of a learner. As we grow in our knowledge of different ways of experiencing God, we can also grow in our ability to serve the worldwide church.

Gisela Kreglinger, in her fascinating study of viticulture[147] and spirituality, compares God to a gardener and the church to a vineyard. To use Kreglinger's

---

145 Owens, 60.

146 A favorite expression of one of my daughters, who favors incarnational spirituality.

147 Viticulture is the discipline of wine-making. See Gisela H. Kreglinger, *The Spirituality of Wine* (Grand Rapids: Eerdmans, 2016), 200.

metaphor, all who are in Christ share the same gardener, our Father in heaven, but it is he who determines the different soils, weather conditions, and general climate differences in order to produce dry sauvignon blancs, sweet rieslings, elegant merlots, or robust cabernets. Each of these wines are enjoyable and serve different tastes, though all come from grapes. God, the true and great vintner, who created each one of us and knows us intimately, knows where we best flourish and bear fruit. Authentic Christian community grows out of such joys and tensions in a diverse and complex living organism. So, "we must learn, like the vintner-craftsman, to see diversity as a gift rather than a threat."[148]

Christ sees us not just in our individuality, as isolated and autonomous consumers doing our own thing in our own way, but as branches in the same vine, held together and nourished individually by Christ, the vine, and tended by a caring vintner, God the Father (John 15). Understanding and respecting our different spiritualities honors and respects how God is building his church. We don't need to feel threatened by our differences, but rather we can rejoice in God's various and creative means of relating to each one of us.

Reflection and Points to Ponder

- Which one of Richard Foster's six different streams of Christian spiritualities do you identify with most closely? Why? In what ways do you think you can nurture your natural spiritual tendencies while on the field?

- How do you view people from other spiritual traditions? Do you see them as fellow believers? Why? What could you do to better understand and appreciate their spirituality?

- You were made to love God. Like a choice wine, you are unique and filled with rich and specific flavor. How can you better understand the personal soil and climate of God's work in your life so you can produce the abundant fruit Christ calls you to?

For Further Reading

Richard J. Foster, *Streams of Living Water: Celebrating the Great Traditions of Christian Faith* (San Francisco: Harper, 1998). An exploration of six rich Christian traditions of spirituality.

Gerald L. Sittser, *Water from a Deep Well* (Downers Grove, IL: IVP, 2007). A historic look at Christian spirituality from early martyrs to modern missionaries.

Gary Thomas, *Sacred Pathways: Discovering Your Soul's Path to God* (Grand Rapids: Zondervan, 1996). Based upon temperament study, this book examines the unique ways in which we grow spiritually.

---

148 Kreglinger, 207.

One of the most powerful tools *in missions is listening. As a new missionary, listening helps us to learn the clues and cues of a new language and culture. To those we serve, nothing is often appreciated more than a skillful and honest listening ear.*

This holds true also in our relationship with our Lord as we take time to listen carefully and prayerfully to him. Listening can be hard work, but it also can be restful. I have found great value in taking time away from people and distractions to simply listen. I have also found that there is often a cross-shaped pattern to God's Voice as he speaks into my silence. As I listen, I am awakened by his Presence, then comforted—or distressed—as he leads me always to the cross, where he speaks words of forgiveness, comfort, healing, truth, confrontation, conviction, direction, and salvation. To listen is to receive, and here I receive his mercy and love and direction. This calls in turn for response, and leads me naturally to repentance, contrition, unburdening, renewal of vows, and worship.

Listening takes time. Often when I hear a word, especially a word of direction or promise, I expect things to happen quite quickly. But the cruciform shape of God's Word leads me from the cross to the tomb. Listening very often requires a period of gestation, where the Word has time to penetrate more deeply toward accomplishing its purpose. This can take hours or days or months or years.

Very often the fruition of the words I have received in quiet listening erupt unexpectedly (and sometimes almost unrecognizably) into new life! This happens often when the waiting has seemed interminable and hope is almost lost. With new life comes a new resilience, a freshness and rested-ness, a new energy, quietness of soul, and the fruit of the Spirit.

Listening in silence and solitude is one of the most generative postures and activities of the soul. At the end of the day, my regret is not that I didn't do more, but that I didn't take the time to do less, so that he might do more for, in, with, and through me.

Howard
global servant in Brazil

Silence and Solitude
The Ancient Pathways toward Emptying and Filling

A friend of mine once told me that wise people see their lives like a reservoir, where wisdom is found most profoundly in the deep, still waters. Jesus was quietly growing in wisdom and stature during his thirty years of obscurity (Luke 2:52). Like Jesus, we need to fill our reservoirs with nourishing water from God. We do this through silence and solitude.

Webster's defines *silence* as the "absence of sound or noise." Silence gives us space away from speaking and away from listening to words, music, and all the noise that can fill up our time. Webster's defines *solitude* as "the quality or state of being alone or remote from society." Solitude involves creating enough uninterrupted distance in a distraction-free environment to be alone with God.

These pathways are by definition individual pursuits, but they are not to be engaged solely for one's own sake. When we withdraw and become quiet, we do so in order to reengage with our communities out of the abundance we have gained through our time alone with God. We notice the benefit of silence and solitude when we look at Jesus' life on earth. Starting with his forty-day withdrawal into the wilderness, over and over he pulled away to prepare his heart for the ministry that lay ahead (Luke 4:1–19). This enabled him to reengage and really hear people, even in the midst of the crowds and noise.[149]

"Be still and know that I am God": Self-Emptying

Henri Nouwen wrote that without the spiritual practices of silence and solitude "it is virtually impossible to live a spiritual life."[150] Both silence and solitude are containers for the practice of other spiritual disciplines. This is the reason why Nouwen claimed they are the keys to spiritual vitality. There is a freedom which comes when we release ourselves to be with the Lord completely and unreservedly. Silence and solitude ask for waiting and patience. To practice them means we must not be in a hurry with unsettled minds, for then we are unable to hear from God. For most of us, this cannot be done without significant quality time, taking the time to unplug and disconnect.

---

149 See the story of Bartimaeus in Mark 10:46–52.
150 Henri J. M. Nouwen, *Making All Things New: An Invitation to the Spiritual Life* (New York: HarperOne, 1981), 69.

So the first thing we need to do is to schedule as much time as necessary to quiet our hearts. How much time is enough? As much time as it takes you, personally, to be at peace before God. It takes at least a day before I can honestly let go of the totality of my thoughts and emotions and center my attention solely upon God. Only then can I begin to hear God's voice.

Like anything else, the more we practice silence and solitude, the easier it is for our minds and bodies to adjust and settle into that space. This is why I like shorter but more frequent retreats, rather than longer but more infrequent times away.

Silence and solitude allow us the space and time to grow in our prayer life. In *The Way of a Pilgrim*, the anonymous nineteenth-century Russian spiritual classic on the Jesus Prayer, the author encouraged letting silence lead us into prayer.[151] This is the example Jesus set for us, as Luke tells us that "Jesus often withdrew to lonely places and prayed" (5:16). When we orient ourselves quietly around God, we naturally grow in his character and graces, deepening our awareness of his will and purposes.

Global servants can lose the sense of intimacy with God, having no experiential love with Jesus. The problem is not that God is distant, but that we are. Being activists, global servants want to be productive and fruitful for God. One of the consequences of such attitudes can be a growing sense of loss in our relationship with Jesus. Thankfully, often the antidote is simply to recommit to spending more uninterrupted time with him.

"Be still and know that I am God": Refilling

God cannot help but shower us with his love and compassion when we are with him. Once we experience God's love and compassion for ourselves, we in turn become channels of that same grace and mercy to others (Matt 9:35–38). The more we experience God's true love, the more we can truly love. The monk and writer, Thomas Merton, told how a time of silence and solitude helped him become a more compassionate person.

> *I met the world and found it no longer so wicked after all. Perhaps the things I had resented about the world when I left it were defects of my own that I had projected upon it. Now, on the contrary, I found that everything stirred me with a deep and mute sense of compassion.*[152]

Pulling away with God also helps us regain and refill our hearts with God's presence. No person can undergo deep stillness with God and remain unchanged. Like an uprooted tree replanted in good soil, we flourish and again become fruitful for the Lord. We regain perspective and Christ's peace and so are ready for whatever next comes our way. Through the habit of silence and solitude, we actually grow in endurance through regular times of rest, recovery, and re-envisioning.

---

151 Olga Savin, trans., *The Way of a Pilgrim* (Boston: Shambhala Classics, 2001), 8.

152 David Teague, *Godly Servants: Discipleship and Spiritual Formation for Missionaries* (n.p.: Mission Imprints, 2012), 119.

How to Practice Silence and Solitude

The greatest challenge to practicing silence and solitude is often practical. How can we, amid busy ministries in which time and money are limited, find a time for quiet and a place to be alone? The key to finding both time and place starts with our mindset. We might need to begin in small ways, but it can be done.

For example, perhaps you can plan to have a period of time when you give up speaking on every issue that comes your way. Try to simply listen without reacting and talking. As you drive to a meeting or commute to work, turn off the radio or your music. Leave electronic media off in the evening at home. Take walks or exercise in silence. Learn how to be alone and quiet in small ways. If you don't have a lot of free time, take what you can, even if only thirty minutes (see Rev 8:1).

Alone times with God can be sweet experiences, but they also can be times of darkness when God seems to remain aloof and silent. If this is the case, my only word for you is to not be afraid. Fear is not of the Lord. Stay with him in the darkness and times of testing. Remember that solitude and silence are gifts. God will eventually reveal his purposes for this time and you can trust him. Remember that we are his beloved.

I know a lot of global servants who are young parents laugh at the thought of any alone time. Exhaustion sets in when we are available and accessible too much of the time. As young parents, you, as much as anyone, need time alone. You simply must make time to be unavailable. If that means sharing parenting roles with your spouse, hiring good childcare, sharing child responsibilities with coworkers—so be it.

When our children were young, I would take sole responsibility for them on Saturday mornings so Debbie could have some time completely to herself. It was life-giving for her and a great bonding experience for me and our children, and a lot of fun too! No matter the circumstances, I have found that most of us are more tired at the soul level than we even know. Be intentional to be alone with God. As Ruth Haley Barton says, "The longing for solitude is the longing for God."[153]

There are also times when we are naturally alone. Maybe you could make the time you spend in the shower each day a time that you are alone with God. As the grit and grime of the day's activities wash off, remind yourself of the dirt that has also accumulated within. Let the water of the shower be the cleansing of your heart before the Lord. Let the warmth of the water warm your heart with God's love as you offer yourself to him for the day.

As we enter into our holy time with our loving God, we gain the perspective so needed in serving him. We empty ourselves so that he can fill us. And even if we don't "feel" such filling, God is faithful and will do what his Word promises. Be creative. No matter your circumstances, it is possible for you to find a way to be alone and quiet before our Father. Figure out a way.

---

[153] Ruth Haley Barton, *Sacred Rhythms: Arranging Our Lives for Spiritual Transformation* (Downers Grove, IL: IVP, 2006), 32.

Most of all, get out of your noise and crowds and find God. Listen to life and to the life-giver. Enter the mystery. God is God and we are not. Listen to him. In quietness and solitude, the Lord comes to us. If you listen very carefully, you will hear God more clearly and feel God more closely than you thought possible. Every quiet moment calls out. Simply be alone and be still before God.

Reflection and Points to Ponder

- We all have different levels of tolerance for noise and people. How do you know you have reached a tipping point and need quiet and time away with God? What signs betray your soul's weariness and need for restoration?

- Do you find yourself resisting either time alone or silence? How or when do you resist such experiences? What troubles you most about being quiet and/or alone? When have you felt most comfortable being still and alone? Can you describe your sense of being alone with God? What do you experience, think about, and feel?

- What is it about silence and solitude that deepens your relationship with God? How do you think God feels about your time alone before him? What does this tell you about developing a pattern of silence and solitude?

- What benefits do silence and solitude provide for you? How does pulling away and being alone aid in your personal life and ministry? How can you give more to people as a result of these practices?

For Further Reading

Ruth Haley Barton, *An Invitation to Silence and Solitude* (Downers Grove, IL: IVP, 2009). An exploration of how silence and solitude restore our spiritual vitality.

Henri J. M. Nouwen, *The Way of the Heart* (New York: Ballantine, 1981). Nouwen's mediations on silence and solitude.

Kyle Strobel, *Formed for the Glory of God: Learning from the Spiritual Practices of Jonathan Edwards* (Downers Grove, IL: IVP, 2013). How Jonathan Edwards used spiritual disciplines, including silence and solitude, in his life.

I remember sitting next to Samuel*

in a training session at a conference we were attending. Samuel, a veteran global servant who had served in the jungles of South America for decades doing Bible translation, surpassed me in age by over thirty-five years. The glee on his face, however, as we studied and learned together at that conference shouted youth and vitality. He was never finished learning, even as he was racing to the finish line in his golden years. I was a student of Samuel that day. I knew what I wanted to be when I grew up.

I continue to be amazed not only at the joy of lifelong learning, but also how it leads me into spaces where God is pursuing his lost sheep. One day as I sat in a taxi in southeast Asia, the taxi driver suddenly asked, "So everyone in your country is a Christian, right?" We proceeded to have a long conversation about truth, and where it comes from; about hope versus despair; and about the meaning of our little lives on this planet at all. I was taking a class during that very season in Christian apologetics and worldview. My heart and mind were bursting with things I had been reading and hearing and studying. The Lord pulled them out in perfect time for that taxi driver on a bumpy dirt road.

Or the time a young teenage girl sat by me on a park bench and suddenly whispered, "Can I ask you something? I am really lost." And she wasn't talking about directions. She began to pour out her heart to me about losing her faith, about feeling she was never "enough," about who she was, and how she just knew that God would never want anything to do with someone as broken as her. I was reading a book just then on God's unending, unshakable love that pursues us all our days. On that park bench that day, all that I was reading and learning poured out in our conversation, as I encouraged this young girl that maybe there was another narrative, that maybe God loved her unconditionally with a passionate, unbreakable love.

The gift of lifelong learning truly is the gift that keeps on giving. The pursuit of learning pours a whole lot into me, for sure. It is stimulating, stretching, challenging, and encouraging to read, learn, and grow. But I'm astounded at how God also uses whatever he is pouring into me to overflow to others around me, from a taxicab driver to a stranger on a park bench.

Renee
global servant in Asia

*Name changed for security.

Lifelong Learning
The Ancient Pathway to Humility

11

Farmers will tell you that there is a law of agriculture that is common to all types of cultivation. You must prepare the ground, plant the seed, and then cultivate, weed, and water. You then patiently nurture the seed's growth and development until it is ripe. It cannot be rushed. Only work and time, in accordance with the ways of cultivation, will lead to success. This is the law of the farm.

Like the law of the farm, our spiritual growth depends upon patient planting and tilling. The processes which shape and form us are mixed and many. We develop in character, in relationships, and in understanding our skill sets and life purposes. Spiritual growth is a lifelong process of learning, in which we open ourselves to the continual in-working of God's Spirit to shape and reshape us. Through an ongoing, voluntary, and self-motivated pursuit of knowledge for either personal or professional reasons, we engage in lifelong development as a person. While lifelong learning is important for everyone, it is especially useful for three types of global servants:

- Younger servants who are culturally formed without much sense of history. We might call them people of the "now," where focus is placed on what is taking place now in real time. While this does have some benefits, without a lifelong context these servants can easily be ruled by the immediate and urgent.

- Emerging global servant leaders who may be so proactive and focused on moving forward that they can be prone to forget there are lessons to be learned from the past and that God is never in a hurry.

- Older, more experienced global servants who may be in a period of change or transition and need a reorientation and reminder that change is a natural process of life. Without a mindset of lifelong learning, they run the risk of plateauing and coasting without pursuing the fullness of their growth in Christ.

While lifelong learning may include formal schooling, it is also more than just going to school. It is about paying attention, reflecting, and applying the biblical concept of *hokmah* (wisdom) in our lives and ministries. Continual learning is crucial for the global servant. Learning is empowering. It creates the energy needed to move forward in our lives and careers.

We typically think of learning on an individual basis, but I believe the most powerful learning experiences can be found in community. Jesus taught in a community of twelve disciples. He was almost always with a crowd or a small group. The disciples learned through a constant habit of action and reflection through his teaching about their life experiences. Gordon Smith encourages the church to see itself as "a learning community that seeks together in faith to know Jesus, to grow together in love for Jesus and to align our lives, mission and way of being in the world to the in-breaking of the reign of Christ."[154]

This is exactly what Paul had in mind when he wrote about true spiritual transformation in Romans 12:1-2: "Therefore, I urge you, brothers, in view of God's mercy, to offer your bodies as living sacrifices, holy and pleasing to God—this is your spiritual act of worship. Do not conform any longer to the pattern of this world, but be transformed by the renewing of your mind. Then you will be able to test and approve what God's will is—his good, pleasing and perfect will." We are called to Christian maturity and holy living through the community action of first presenting our bodies (vs. 1) and second the renewing of our minds (vs. 2). Only a renewed mind can test and approve what is God's good, pleasing, and perfect will. But notice these acts of worship in presenting our bodies and renewing our minds are to be done in community—the use of brothers in verse one.

However, what matters most is that a commitment to learn is embodied in our daily routines and rhythms, and in the circular seasons of life. Such an attitude of curiosity and willingness to change and grow, practiced over a lifetime, gradually and incrementally leads to transformation. This is why the monastic vision of education was so effective, because the monks learned together over a lifetime. Such personal and professional development is often a slower process than what we want, but it is effective, because small things accomplished matter much more than big things only dreamed of.

The Posture of a Learner

Lifelong learners have a refreshing humility. They admit the limitations of their knowledge and are continually asking questions of themselves, their world, and God. They are curious people, constantly adding new insights and making course corrections in their spiritual growth. They view learning as a driving force to transformation. They believe they have not "arrived" spiritually. There are always new things to learn and fresh challenges in learning them. We all have experienced the need to recalibrate in our Christian growth, realizing that our learning and growth is circular as well as progressive. In other words, we are open to revisiting life lessons once learned before yet forgotten. We are not afraid to review and go back to reacquire some knowledge or behavior which we had thought we had already conquered or put into practice. This takes both humility and wisdom.

---

154 Gordon T. Smith, *Called to Be Saints: An Invitation to Christian Maturity* (Downers Grove, IL: IVP, 2014), 39.

Humility is the basic posture of both the learner and missionary. To become contextually sensitive to and have compassion for new people requires a learning posture from first arriving on the field. Learning to adapt and integrate well decreases initial cross-cultural stress.[155] Bonding with a new culture requires the posture of a learner. We must learn the ins and outs of life in our host country, including new language skills. We do this by immediately becoming immersed in the new culture: eating local foods, dressing in the local dress, perhaps even living with a family.

Moving into cultural immersion might produce increased short-term stress, but a global servant who is able to handle such short-term distress can hopefully adjust to their new culture more completely in the long run. We can read national literature and look for opportunities to attend cultural and family events such as plays, movies, weddings, and funerals. No matter how long we've been on the field, it is important not to become stagnate, but always growing in our knowledge of local customs.

It's good to remember that when we take the posture of a humble learner we also make a commitment not to take ourselves too seriously. Learning, by definition, means we don't know everything; and therefore, we can relax into the learning process, realizing that we can accept failures and laugh at our mistakes. One of the greatest sources of humor for global servants is our language mistakes.

I once spent a whole semester telling my students to "turn around in their Bibles" rather than to "turn to their Bibles." I was embarrassed when I found out, but I was able to laugh at the confusion I caused. Humor helps us to be teachable, flexible, and humble in spirit. Richard Foster reminds us that learning can also be enjoyable. "Study produces joy. Like any novice we find it hard work in the beginning. But the greater our proficiency, the greater our joy."[156]

Vulnerability and Transparency

When we take the posture of a learner, we also commit to being vulnerable and transparent as authentic people before one another. Remember, we are ambassadors of Christ alone. It is on his authority, not ours, that we proclaim the gospel.[157] When we derive authority for our ministry from anything other than Christ, we put ourselves in a position of lording over others rather than learning from them.

Ministering cross-culturally is a very difficult task, and no one is up to the job in their own strength. Paradoxically, this understanding of our weakness is the source of our strength. The gospel is full of paradox—we are strong when we are weak, we are rich when we are poor, we are mature when we are childlike, we are fully free

---

[155] Myron Loss, *Culture Shock: Dealing with Stress in Cross-Cultural Living* (Winona Lake, IN: Light and Light Press, 1983), 55.

[156] Richard J. Foster, *Celebration of Discipline: The Path to Spiritual Growth* (San Francisco: Harper and Row, 1978), 66.

[157] See 2 Cor. 5:20.

when we are not in charge.[158] At first glance these statements can seem like utter nonsense. But the Bible tells us that our brokenness and woundedness is where we can find healing and strength for ourselves and others. As Jesus conquered through the cross rather than the crown, we, as his disciples, must follow his example.[159] We must bear the hallmark of Christ and be people of integrity through transparent openness and vulnerable weakness.

While both transparency and vulnerability are essential, there are some differences between the two terms. Transparency is based upon our ability to share openly, while vulnerability is based upon our ability to share riskily. It is possible for someone to be transparent without being vulnerable. We retain control when we are transparent, but not when we are vulnerable. For both, however, humility is the key. Humility is the quality that enables us to live truthful, authentic lives.[160] And living truthfully and authentically enables us to be free to learn about ourselves, others, God, and the world (see John 8:32).

Parker Palmer says it this way:

Afraid that our inner light will be extinguished or our inner darkness exposed, we hide our true identities from each other. In the process, we become separated from our own souls. We end up living divided lives, so far removed from the truth we hold within that we cannot know the "integrity that comes from being what you are."[161]

Hiddenness is a real temptation for global servants, partly because it is so easy for us. Our support base is thousands of miles away. What people know is only what we tell them in our reports. What is really happening can be concealed when we visit people back home in short bursts after long periods of separation. Coming from a culture that rewards and promotes instant success, we are tempted to conceal our ministry results because they seem so ordinary. The slowness of our work causes us to fear that people may want more bang for their buck.

Every year I receive from several of my supporting churches evaluation forms asking me some very pointed questions regarding my effectiveness in ministry. The pressure I feel to give a good account is real, even when things aren't going so well. I wonder if my answers will dictate whether my churches will call our ministry into question or even stop their financial support. While my fears probably aren't rooted in reality, it's easy to let those fears overtake me when I respond. I am tempted to hide.

When we realize that no one and no ministry is perfect, and that there is always room to learn and improve, then we are free to come out of hiding. As I was coming out of my cloud of spiritual darkness and clinical depression some years ago, I was determined not to hide it from our donor base. Although I didn't make

---

158 2 Cor. 12:9–10.
159 See John 13:14–17.
160 *The Rule of Saint Benedict*, ed. Timothy Fry (New York: Random House Vintage Press Reprint, 1998), 7:10.
161 Parker J. Palmer, *A Hidden Wholeness: The Journey Toward an Undivided Life* (San Francisco: Jossey-Bass, 2004), 4.

it a major point of emphasis, I did share openly and freely with individuals, our mission committees, and even from the pulpit in each of our supporting churches. I felt this was necessary for me, and instead of being punished by taking such a risk, I found great freedom in the love and encouragement I received back from such gracious and caring people. This process helped greatly in my recovery.

True humility through transparent honesty and vulnerable truthfulness asks God to save us from the distraction of trying to impress others. It cries out to save us from the dangers of seeking praise from others, whether or not deserved. It teaches us to learn from criticism with a clear head, resisting the urge to defend ourselves. It helps us understand that true freedom comes when we let go of the need to be at the center of the universe and are willing to learn from everything and everyone. When we are open and vulnerable, we become liberated from our need to be right all the time. We are learners of Christ (see Matt 11:29).

The Attentive Life

One of the ways we live a life of learning is by being a student of the world around us. This can be a struggle, of course, for a busy and hurried global servant. But a posture of lifelong learning teaches us to pay attention. Jesus is always calling out to us, "Look! Listen! Take notice! There is so much to learn and discover!"[162]

Paying attention is characteristic of those with a teachable spirit. They are willing to be taught by anything they encounter in life—a child, a smile, a word of correction, a sunflower, a nesting robin. Paying attention is not a way of making something happen, but a way to see what has already been given to us. I find it helps me to maintain this posture by starting each day asking God, "Lord, what am I missing? What are you already doing today?"

It isn't easy to practice paying attention. Leighton Ford puts this challenge into perspective:

> *From the time we were children we were told to "pay attention," as if this were the simplest thing in the world. But in fact, attentiveness is one of the most difficult concepts to grasp and one of the hardest disciplines to learn. For we are very distractible people in a very distracting world.*[163]

Early in my missionary career I was faced with a crisis of calling. After about two years on the field I sensed God calling me into a deeper and harder work than I thought I could handle. During this struggle, I started to evaluate what I had accomplished and found little fruit. I asked God, "If you really want me to sacrifice even more, will you let me know it is worth it?" I wanted a clear affirming sign that God was at work. But guess what? Things only got worse, and my sense of failure grew even more. I wondered what was happening and if we should consider returning home.

But then I started to pay attention to what was really going on in my life. I could see that every difficulty I encountered, every failure I experienced, became something God was addressing and solving. Rather than my problems being a

---

[162] See Matt 6:25–34, where Jesus calls us to pay attention to the birds and the lilies to help combat our worries.
[163] Leighton Ford, *The Attentive Life: Discerning God's Presence in All Things* (Downers Grove, IL: IVP, 2008), 23.

barrier too difficult to surmount, I saw amazing ways in which God was present with me. I started seeing God in all my circumstances, and I regained perspective on God's calling and my commitment to stay. The key to paying attention is the willingness to open up to God, even when he acts mysteriously.[164]

Brother Lawrence, who served in the kitchens of his monastery, longed to converse with God no matter what he was doing, from washing pots to singing the Psalms.

> *I make it my business to rest in [Christ's] holy presence which I keep myself in a habitual, silent, and secret conversation with God. This often causes in me joys and raptures inwardly, and sometimes also outwardly, so great that I am forced to use means to moderate them and prevent their appearance to others. . . . I honestly cannot understand how people who claim to love the Lord can be content without practicing His presence.*[165]

When we practice Christ's presence, we start to learn how to let go of our need to manipulate, control, and compete with the world around us. When we learn to accept each moment as sacred, we start to see life through Christ's eyes, learning what he wants to teach us through each encounter of the day. Christ becomes our joy, sorrow, emptiness, and fullness. We become teachable in every moment.

Poet Wendell Berry wrote, "There are no unsacred places; there are only sacred places and desecrated places."[166] Likewise, when we are paying attention, there are no places of ignorance, but only places where we choose to learn and places where we stay unfocused and ignorant. When we are open to learning in every moment, we learn to pray prayers we would otherwise not pray.

Immediate Obedience

The Rule of Benedict tells us that "the first step of humility is unhesitating obedience."[167] I believe one of the reasons some of us are unable to learn is that we have forgotten the importance of humble obedience. I am not referring so much to a list of dos and don'ts, but to obeying the promptings of the Holy Spirit when the Lord speaks to us.

The writer of the letter to the Hebrews makes this very point when he talks about Abraham. "By faith Abraham, when called to go to a place he would later receive as his inheritance, obeyed and went, even though he did not know where he was going" (Heb 11:8). Abraham demonstrated what it means to walk by faith, by obeying the voice of God even when he didn't know his end destination.

---

164 Some practices that can especially open us up to seeing God working in our lives are journaling, examen, practicing God's presence in daily activities, retreating, practicing simplicity, and praying during fixed hours every day.

165 Brother Lawrence, *The Practice of the Presence of God* (New Kensington, PA: Whitaker House, 1982), 31.

166 Wendell Berry, "How to Be a Poet (to remind myself)," *New Collected Poems* (Berkeley, CA: Counterpoint, 2013), 354.

167 Rule of St. Benedict (5:1), Lonni Collins Pratt and Father Daniel Homan, *Benedict's Way* (Chicago: Loyola Press, 2000), 199.

Yet, if we are honest, we have trouble obeying. We don't usually struggle with willful disobedience; it is simply that we have filled up our lives with so much stuff—our own thoughts, agendas, and desires—that we have lost the ability to discern what God is saying. Or it may be that we simply don't want God to interfere with our own plans for the day.

The Latin root of the word *obedience* is *ob-audire*, which means "to listen." We get the word *audio* from this root. If we understand this nuance, we can find obedience to be less arduous. Obedience is just listening to God each day and following his path for us. Quaker writer Thomas Kelly describes this relationship in terms of our lives as lost sheep looking for the Shepherd.

> *It is the drama of the lost sheep wandering in the wilderness, restless and lonely, feebly searching, while over the hills comes the wiser Shepherd. For His is a shepherd's heart, and He is restless until He holds His sheep in His arms. . . . It is the life of absolute and complete and holy obedience to the voice of the Shepherd. But ever throughout the account the accent will be laid upon God, God the initiator, God the aggressor, God the seeker, God the stirrer into life, God the ground of our obedience, God the giver of the power to become children of God.*[168]

The focus here is simply following the Shepherd who knows what is best for our lives and for our ministries. Obedience maintains a lasting and healthy relationship with God. Jesus makes this plain when he says that obedience is a marker of love. "If you obey my commands, you will remain in my love, just as I have obeyed my Father's commands and remain in his love" (John 15:10).

Obedience requires active response. When we believe the Holy Spirit is saying something to us, we must act on it right away. But too often we are afraid to act because we fail to see God at work teaching us in the moment how to obey.

I think this was one of the greatest disappointments Jesus experienced in relation to his disciples. He often gave them opportunities for growth, and when they failed to follow they lost God-moments to learn from him. At the Garden of Gethsemane, he asked the disciples to watch and pray with him. But they fell asleep—not just once, but repeatedly. What was Jesus' response? "Watch and pray so that you will not fall into temptation" (Matt 26:41) and "Are you still sleeping and resting? Look, the hour is near, and the Son of Man is betrayed into the hands of sinners" (v. 45). Notice what the disciples could have learned if they had been immediately obedient: 1) power against temptation; and 2) the timing of God's redemptive plans. Pretty heady and important stuff. When we fail to be obedient, we are ultimately the ones who lose out.

---

[168] Thomas R. Kelly, "*A Testament of Devotion,*" in Richard J. Foster and Emilie Griffin, eds., *Spiritual Classics* (San Francisco: Harper, 2000), 177.

Proverbs 9:9 says, "Instruct a wise man and he will be wiser still; teach a righteous man and he will add to his learning." Wise and righteous people can never get enough learning. We become wise as we learn to obey in all the circumstances in our seasons of life. It takes intentionality and effort to take what we experience and convert it to applied understanding.

Truly learned persons are probably quite different in their sixties than they were in their twenties. It takes habits of obedience and patiently paying attention to become a lifelong learner. We cannot go faster in our growth than grace allows. As Brother Lawrence rightly observed, "It is not possible to spiritually mature all at once."[169]

In Proverbs 10:14 we are told that "wise men store up knowledge." The phrase "store up" literally means to hold a treasure. That treasure brings not only knowledge, but great peace. Paul says this peace comes from reflecting on

whatever is true, whatever is noble, whatever is right, whatever is pure, whatever is lovely, whatever is admirable—if anything is excellent or praiseworthy—think about such things. Whatever you have learned or received or heard from me, or seen in me—put into practice. And the God of peace will be with you.
—Philippians 4:8–9

True learning is not just to "think about such things," but also to put them "into practice."

---

[169] Brother Lawrence, 45.

Reflection and Points to Ponder

- What new things have you learned about life, yourself, and/or God in the last year? Have you rethought or changed positions on anything in the last few years? What do you think this says about you and your life journey as it stands right now?
- What qualities do you feel are exhibited in a person who has a teachable heart? How does humility relate to learning? How does being humble help you to reach people in a new culture as a global servant for Christ?
- How honest are you with others when you don't know an answer to a particular question? How hard is it to share your limitations with others in transparency and vulnerability? How do people feel about disagreeing with you? What steps can you take to be more transparent and honest in your community? If you don't have a safe place to be honest and transparent, what resources or steps can you take to find one?
- How can you practice the presence of God better in your daily life? What might you do or not do to pay better attention to God-moments? To learn daily obedience?

For Further Reading

Mark Buchanan, *Spiritual Rhythm* (Grand Rapids: Zondervan, 2010). Being with Jesus every season of your life.

Leighton Ford, *The Attentive Life* (Downers Grove, IL: IVP, 2008). A journey in paying attention to God in the daily rhythms.

Douglas Kaine McKelvey, *Every Moment Holy* (Nashville: Rabbit Room Press, 2017). A beautiful book of liturgies for special but also everyday moments in our lives. It teaches us that every moment is sacred and an opportunity to hear from God.

Parker J. Palmer, *A Hidden Wholeness* (San Francisco: Jossey-Bass, 2004). Learning how to live an undivided life.

Carolyn Weber, *Holy Is the Day: Living the Gift of the Present* (Downers Grove, IL: IVP, 2013). A collection of reflections on seeing God in the everyday of life.

As a young mother, our ministry of church planting took all the "extra" time I had. I was astonished one day to have a young woman ask to meet with me for confession. Not only did I not practice any sort of verbal, witnessed confession, my background offered me no method to pursue it. But I was committed to the young woman in a discipleship relationship, so I agreed. My trepidation was that I would fail her, and that it would become an unwieldy time-taker. Her first words when we met were that God had told her to confess to me.

That intrigued me, and we explored that a bit. She confessed to me a sin that was keeping her from an open relationship with God. After praying with her, I suggested we meet once a month or so to check on her spiritual state. Little did I know that this was a clear example of God equipping and calling me to a ministry of spiritual direction. Several years later I applied for spiritual direction training, and in filling out the application I realized that I had been in spiritual direction relationships for quite some time.

My husband and I served as global servants in Europe for twenty years, and I found that all my relationships with the believers there were centered around discerning how God was at work in their hearts and souls. It was natural for me to press into the questions they had and look together for where God was inviting, where he was present, and how they might respond. I am grateful for my training in spiritual direction, and for the opportunity to practice it in our ministry to global servants. Over and over, the spiritual direction relationship is the key for robust spiritual health and for grounding in the love and purposes of God. It is a deep blessing to be part of God's desire to make his Son known to all people by helping global servants thrive in their lives and ministries.

Sarah
global servant in France

Spiritual Direction
The Ancient Pathway toward Discernment

Former missionary in Nigeria and International Director of SIM, Jim Plueddemann, describes the current paradigm for missions as that of an efficient machine. He says that while statistical measurements might work in a factory, they don't measure personal growth. Without a paradigm shift, the church will end up only making converts but not developing discerning disciples.[170] Eternal, inward change cannot be predicted, nor easily measured. Like Plueddemann, I believe missions must make sure there is a renewed focus on spiritual formation that makes use of three graces that God uses in the process of spiritual maturity: the Word of God, the Spirit of God, and the people of God. One of the best ways of utilizing all three means of grace is through the ancient pathway of spiritual direction.

What Is Spiritual Direction?

A simple definition of spiritual direction is when a person (the director) listens to a person (the directee) in a compassionate, attentive, prayerful, and confidential way in order to help the directee see God's presence more fully. Spiritual direction is neither "spiritually" more important than any other practice, nor is it necessarily "directive." Spiritual directors typically do not tell another person what to do. The focus is always on the directee and what they are feeling and thinking. The director's role is to simply ask good questions and offer invitations to understand God's workings.

Spiritual direction is utilizing what Jesus said in John 16:12–13: "I have much more to say to you, more than you can now bear. But when he, the Spirit of truth, comes, he will guide you into all truth." Or, as James tells us, "Come near to God and he will come near to you" (Jas 4:8). The Holy Spirit is the true director of the time together, as both the spiritual director and directee pay attention to the Spirit's invitations.

While some evangelicals prefer to use other terminology for spiritual direction, the universal markers for it are sharing and support through spiritual guidance. Though we all need spiritual wisdom, global servants living amid the ambiguities of life and ministry in unfamiliar and lonely outposts could especially benefit from an additional wise perspective. Spiritual direction provides empowerment to respond to the Spirit in times of cultural uncertainty and overwhelming stress and workloads.

---

170 James E. Plueddemann, *Leading Across Cultures: Effective Ministry and Mission in the Global Church* (Downers Grove, IL: IVP, 2009), 189.

The Difference between Spiritual Direction and Other Helping Relationships

Spiritual direction may sound trendy, but in fact it has a long and honored history in Christian soul care. However, spiritual direction can be confused with other well-known and treasured Christian guidance. So how might we differentiate spiritual direction from other Christian practices such as psychotherapy, pastoral counseling, and discipleship ministries?

The following chart simplifies the different approaches of four major counseling relationships.[171]

	Spiritual Direction	Psychotherapy	Pastoral Counseling	Discipleship
Presenting Problem	Desire for God: desire to know God and to make one's faith heartfelt; relational development with God	Desire to heal an emotional wound: trauma, emotional needs, mental illness, problem behaviors, addictions, anxiety, depression, fear	Desire for help with personal problems: a specific life challenge or problem; seeking biblical wisdom for parenting, marriage, or life issues	Desire to mature in the Christian faith: ignorance of Christian life and practice, mentoring in spiritual assessment, Bible study, prayer, tithing, etc.
Goals	Experience the presence of God: in one's heart and realities of life, finding God's will, and conforming to Christ—becoming Christlike	Curing the disease: integration, personal wholeness, and social harmony	Resolving the problem: applying biblical wisdom from Scripture to the specific problem, dealing with sin, and finding Christ	Growing in knowledge of God and Christian practices: discovering what it means to be a Christian through spiritual growth, fellowship, and worship
Procedures	Threefold listening, to oneself, the Holy Spirit, and the director: listening, prayer, and directive response as needed by suggesting appropriate spiritual discipline	Therapeutic listening, testing, and assessing: crisis intervention, group therapy, reframing, developing plan of action, medication	Individual, couple, or family counseling: working through a specific problem by listening, giving information, scriptural counsel, and prayer	Teaching specific discipleship material: some listening, but mainly information-based teaching through a program of material

---

[171] For a more detailed look at the differences between spiritual direction, mental health counseling (psychotherapy), and pastoral counseling, see Gary W. Moon and David G. Benner, "Spiritual Direction and Christian Soul Care," in *Spiritual Direction and the Care of Souls: A Guide to Christian Approaches and Practices*, eds. Gary W. Moon and David G. Benner (Downers Grove, IL: IVP, 2004), 11–28.

Ignatian Spirituality

In chapter 3 we explored the spirituality of St. Ignatius of Loyola and the Jesuits. Now let's look at Ignatian influence on spiritual direction. Probably no other figure in church history, outside of Jesus himself, was as influential in the development of spiritual direction as Ignatius.[172] First, let's summarize the history of how Ignatius developed his use of spiritual direction for the Jesuits:

- Ignatius' own personal life exhibited radical and fundamental transformation, godly submission, and obedience to the lordship of Jesus Christ.
- Ignatius developed spiritual practices, including spiritual direction, which shaped his affections, intellect, and will.
- Ignatius' spiritual practices and personal humility influenced a group of like-minded men, who formed the early Jesuit society.
- This society, the Friends of Jesus, used the spiritual direction found in the *Spiritual Exercises of Ignatius* to move out in mission to the known world.[173]

The key understanding for Ignatius was the balance between being and doing—what Ignatian spirituality calls contemplation in action. This tension between waiting and acting is one of the most difficult challenges we face as global servants.

I recently interacted with a national mission leader from Eastern Europe who was struggling to find the balance between time with God, his family, and ministry demands—something many Eastern European ministers fail to even address. He shared that many pastors in his country are subject to burnout because they live beyond their personal capacities and knowledge of God. I mentioned that he might have the opportunity to influence a whole generation from his country if he was willing to listen to the Holy Spirit's counsel and set up conscious balance between being and doing. These rhythms are what Ignatian spirituality calls contemplation in action.

What we need to see is that the two—contemplation and activism—are not opposites, but rather counterparts to one another. Ignatius knew how to meet the demands of ministry while also being connected to Christ. Through his own life experience he elaborately, and often at the risk of church censorship, forged a clear pathway between spiritual reflection and Spirt-led action. He was able to lead others because he had first done it well for himself. The processing of his spiritual life and contemplation was recorded in *The Spiritual Exercises*. These exercises were created not so much to be read but to be experienced. Ignatius believed spirituality is better caught than taught, and he developed a process which enabled others to experience God's direct and personal guidance.

---

172 A lone possible exception in church history was Count Zinzendorf and the Moravians, who used an informal practice called "speakings" to influence missionary candidates. This was an adapted method of spiritual direction which called upon community discernment for missionary activity. For a detailed look at Jesus' method and examples of spiritual direction, see Bruce Demarest, *Soulguide: Following Jesus as Spiritual Director* (Colorado Springs: NavPress, 2003).

173 Ignatius of Loyola, *The Spiritual Exercises of St. Ignatius,* trans. Louis J. Puhl (New York: Vintage Books, 2000).

Let's illustrate by using Ignatius' discussion of decision-making.[174] His writing is centered upon the rhythms of consolations and desolations, which he claimed are integral to spiritual growth. Ignatius believed that there are movements in the heart that lead either toward God or away from him. For example, I might go for a walk in the woods one day and become overwhelmed by God's beautiful creation. This is a consolation.

Conversely, I might find myself frustrated and irritated due to a multitude of interruptions which is slowing my work. This is a desolation. One moves me closer to God and the other moves me away. When I observe these conditions of my soul, I am better able to see where God is present or absent in my life. I can then discern how to make choices that will move me toward greater spiritual growth.

But often it takes another person, a spiritual director, to help us see the differences. For global workers, even if isolated, there are four possible ways we can experience spiritual direction. I will list them in order from individual to communal opportunities.

Spiritual Direction through Reading the Bible and Spiritual Classics

Seeking biblical wisdom through the reading and study of the Bible is the priority of every global servant. Two major passages that speak to the leading of the Holy Spirit are Romans 8 and Galatians 5. These passages speak not to specific guidance, but rather of daily godly living, defeating sin, and developing the fruit of the Spirit (Gal 5:18–25). I would also suggest contemplative reading in the Psalms. God's Word is a powerful guide and a primary director in our lives.

Many of us will find ourselves in places where, after time in the Word, we feel the Spirit prompting us toward action. It is best to respond immediately. However, let us not be over-scrupulous. God knows our motivations. The move toward action is what is key, not the nitpicking details. Perhaps the best way of finding individual spiritual direction is to learn to discern the genuine workings of grace through the careful saturation of the Holy Scriptures into our minds and hearts. In being filled with scriptural truth, we are better equipped to instinctively know when the Spirit is speaking.

There are also a great many Christian devotional classics which inform and shape us when we read them to recharge our spirituality. Become familiar with some of the time-tested spiritual classics that the church has produced over the centuries.[175] Just beware that everything the classical writers taught are also subject to discernment under Scripture's authority.[176]

---

174 St. Ignatius of Loyola, *The Spiritual Exercises*, 115–21.

175 Richard J. Foster and Emilie Griffin, eds. *Spiritual Classics: Selected Readings for Individuals and Groups on the Twelve Spiritual Disciplines* (San Francisco: HarperCollins, 2000); and Richard J. Foster and James Bryan Smith, eds. *Devotional Classics: Selected Readings for Individuals and Groups* (New York: HarperCollins, 1993).

176 The best resource I know of for reading the spiritual classics is Jamin Goggin and Kyle Strobel, eds., *Reading the Christian Spiritual Classics: A Guide for Evangelicals* (Downers Grove, IL: IVP, 2013).

Spiritual Direction through Personal Spiritual Directors

The common approach to spiritual direction is through regular meetings with a spiritual director. Generally speaking, spiritual directors should be available to meet with directees at least once a quarter for about an hour to discuss the directee's prayer life. Face-to-face meetings are best, but because this is often impossible on the mission field, the global servant may find it works best to meet with their spiritual director online, over phone calls, or via email. Letter writing has also been a traditional source of spiritual direction throughout the history of the church.[177]

How do we go about finding a spiritual director? In addition to prayer, you may have certain personal preferences that will help you determine what you want in your director. For example, you may prefer a director of your own gender. Or perhaps you would like someone who is a little older than you or has walked with Jesus longer. A young mother may prefer another woman who has already raised her own children. You may desire someone who is from your own particular church tradition, or maybe the opposite—someone whose background is totally different from yours. Take some time to think through what you would like in a potential director.

It is possible that there is someone already in your present circle of contacts that meets your criteria for a spiritual director, or someone you are drawn to as a mature and wise person. Maybe this person is someone you already go to when faced with a difficult or unanswered question. This does not mean that this person is a trained spiritual director, but their life experience and winsome spirit is already benefitting your spiritual growth. If this is the case, you could ask them if they would be open to meeting with you on a regular basis to discuss your ongoing relationship with God.

Many ancient writers list a variety of characteristics for a spiritual director. For example, Jesus points us to humble people (Matt 5:3–10). Paul wants us to be filled with the fruit of the Spirit (Gal 5:22), people who please God not man (1 Thess 2:4), and those who attend to the whole person (1 Thess 5:23).

Many of the desert fathers and mothers explain that spiritual guides must have a spirit of *metanoia*—that is, one of repentance and purity of heart. St. John of the Cross adds that a director needs to be able to hear God's distinctive ways. Teresa of Avila saw the importance of good judgment and experience. She also valued kindness. Francis de Sale saw friendship as the key quality.

More recent writers have added such things as simplicity, lifelong learner, willingness to hold confidences, the ability to balance strength and gentleness, mental clarity, objectivity, awareness, and the ability to attend to one's own spiritual life.[178] These characteristics are honorable but daunting, and no one can meet them all.

---

[177] C. S. Lewis is famous for providing spiritual direction through this method. See Lyle W. Dorsett, *Seeking the Secret Places: The Spiritual Formation of C. S. Lewis* (Grand Rapids: Brazos Books, 2004), 113.

[178] All these characteristics are listed in Tilden Edwards, *Spiritual Director, Spiritual Companion: Guide to Tending the Soul* (Mahwah, NJ: Paulist Press, 2001), 94–96.

There are evangelical training programs for spiritual direction, and a simple Internet search will provide help in locating directors, either near you or ones who are available online. However, caution is advised since not everyone who calls themselves a spiritual director stands in the Christian faith. If you do not know the person, it would be wise to find out about their own personal beliefs about Christ and the Bible before you commit to a long-term relationship with them as your spiritual director.

Spiritual Direction in a Group Setting

A helpful and viable way to get spiritual direction is through group meetings. Within a community of peers, we can offer spiritual companionship and prayers. Most spiritual direction groups focus primarily on praying for guidance for one another. If God speaks to the group, we are not afraid to confirm this, but it must always be done in a spirit of careful listening and prayer. Every group is different, but generally they should number somewhere between four to eight, with leadership shared as much as possible. Meetings can take place monthly or as often as possible, but regularly enough to keep current with one another's lives.[179]

It is important to note that a spiritual direction group should never replace the need for church. This group's purpose is spiritual accompaniment. It does not provide the needed elements found elsewhere in the body, such as worship, the Word, and evangelism. It is not superior to other ministries within the body, but a companion to them.

Spiritual Direction within a Formal Mission Agency Context

I recommend that mission agencies develop a culture of discernment by promoting ongoing spiritual direction for every person in the organization. This opportunity should start at the very beginning of a missionary's career while the newly appointed global servant is raising prayer and financial support. Such a process would not only be a discipling tool for the new missionary, but also a means for discerning where God is leading them in discovering their prayer and financial partners.

After the global servant arrives on the field, annual meetings with designated spiritual directors would reinforce God's guidance in their first term. Historically, spiritual direction is not new to the mission field. Arguably, two of the greatest missionary movements were the Jesuits in the sixteenth century and the Moravians in the eighteenth century. It is interesting to note that both the Jesuits and the Moravians had systems in place to provide regular spiritual direction for their missionaries—whether through formal meetings with superiors for the Jesuits, or the informal meetings with peers for the Moravians.

---

179 For a simple format for group spiritual direction, see David G. Benner, *Sacred Companions: The Gift of Spiritual Friendship and Direction* (Downers Grove, IL: IVP, 2002), 165–83. Also see Rose Mary Dougherty, *Group Spiritual Direction: Community for Discernment* (Mahwah, NJ: Paulist Press, 1995).

For spiritual direction to be maximized, it must be done regularly and ingrained into the life of the mission and its personnel. This means that mission agencies need to promote, identify, and train those with a calling for spiritual direction within their own ranks. However, until this is fully accomplished, spiritual direction could be outsourced to those who are qualified by their training and experience in missions.

Spiritual direction is a forgotten spiritual practice which has been recently resurfacing, especially within Protestant churches. As we care for souls, we do not seek to solve problems so much as to hear from the Lord as he speaks into our lives with his loving care. There is no port of arrival in spiritual direction, only the journey. The stories of our lives with God are continually unfolding through each and every day. Spiritual direction honors that journey.

Reflection and Points to Ponder

- How do you respond when you hear the term *spiritual direction*? What would you like to know more about spiritual direction?

- Choose a story about your faith walk that you have never told anyone. As you write or share about it, answer these questions: Why is this story significant? Where was God present? How would you describe your emotions? What fruit came from this situation? Why have you never shared this story with anyone? How might sharing this incident with a spiritual director be beneficial?

- How would you go about starting a spiritual direction small group with those in your circle? Or, conversely, how would you go about finding a spiritual director for yourself?

For Further Reading

Jeannette A. Bakke, *Holy Invitations: Exploring Spiritual Direction* (Grand Rapids: Baker, 2000). A practical and well-informed resource in regard to spiritual direction.

Morris Dirks, *Forming the Leader's Soul: An Invitation to Spiritual Direction* (n.p.: SoulFormation, 2013). Written from a pastoral perspective, the book challenges pastors to move into relational ministry through the practice of spiritual direction.

Margaret Guenther, *Holy Listening: The Art of Spiritual Direction* (Cambridge, MA: Cowley, 1992). A series of reflections on the art of spiritual direction from an experienced spiritual director.

Gordon T. Smith, *Spiritual Direction: A Guide to Giving and Receiving Direction* (Downers Grove, IL: IVP, 2014). A brief introduction to the basics of spiritual direction from an evangelical perspective.

Thursday morning had finally arrived.

I was picking up the toys of my two toddlers and straightening up the house. In my heart was a growing anticipation of the women who would soon be arriving to my home in Quito, Ecuador.

Several months earlier I had decided to invite a few moms from our community to our home on a Thursday morning to work on our scrapbooks together. They brought their kids, who quickly ran off to play, and we sat around my butcher-paper-covered table to cut paper and pictures, but even more to share the stories of our lives. Out of that initial meeting, word got around, and we had different women around the table each week.

For me to open my home to these women was a treat. I wanted my home to be a warm and inviting place where women found rest and fellowship. I loved preparing special snacks and having fun things for the kids to do. Some weeks there was uproarious laughter around my table, and other weeks there were honest tears. We became a group that prayed for each other, took meals when someone was sick, cared for each other's kids, and grew to love each other deeply. I never could have dreamed that my desire to offer hospitality in this simple way would be something the Lord would use to show me the true passion of my heart, which is caring for others and shepherding their hearts.

Jen
global servant in Ecuador

Hospitality
The Ancient Pathway to Space and Freedom

Henri Nouwen wrote that "hospitality is ministry and all ministry is hospitality."[180] Though hospitality is a waning practice in the Western church, it is still a large part of ministry on the mission field. Missionaries are, at times, defined by how they host and are hosted. Global workers, whether at home or abroad, usually travel to visit people and churches. Those of us who work in faith missions are required to raise our own financial support, which means we must interact with many people in homes. When on the field, we often need to travel and visit ministries and churches, just like in the New Testament (3 John 8).

Hospitality is a mark of biblical love within the Christian community. To offer hospitality is to welcome, accept, and receive one another. It's not as much about food and lodging (though that is included) as it is about having a heart of generosity. When we receive another not as a burden, but in love, we are receiving Christ. "He who receives you receives me, and he who receives me receives the one who sent me" (Matt 10:40). Gordon Smith says hospitality is a marker of Christian presence in the world. He believes it is an integral part of vocational holiness.[181]

The importance of hospitality is in the vividness it brings to one's relationship with God. I often hear missionaries complain about their lack of intimacy with the Father. "I feel so dry in my prayer life." "I wonder where God is, because he seems so distant and I am so lonely." Isolation can be the reality for a global servant. We can be surrounded by people and yet feel that no one really sees or understands us. There can be many explanations for this emptiness in our lives, but one remedy is to practice the art of hospitality.

Biblical Hospitality

Hospitality was a high cultural value in both the New and Old Testament. It was at the foundation of God and man's relationship. God created the Garden of Eden to be a hospitable place and welcomed humankind to live in the sacred space of his presence.

---

180 Henri Nouwen, "Education to Ministry," *Theological Education* 9 (Autumn 1972), 50.
181 Gordon T. Smith, *Called to Be Saints: An Invitation to Christian Maturity* (Downers Grove, IL: IVP, 2014), 123.

Middle Eastern hospitality is reflected often in the Old Testament (Gen 18:19; Deut 10:18–19; Lev 19:33–34; 1 Sam 25:8; Job 31:31–32). Throughout the pages of Scripture, the responsibility of caring for the traveler and those in need is largely taken for granted because it was the norm. But hospitality was also more than mere custom. It was a demonstration of faithfulness to God. The prophet Isaiah described true "fasting" to the people of Israel:

> *Is it not to share your food with the hungry and to provide the poor wanderer with shelter—when you see the naked, to clothe him, and not to turn away from your own flesh and blood. Then your light will break forth like the dawn, and your healing will quickly appear; then your righteousness will go before you, and the glory of the Lord will be your rear guard. —Isaiah 58:7–8*

In the New Testament, hospitality was described by the Greek words *philoxenia* (love of strangers), *xenizo* (to receive as a guest), *synago* (entertain, Matt 25:35), and *lambano* (receive, 3 John 8). The washing of guests' feet (John 13:1–17) and a kiss of welcome (Luke 7:44–46) were customary. Jesus certainly invited his disciples to practice hospitality. He opened his life to strangers (Matt 25:35). He invited the poor, crippled, and lame (Luke 14:13). He offered a cup of cold water (Matt 10:42). Jesus also emphasized that a special responsibility for hospitality should be given for those serving God.[182]

Acts and the New Testament letters reveal that hospitality was seen as a mark of Christian discipleship in the early church. In fact, both itinerant teachers in the first century and modern missionary expansion has been dependent upon entertaining guests.[183] "Do not forget to entertain strangers, for by so doing some people have entertained angels without knowing it" (Heb 13:2). "Offer hospitality to one another without grumbling" (1 Pet 4:9).

Hospitality is, at its core, outward-looking, instantaneous, and generous in meeting the needs of others. Within the church, it is actually a gift (*charisma*) from God (1 Pet 4:10–11). It is an essential characteristic of being a Christ-follower. After the New Testament era, the early church practiced hospitality not just for individual travelers but also through the establishment of hospitals, way stations, food programs, alms (giving to the poor), and the building of monasteries which served as accommodations for travelers.

Community Hospitality: Invitation to Safe Space

"Hospitality is a practical outworking of the call to love and creates a space for formation."[184] Hospitality is the warmth of acceptance, being known and welcomed. This opens us up to be ourselves, freeing us to discover God, his gifts in our lives, and the others who will journey with us. It fosters our spiritual growth through mutual shepherding, caregiving, transparency, accountability, and

---

[182] See Matthew 10:14; Luke 9:5.

[183] See Acts 9:43; 11:18; 16:15; Rom 16:23; Titus 3:13.

[184] James Wilhoit, *Spiritual Formation as if the Church Mattered: Growing in Christ through Community* (Grand Rapids: Baker, 2008), 198.

intentionality. At a basic level, through hospitality we become spacious people by offering grace, shelter, and the welcoming presence of Jesus.

Our world desperately needs safe people and safe places. Hospitality is one of the ways God creates space to be safe in a hostile world. Henri Nouwen taught that hospitality was not effecting change in people, but lavishly providing space where change can take place. Without this critical element of space, hospitality is less than authentic. Nouwen defines hospitable space as free, friendly, welcoming, open, empty, and fearless.[185]

We create a safe place for our guests, but at the same time we also maintain proper boundaries for ourselves so that genuine love, friendship, and care can be freely given with no strings attached. In true fellowship there must be a mutuality of sharing which allows us to present ourselves authentically. Nouwen says, "Real receptivity asks for confrontation because space can only be a welcoming space when there are clear boundaries, and boundaries are limits between which we define our own position. Flexible limits but limits nevertheless."[186] Hospitality with boundaries frees us to be ourselves with others.

Community Hospitality: Invitation to Freedom

True spiritual community in Christ has a spirit of freedom. In this spirit, we are inclusive, declaring there is room at the table for everyone. Invitation, care, recognition, and respect are deeply human and holy elements. We are not free when we exclude or separate others from joining us in fellowship. Freedom offers the ability to love and to give generously to all according to our individual gifts (1 Cor 12).

In genuine hospitality, we must guard against a scarcity mentality. There is no liberty in this. Missionaries struggle with spending their precious dollars on anything that is not recognized ministry. We can therefore become stingy and hoard our resources for ourselves. When gripped by the love of Jesus, however, we grant dignity by freely giving to others as needed.

When we lovingly provide for others, we free them to share their lives honestly. We create opportunities for transforming shalom rest. In hospitality, we do not rush. It is like a truly splendid meal where both host and guest linger over dessert and coffee, savoring every moment of the whole experience. When we take the time to loiter together, we offer God the opportunity to shape us into a stronger community.

Hospitality sets the table, but God provides the food. It is foolish to believe that hospitality itself can produce lasting transformation. This is a ministry and blessing that can only be explained by the blessing of the Almighty God. Therefore, in hospitality we invite not only one another into space and freedom, but also the Holy Spirit to come upon us in the fullness of grace and love. The fruitfulness of hospitality is the result of the work of the Triune God having the space to move among his people.

---

185 Henri Nouwen, *Reaching Out: The Three Movements of the Spiritual Life* (New York: Doubleday, 1975), 60.
186 Nouwen, 60.

Welcoming Presence: The Spirit of Hospitality

"Therefore welcome one another as Christ has welcomed you, for the glory of God" (Rom 15:7 ESV). As we share our goods and resources, our homes and food, our lives and love, we create a welcoming presence so others may experience the reality of God's open heart toward them. Being servants with hospitable hearts creates pathways for trans-formation, and God is glorified. This is about loving people, not merely entertaining them.

Hospitality also teaches us many lessons. When my wife and I first arrived on the field our son was only two years old. We had brought some of his toys and playthings along to the field with us. The Serbian stores we shopped at had little for young children, and what they did have was poorly made and prone to break easily. Our English children books were something precious and dear to us. So it was with strong angst when one day I looked out at our front yard and saw neighborhood kids taking our son's toys home with them. I quickly sprung from my office to rescue the toys! This continued so much so that I soon found I was spending an inordinate amount of time guarding our toys.

I prided myself on leaving everything behind to come to the mission field, only to find a deep possessiveness in my heart. How were neighbors to see a welcoming presence of Christ in my life when all I was doing was chasing after things! In the early church, possessions were shared among all believers (Acts 2:32–47). Could it be that our posture—what we do or don't do—toward our possessions are indicators of whether the Spirit is truly in our midst?

The early Jerusalem church "ate together with glad and sincere hearts" (Acts 2:46). The word used for *sincere* in this verse can mean single-minded devotion, the absence of pretense, sincerity, and generosity—all earmarks of hospitality.[187] Impressing others was not the goal because their attitude toward one another was one of respect, love, openness, space, and freedom, which enabled them to truly enjoy each other.

Early church father John Chrysostom beautifully described the hospitality of the church in Acts: "This was an angelic commonwealth, not to call anything of theirs their own. Forthwith the roots of evils were cut out . . . none reproached, none envied, none grudged; no pride, no contempt was there . . . the poor man knew no shame, the rich no haughtiness."[188]

John the apostle writes in his first letter these supporting words: "If anyone has material possessions and sees his brother in need but has no pity on him, how can the love of God be in him? Dear children, let us not love with words or tongue but with actions and in words of truth" (1 John 3:17–18).

---

187 F. F. Bruce, *The Book of Acts, The New International Commentary on the New Testament* (Grand Rapids: Eerdmans, 1980), 81; John R. W. Stott, *The Message of Acts, The Bible Speaks Today* (Downers Grove, IL: IVP, 1990), 82–83.

188 John Chrysostom, "The Homilies on the Acts of the Apostles," in *A Select Library of the Nicene and Post-Nicene Fathers,* ed. Philip Schaff, vol. XI (Grand Rapids: Eerdmans, reprint 1975), 47.

Creating space and freedom for spiritual conversation, meeting material needs, and inviting people into the welcoming presence of Jesus are vital to our spiritual formation. Missionaries need to be people who practice hospitality as well as people who receive hospitality. We need our tables to welcome both friends and strangers. We need to listen and attend well to others. James tells us, "My dear brothers, take note of this: Everyone should be quick to listen, slow to speak and slow to become angry" (Jas 1:19). This is the spirit of hospitality which creates the space and freedom to welcome Jesus in our midst.

Reflection and Points to Ponder

- When have you felt deeply received and welcomed by someone? How did that touch your soul? When did you experience woundedness and hurt because you were not received or welcomed by someone?
- How has Jesus touched your life and healed your wounds? How can you be hospitable to others in the way Jesus has been to you?
- How comfortable are you when guests come calling—invited or uninvited?
- Do you struggle with performance and perfectionism? What things could you do to shift your focus, even being more hospitable toward yourself?
- How might Jesus want to use your home and resources and your heart and love as a shelter for others?

For Further Reading

Karen Burton Mains, *Open Heart, Open Home: The Hospitable Way to Make Others Feel Welcome and Wanted* (Downers Grove, IL: IVP, 1997), revised ed. An exploration of the deeper concepts of Christian hospitality, using our home and opening our heart to care for others.

Henri J. Nouwen, *Reaching Out: The Three Movements of the Spiritual Life* (New York: Doubleday, 1975). Nouwen presents three movements of the spiritual life. The second involves moving from hostility to hospitality.

Dustin Willis and Brandon Clements, *The Simplest Way to Change the World: Biblical Hospitality as a Way of Life* (Chicago: Moody, 2017). The authors write about how a life of biblical hospitality can make a difference for the gospel.

I struggled throughout grade school

with epilepsy. My life was full of periodic seizures, lonely lunch hours, and being the last kid picked for kickball. I was sad much of my childhood.

And I wondered, why do I even exist? The world is full of such amazing people, why did God create me? I wished I had some great dream to pursue, but mostly I just tried to make it through from day to day without being too depressed.

In desperation, I gave my heart to Jesus when I was twenty-four. Immediately I was filled with a new sense of gratitude and my life took on new meaning. It's like I had been living life in shades of grey and suddenly the color was dialed up. My life felt like it had new value. All I wanted to do was to somehow give back the special gift I had received.

That's when I discovered the real joy of submitting to Jesus and serving others. When I felt his Spirit impress me to hold out my hand to help someone else, the color in life became more vivid. It's like he heightened all my senses. And then something inside me began to shine. Like golden nuggets in a clump of clay, I discovered that I had new and special gifts I could give others.

Like an elixir to my soul, a true joy thrills my heart when I can reach out to give others what God's given me, to fulfill something that they are lacking. Sometimes it gets really hard to do and it costs me more than I think I have to offer, but somehow there's always a reserve tucked away, hidden inside of me that I didn't know was there. And then God refills me again and the freshness of being renewed makes me willing to start all over again, for his glory.

It's like eating potato chips. Once you reach inside the bag and eat one, the craving increases and it's hard to stop.

Jim
global servant in Germany

Submission
The Ancient Pathway of Following

I have been a missionary for almost forty years, serving as both a leader and a follower during that time. One of the most disappointing observations I have witnessed during these years has been the struggle many global servants have working together in teams. Unfortunately, interpersonal conflict stemming from poor team dynamics seems to be the norm rather than the exception in the mission community. I have been a part of teams torn apart by conflict, and as a member-care worker I have witnessed devastating strife in many other groups. In fact, my personal belief is that world evangelism is harmed more from inner fighting than outside persecution. We are our own worst enemy!

What can be done to lessen the occurrence and intensity of these conflicts? Learning the discipline of proper submission is a good starting point. Submission is a spiritual act, because as Adele Calhoun says, "True biblical submission is not linked solely to hierarchy and roles. It begins in the very center of the Trinity where the Father and the Son and the Holy Spirit all mutually honor and defer to each other."[189]

The Missionary Call

Understanding biblical submission requires us first to look at the missionary call. Missionaries need to have a sense of calling. In fact, many organizations refuse to appoint someone unless there is a stated call to the mission field. This calling is what gives a global servant a strong vocational commitment to serve for the long haul. It is an anchor for their lives and ministry and keeps them pressing onward when difficulties and challenges arise (Phil 3:12–14).

But a missionary call can also have a dark side. This happens when we own our ministry so much that we refuse input and accountability from others. As Os Guinness says, the wonder of calling has grown into the "horror of conceit."[190] A global servant's inordinate pride leads to losing sight that each one of us is part of a bigger body (1 Cor 12:12–31).

---

[189] Adele Ahlberg Calhoun, *Spiritual Disciplines Handbook: Practices That Transform Us* (Downers Grove, IL: IVP, 2003), 119.

[190] Os Guinness, *The Call: Finding and Fulfilling the Central Purpose of Your Life* (Nashville: W Publishing, 2003), 113.

Thankfully, global servants do not need to doubt God's calling; they only need to recognize and modify their ownership over that call. "Vocation does not come from willfulness," says Parker Palmer. "It comes from listening. I must listen to my life and try to understand what it is truly about—quite apart from what I would like it to be about—or my life will never represent anything real in the world, no matter how earnest my intentions."[191]

In other words, calling is not a goal to be achieved, but rather a gift to be received. The global servant must always keep in mind that he or she is first called not to a place or a ministry or a people group, but to a person—Jesus Christ.

Submission is the means God uses to affirm our calling and accomplish unity among missionaries. Our submission to God allows him to form our choices, vocations, callings, and persons. God owns our ministry, not us. It should not lessen our passion and steadfastness for our ministries, but our commitment becomes not to our work but to the God who calls us to that work.

Leadership Defined

Because leadership skills fluctuate over time and according to organizational needs, leadership is a highly complex and diverse phenomenon. When we ask what kind of leadership we need, "It all depends" is a valid answer, because different skills are needed at different times. One thing that never changes, however, is the biblical truth that relationships are at the center of a leader's responsibility.

When we as leaders focus only on tasks, goals, and results, we can easily be tempted to use people to accomplish agendas and to let the ends justify the means. We can steamroll over people to get what we want, and in doing so deeply hurt others. But Jesus brings us back to the essence of Christian community when he says, "By this all men will know that you are my disciples, if you love one another" (John 13:35). "A loving community, says Jesus, is the visible authentication of the gospel."[192] Our genuine love for one another sets Christian community apart from the world and draws seekers to Jesus.

Leadership is mentioned as a spiritual gift in the New Testament, but Paul says it is neither higher nor lower than other gifts (Rom 12:1–8). The Bible focuses more on a person's inner life than on his or her titles and skills. There must be an element of relational knowledge and love between followers and leaders. This is often missing from the world's definition of leadership. Jesus describes leading like this:

The watchman opens the gate for [the shepherd], and the sheep listen to his voice. He calls his own sheep by name and leads them out. When he has brought out all his own, he goes on ahead of them, and his sheep follow him because they

---

191 Parker J. Palmer, *Let Your Life Speak: Listening to the Voice of Vocation* (San Francisco: Jossey-Bass, 2000), 4.
192 Bruce Milne, *The Message of John: The Bible Speaks Today* (Downers Grove, IL: IVP, 1993), 206.

know his voice. But they will never follow a stranger; in fact, they will run away from him because they do not recognize a stranger's voice. . . . I am the good shepherd. The good shepherd lays down his life for the sheep. . . . I am the good shepherd; I know my sheep and my sheep know me. —John 10:3–5, 11, 14

This leader-follower dynamic has a mutual sharing of life and work. It requires leaders who do not think of themselves more highly than they ought (Rom 12:3), but instead consider others better than themselves (Phil 2:3). This is especially important in mission structures which are constrained by geographic and time distances between leaders and missionaries who are spread around the globe. Since trust is so important, mission leadership requires some informality. Leaders must not rely solely on dictating policies from a central headquarters, but rather on creative, fresh relationships that resemble more of an organism than an organization. Such a focus supports the biblical doctrine of the priesthood of all believers (1 Pet 2:9), where there is a recognition that everyone contributes in Christian ministry.

Leaders and followers who want to maintain healthy and strong relationships must be mutually candid with each other. This means that everyone can give honest input on directions and decisions, even if the leader still has the final say. Without relational openness, true spiritual community cannot exist. Honest sharing builds credibility, which in turn builds trust and confidence in one another. When we are honest even about our mistakes, we echo the words of the anonymous fourteenth-century author of *The Cloud of Unknowing*:

> *Take a good look at yourself. Who are you? What makes you worthy of your calling from God? Never forget your spiritual vulnerability. . . . Instead of feeling proud of yourself, exercise humility. . . . Remember your spiritual needs rather than your spiritual achievements.*[193]

A healthy leader leads by giving attention to the quality of interpersonal relationships and is intentional about developing places of safety for others. Sadly, such leaders are rare. In a meeting I attended, the leader of a mission organization told the group that he was tired of hearing about being a safe person. He said he wasn't interested in people feeling safe when they came to him. It was no surprise, then, that people avoided going to him with any feedback on his decisions and polices.

When leaders are open, they become safe people for others because they aren't afraid to look at themselves in the mirror. They are willing to learn and grow, both in position and personhood. Leaders should not fear personal imperfections.

Jesus didn't choose the future leaders of the church because they were perfect. "There is no suggestion in the Gospel stories as written that Jesus was going after the brightest and the best."[194] The apostle Paul also spoke out against this type of thinking. "God deliberately chose men and women that the culture

---

[193] *The Cloud of Unknowing*, ed. Bernard Bangley (Brewster, UK: Paraclete Press, 2006), 6.

[194] Eugene Peterson, *Tell It Slant: A Conversation on the Language of Jesus in His Stories and Prayers* (Grand Rapids: Eerdmans, 2008), 115.

overlooks and exploits and abuses, chose these 'nobodies' to expose the hollow pretensions of the 'somebodies'" (1 Cor 1:28, The Message).

Leaders who trust not in their own understanding alone, but in all their ways acknowledge the Lord, will see their path directed (Prov 3:5–6). First Samuel 13:14 tells us that the foundational understanding of biblical leadership is the searching, calling, and empowerment of the Lord himself, for "the Lord has sought out a man after his own heart and appointed him leader of his people."

Followership Defined

Most North American global servants have been raised in a pervasive culture of "me first." Being a follower, therefore, is almost always viewed negatively. Our society tends to overvalue leaders and undervalue followers. Being called a follower often connotes being among the timid and mindless herd. Leaders are the ones who get the status and rewards; followers are second-rate, lacking the necessary skills, abilities, or character to lead. But this is not the case for those who follow Christ. Jesus turned everything upside down when he said, "The one who rules [should be] like the one who serves" (Luke 22:26). True biblical submission, learned through the slow formation of following Christ's authority, is a key factor for abiding, fruitful ministry.

The Bible actually has more to say about followership than leadership. Ken Williams of Wycliffe Bible Translators corrects misunderstandings about biblical followership by teaching what followership does *not* mean.[195] First, being a follower does not mean that someone is inferior. Notice what Paul said in the midst of proclaiming what God will do at the end of this age: "When he has done this, then the Son himself will be made subject to him who put everything under him, so that God may be all in all" (1 Cor 15:28). Though Jesus is subject to the will of the Father, he is not inferior to God. He is subject in function or role, but not in person.

Second, followership does not mean that a person lacks insight, good ideas, skills, or other gifts and abilities. In the book of Genesis, Joseph possesses great abilities, although for a period of his life he was only a slave. Another example in the New Testament is the mentorship of Timothy under the apostle Paul. Timothy was serving Paul, but he was encouraged not to neglect his own personal giftedness (2 Tim 1:6).

Finally, a follower need not always give blind, unthinking obedience without honest feedback to a leader. Whether considering education, natural giftedness, or previous experience, everyone has a unique set of gifts, abilities, and life-lessons that can contribute to a team's purpose and project. In fact, both leaders and followers orbit around a common purpose, and both should submit to that purpose. Abraham (Gen 18:16–33) and Moses (Ex 32:9–14) are examples of those who responded to God with open communication, often discussing and even arguing with God when they disagreed with what they perceived his directives were to be.

---

195 Ken Williams, unpublished notes on biblical followership (Wycliffe Bible Translators Counseling Department, 1990).

A teachable spirit, purity of life, heart for the Word of God, commitment to Christ's body, deep prayer, and demonstration of the fruit of the Spirit are all characteristics of a follower of Jesus.[196] Without such characteristics, followership will be poor. However, does being a follower mean we must always totally submit to our superiors under all circumstances?

Submission and Obedience

The stories of abusive leadership, even among mission agencies, are legend. The misplaced appeal to authority has been used to manipulate and destroy in the name of God. Due to such abuse, the concept of total submission—of surrendering to anyone—has become suspect, and understandably so. Certain teachings on Christian leadership, when carried to an extreme, teach harmful forms of control and manipulation.[197] The major error of such teaching "rested upon the false assumption that submission was the equivalent of unconditional obedience and that God vests certain people with unquestioned authority over others."[198]

So how do we draw the line between the benefits and demands of biblical submission and the harm and abuse of unbiblical authoritative leadership? The answer lies in understanding the differences between obedience and submission. On the surface, both appear to be the same; both are biblical commands and foundational practices for Christians.[199] But there is a subtle difference between the two. This difference centers on motivation. David Benner draws out this slight but nevertheless key distinction:

> *Christians focus on obedience more than surrender. But while the two concepts are closely related, they differ in important ways. . . . Surrender is foundational to Christian spirituality and is the soil out of which obedience should grow. Christ does not simply want our compliance. He wants our heart. He wants our love, and he offers us his. He invites us to surrender to his love.*[200]

Benner says, "Those who surrender obey. But not all who obey surrender."[201] Love is the motivation behind our submission. Those who love, obey; but not all who obey love. Many missionaries obey out of behavioral responses but not heart responses. Motivations such as fear, guilt, shame, or manipulation are often the true reasons we toe the line. But love should be at the root of any obedience, and

---

196 See Pss 27:4; 42:1–2; Prov 9:8–10; Matt 4:19; 6:9–33; Luke 9:23; 11:1–4; John 6:5–66; 13:13; 17:22–26; Acts 2:42, 44–47; 4:31–33; 1 Cor 5:15; 13:4–7; Gal 5:22–25; Eph 4:1–3, 22; 5:5; Col 3:5–10, 16; 1 Thess 4:3–7; 2 Tim 2:15; Heb 10:24; 1 Pet 2:13–25; 1 John 1–3.

197 See, for example, the critique of such manipulation by church authorities in Frank A. Viola, *Who Is Your Covering? A Fresh Look at Leadership, Authority, and Accountability*, rev. ed. (Brandon, FL: Present Testimony Ministry, 1999).

198 Viola, 50.

199 Many passages in the Bible speak of obedience and submission. Here are some key Scriptures on obedience: Ex 19:5; 2 Chr 31:21; Isa 1:19; Jer 7:23; John 14:15, 23; 15:10; Acts 5:29; Rom 1:5; 6:17; 2 Cor 10:6; Phil 2:12; Phlm 21; Heb 5:8; 1 Pet 1:2, 14; 2 John 6. On submission: Matt 26:39–42; Mark 14:36; Luke 22:42; Rom 13:1; 1 Cor 16:7, 16; Eph 5:21–24; 1 Tim 2:11; Heb 12:9; Jas 3:17; 4:7; 1 Pet 3:1; 5:5.

200 David G. Benner, *Surrender to Love: Discovering the Heart of Christian Spirituality* (Downers Grove, IL: IVP, 2003), 10.

201 Benner, 55.

this surrender to love is what defines true submission. God is love, and obedient service is offered out of a response of love for him. This interweaving of love and submission is at the core of our spirituality.

It is no surprise then that the foundation to a missionary's spirituality is a submissive response to God's initiation of love for us and for his kingdom. A missionary is always called to submit to God, but he or she is not always called to obey others when faced with a decision that does not conform to the love of God and his truth.[202] Such obedience is not biblical because it works against both love and justice. Of course, this kind of circumstance involves mature discernment on the part of the person experiencing it.

Watchman Nee, in his well-known but equally misunderstood book, *Spiritual Authority,* writes, "Submission is a matter of attitude, while obedience is a matter of conduct."[203] As Nee explains, submission is the general heart attitude, while obedience is only the outcome and application. "Sometimes obedience is submission, whereas at other times an inability to obey may still be submission."[204]

True submission is always willing to suffer the consequences of any action. It does not, therefore, demand its rights, even when appropriate. It surrenders to God's love and lets God justify or not.[205] The key is to practice inward submission but not slavish obedience. Difficulties within mission agencies arise when we confuse the two, because most conflicts are related to a lack of inward submission rather than to simple disobedience.[206]

Power and Control

All global servants should be disciples of Jesus Christ, under his authority. However, God places certain people, such as those with the gift of leadership (Rom 12:8), as his representative leader. This always has the potential for spiritual abuse. Through inappropriate means of power and control, both followers and leaders can be guilty of instigating as well as being victims of abuse.

Followers can unfairly mistrust their present leaders because they have previously suffered abuse from the hands of other supervisors. When followers jump to conclusions too quickly and negatively react to authority, problems arise. On the mission field, this is compounded by missionaries who come from cultures that value self-determination and independence. But Jesus did not come to abolish the law (Matt 5:17), though he did redefine it as an authority of function, not status or position. "You know that the rulers of the Gentiles lord it over them, and their high officials exercise authority over them. Not so with you. Instead,

---

202 See Acts 4:19.

203 Watchman Nee, *Spiritual Authority* (New York: Christian Fellowship Publishers, 1972), 107.

204 Nee, 108.

205 The supreme biblical example of such submissive attitudes are found throughout the book of Daniel. For example, we see this in Daniel 1 (with the eating of rich and non-kosher foods) and Daniel 3 (Nebuchadnezzar's statue). In both cases, Daniel and his friends disobeyed authority by not following their orders, but they also submitted to their authority by being willing to suffer the consequences of their disobedience.

206 I have found that most missionaries will not outright go against their mission leadership, but inwardly they are angry and harbor hurt and resentfulness, which, if unaddressed, hinders team function.

whoever wants to be first must be your slave" (Matt 20:25). For Jesus, authority rested not in a title but in a towel (John 13:1–17).

Of course, to submit is easier said than done. Anyone can submit to a decision when one agrees with it; the difficulty comes when we disagree with a decision. When there is a difference of opinion, how will the global servant respond? Submission in these cases is a choice to surrender first to Christ and then to his functional authority in the church.

We must also work against selective submission. This is malicious compliance in which we practice obedience, but we still maintain control of the decision. An example of this kind of selective submission is the "it is better to beg forgiveness than ask approval" approach, which seems to be rampant in missions today. Due to the pressure of distance and time, global servants often find it easier to go ahead with something and present a de facto decision to their leaders. They retain control while feigning compliance.

In a similar way, leaders who struggle with power and control can be experts at exerting pressure in inappropriate ways. In fact, this abuse of authority is all too endemic in mission circles. Some leaders abuse their authority through the misuse of Scripture to boost their position or decisions, bullying others from the pulpit. Through such pressure a leader motivates guilt or shame, not love. The playing field is never level, because when a leader sets himself or herself up as the one who speaks for God, who would dare to question it?

A central feature of all these scenarios is the issue of power and control. Seeking control is a basic hindrance to maturity in Christ. As a disciple we need to remember we cannot control how Jesus will work in our lives. Power struggles only turn people away. The church cannot be revealed in all its attractiveness and glory to the unbelieving world if it refuses to acknowledge the true meaning of submission, obedience, and surrender. True intimacy, true incarnational presence, and true mission requires sacrifice and surrender because, paradoxically, the abundant life promised by Christ comes not by grasping but by releasing.[207] Love increases when power decreases.

Those who grasp at power, ironically, powerfully resist being grasped by God.[208] But by following the ancient pathway of spiritual submission we discover the truth of the great reversal. It is only when we give up power and control and surrender to love that we are then able to be shaped by the presence, purpose, and power of Jesus. Only then does the peace of God which surpasses all understanding come upon us and we are able to know God's perfect will (Phil 4:7; Rom 12:1–3).

---

207 See John 10:10 and Philippians 2:5–11.

208 The Jacob narratives in Genesis 27–35 aptly demonstrate this.

Reflection and Points to Ponder

- What are your reactions to the words *leader* and *follower*? How do you identify yourself as a leader? How do you identify yourself as a follower? What does this say about your understandings of leadership and followership?

- Reflect upon past experiences of submission you have had. Were they negative and abusive experiences or positive experiences? What outcomes and effects came out of these experiences?

- Write out your understanding of the differences between submission and obedience. Reflect upon both your personal and work relationships and where you have wrongly misapplied one for the other.

- Submission, like other disciplines, is gained by daily practice. In what areas of your life are you already living in surrender, and how can you grow deeper in obedience? What areas of your life can you allow others to mentor, disciple, teach, correct, and guide you toward being a better follower?

For Further Reading

David G. Benner, *Surrender to Love: Discovering the Heart of Christian Spirituality* (Downers Grove, IL: IVP, 2003). A brief but excellent look at how love and surrender lies at the core of the Christian life.

Allen Hamblin Jr., *Embracing Followership: How to Thrive in a Leader-Centric Culture* (Bellingham, WA: Kirkdale Press, 2016). Though written to a worldwide secular audience, Hamblin is a global servant writing in support of the honor and value of followership.

Watchman Nee, *Spiritual Authority* (New York: Christian Fellowship Publications, 1972). A seminal work on spiritual authority by the famous Chinese church leader.

James E. Plueddemann, *Leading Across Cultures: Effective Ministry and Mission in the Global Church* (Downers Grove, IL: IVP, 2009). Written by a veteran mission leader, this book looks at cross-cultural leadership development in the global church.

Among the eight thousand refugees

in the Moria refugee camp in Lesvos, Greece, were two young Afghani men. Julianna, a volunteer at the camp, was tasked with telling them to move from the illegal structure they built and to assist in returning them to their registered tent. I went along to assist. When we arrived and Julianna told the men that they needed to return to their registered tent, they would not listen. We kept talking with them for a while, hoping they might change their minds, but they continued to reject our pleas and attempts to reason with them.

The situation was made more difficult by the language barrier. They spoke Farsi, we did not, and no translator was available. The situation was becoming tense. Something had to give, so I went to look for Ahmed, who was a Farsi speaker. Ahmed was also a refugee in the camp and was one member of the small pool of volunteer translators for our NGO. When I found him, we quickly returned to Julianna and the two men.

An hour had passed by this time, and as we returned the situation had continued to deteriorate. She was frustrated, and a happy ending seemed unlikely. One of the men had even threatened suicide. Looming over us was the threat of asking the police to intervene. This was not a desirable scenario; the use of force would almost certainly have been a lose-lose outcome.

We had been trained and told daily to remain calm and not to raise our voices, even in the face of opposition. So we each prayed silently (and quietly, with a whisper) that they would listen and comply. It was 4:30 p.m. by now; our shift was ending soon and darkness was rapidly encroaching. Ahmed was a great help in translating—and suddenly, after two hours, they agreed to move back to their registered tent.

We spent the next thirty minutes helping them gather their belongings and moving them up the hill, back to their tent where they were registered to sleep. Yay, God! As we left and walked back to report to our supervisor, Ahmed told us there was no way that he could have done what we just did. Our patient demeanor and persistence amazed him. The only word he had to explain this was Jesus! I looked at him and smiled and said, "You're right!"

John
global servant in Europe

Incarnational Ministry
The Ancient Pathway to Presence

Evangelicals believe that only a personal God can be present to an individual. We also believe that because human beings are made in God's image (Gen 1:27), we can be present to one another in a way other forms of creation cannot. The apostle John teaches us that this presence with one another—this being with, being for—is love. This love is demonstrated in the incarnation and in the sacrificial death of his beloved Son.

> *Dear friends, let us love one another, for love comes from God. Everyone who loves has been born of God and knows God. Whoever does not love does not know God, because God is love. This is how God showed his love among us: He sent his one and only Son into the world that we might live through him. This is love: not that we loved God, but that he loved us and sent his Son as an atoning sacrifice for our sins. Dear friends, since God so loved us, we also ought to love one another. No one has ever seen God; but if we love one another, God lives in us and his love is made complete in us. —1 John 4:7–12*

Like Jesus, we commit to loving people incarnationally by being fully present to them. As missionaries, who we are is as important as what we do. We must embody Jesus to others through love and truth. This is called the incarnational ministry of presence. As I have spoken with global servants, they have expressed to me that when they are present with people, especially during moments of crisis or hardship, they are met with gratitude for simply being there. Presence, over deeds, is what is remembered. This presence is love.

Being and Doing

Regrettably, global servants receive no training in incarnational presence. David Teague says this is because "it is not an academic subject that can be tested and graded, but rather a by-product of our own spiritual formation."[209] Such ministry requires us to learn to *be*, not merely *do*. It is the overflow of God working in our lives, which cannot be planned or prepared for.

---

[209] David Teague, *Godly Servants: Discipleship and Spiritual Formation for Missionaries* (Mission Imprint, 2012), 133.

Paul states, "May the God of hope fill you with all joy and peace as you trust in him, so that you may overflow with hope by the power of the Holy Spirit" (Rom 15:13). As God's hope, peace, and joy flood our being, we overflow with the power of the Holy Spirit, and this hope, in turn, flows to others. We are the conduit, not the source.

Global servants are often focused on accomplishing objectives, meeting deadlines, and crossing things off to-do lists. We prefer results over process, action over deliberation, and the practical over the theoretical. A mission leader shared with me that in the absence of an agenda, his tendency is to act—to do something. How many of us are just like my friend: needing to act, not able to wait? We are impatient people. We say we are committed to listening and following God's lead, but we seem to need him to speak only on our timeline and for our desired results.

Our need to hurry is a disguised need to control. It reveals our anxiety and lack of trust in God. But we can trust in the presence of Christ to be with us. Jesus reminds his followers of this truth: "My Father is always at his work to this very day, and I, too, am working" (John 5:17). Our task is to seek and find where the Spirit is already working and respond to his initiatives. The most important factor to God is not what we do for him but who we are in him.[210] This doesn't mean we must be perfect before we serve Jesus—but only that we are aware of who we are in Christ.

If we don't have a growing awareness of Christ's presence in us, we will struggle with being effective in a ministry of incarnation. David Teague says it this way:

When we begin a ministry of "being," we find ourselves constantly getting in the way. We steer conversations to suit our own interests. We visit to suit our own needs. We arrive with our own anxieties, fears, and prejudices that prevent Christ from working through us. We are still trying to control the situation instead of allowing the God who is present within us to work through us.[211]

To dwell in Christ's presence empowers us to remain in the presence of others. Henri Nouwen says this must be our first priority: "The central question is, are the leaders of the future truly men and women of God, people with an ardent desire to dwell in God's presence, to listen to God's voice, to look at God's beauty, to touch God's incarnate Word, and to taste fully God's infinite goodness?"[212]

This dwelling in the presence of God naturally leads toward seeing ourselves in truth—that we are sinners in need of a Savior—as Isaiah and Peter did.[213] We become like Jesus himself: people of no reputation who, unlike the animals of this earth who have homes, instead have none (Matt 8:20).[214] The attitude of not caring for one's reputation is modeled in Philippians 2:7, where Paul says Jesus

---

210 See 1 Samuel 16:7, where God reminds Samuel that he judges people's outward appearances differently than how we view them.

211 Teague, 134.

212 Henri Nouwen, *In the Name of Jesus* (New York: Crossroads, 1996), 29–30.

213 See Isa 6:5; Luke 5:8.

214 See also Matt 13:53–58; Mark 6:1–6.

made himself nothing (or of "no reputation," KJV). This doesn't mean that Jesus didn't have significance or divinity, but that he didn't regard it as something to be seized or grasped in his incarnational presence among us. It means taking on the status of nothing (or as Paul says in the passage—the form of a servant) for the sake of others.

This is "being," as opposed to "doing." Jesus dismissed reputation. He became of "no reputation"—not by accident, but by intention. His design was to live a life of incarnational presence among us ("tabernacling").[215]

Being with People

What does it mean to be present with those we have been sent to? The key is to trust the presence of God within us. We are not called to solve problems, fix people, or care beyond our strength. We are called to be witnesses to the presence of God and servants to the people in our lives (Acts 26:16).

At one time in our life and ministry, Debbie and I were able to live for several years in one neighborhood. We prayed and sought out how we could share Christ with those around us. Rather than "preaching" to our neighbors, eventually we decided to basically do just two things. First, we would be neighborly—get to know people by name and try to understand their lives. We would help out in little ways, such as shoveling snow, watching homes when people were gone, loaning tools, etc. Second, we hosted two informal parties each year—a neighborhood barbecue each summer and a Christmas cookie exchange each December.

We didn't share the gospel at either event, but sometimes after asking for permission I would pray a blessing over our neighborhood. People came to know us and understand that we were "faith people." By just being present in their lives, we began to see changes. One couple, after living together for thirteen years, decided to get married and came to us to ask what it means to have a Christian wedding. This led to all kinds of discussion and, eventually, time in the Word together. What joy to celebrate with them not just their marriage, but their new lives in Christ! A single woman decided to visit our church to see what it was about. A third family was not well-respected because of their lifestyle. We discovered they had very difficult backgrounds with no real mentoring from family, and it was our pleasure to begin to help them grow in social graces. This opened many doors to sharing Christ as well.

We were just present in people's lives. But in order for this presence of Christ to be felt, we truly had to be people who were available. St. Benedict is very clear on this point when he states, "Let all guests who arrive be received like Christ, for He is going to say, 'I came as a guest, and you received me.'"[216] People need to sense that we are welcoming, available, and safe.

Consider some of the issues first-term missionaries might face when they arrive on the field. Loneliness, pressure of adjusting to a foreign culture, learning a new language, constant demands on one's time, lack of adequate health care, and

---

215 See John 1:14. "Tabernacling" is the literal word John uses in the Greek.
216 Lonni Collins Pratt and Father Daniel Homan, OSB, *Benedict's Way: An Ancient Monk's Insights for a Balanced Life* (Chicago: Loyola Press, 2000), 65.

overwhelming workload. There is also pressure to always be positive and supportive of national workers, confusion over work roles, frequent lack of privacy, inability to get away for recreation or holiday, financial and support needs, the constant need to communicate with family and supporters back home, and a lack of mentors. The list could go on, but I think it is evident that unless we cope with these stressors well, not only will our joy be depleted, but we will be robbed of being welcoming people to others.

In 2 Corinthians, Paul wrote about the pressures he had felt in ministry:

As servants of God we commended ourselves in every way: in great endurance; in troubles, hardships and distresses; in beatings, imprisonments and riots; in hard work, sleepless nights and hunger; in purity, understanding, patience and kindness; in the Holy Spirit and in sincere love; in truthful speech and in the power of God; with weapons of righteousness in the right hand and in the left; through glory and dishonor, bad report and good report; genuine, yet regarded as impostors; known, yet regarded as unknown; dying, and yet we live on; beaten, and yet not killed; sorrowful, yet always rejoicing; poor, yet making many rich; having nothing, and yet possessing everything. —2 Corinthians 6:4–10

In this brief passage, Paul mentions nineteen distinct stressors he had faced as a missionary. Yet this didn't stop him from saying in the next verse, verse 11, that he and his traveling team had still "opened wide our hearts to you." Indeed, the missionaries were not "withholding [their] affection" from the Corinthians (v. 12). The key was not for Paul to prepare more, try harder, or do more, but for the Corinthians simply "to receive God's grace" (v. 1), and for Paul and his team to be present there with the church, allowing God to work. We must ask ourselves the question, "Am I here for myself, or for these individuals before me? Am I asking for God's presence to overflow into their lives through me at all times?"

Listening to People

One of the most effective ways to be present with others is through the art of listening. Listening, which is a desperately needed skill for global workers, is a powerful way to bring Christ into conversations and to let the Holy Spirit be at work.

To listen well means we put aside the temptation to always solve things for others. It means we can validate their feelings, even if we can't affirm their thinking. We listen and reflect back what we are hearing someone tell us. This is empathic listening, which might be called the highest form of listening. Empathic listening allows us to evaluate without being judgmental. It unlocks God's presence and truth to the situation at hand. When we listen well, we become conduits of God's wisdom—able to give compassionate encouragement and practical input.

People long to be known, to be who God made them to be, but they are also fearful of it. Many have opened themselves to others only to be deeply hurt. They may have been victims of those who think that to help another, they need to fix them—i.e., to cause them to think and act more like they do.

Incarnational Ministry

Abba Paphnutius wrote, "I have seen a man on the bank of the river buried up to his knees in mud and some men came to help him out, but they pushed him further in up to his neck."[217] Whatever we, as global servants, do, we should never push anyone further into the mud. What a gift, however, to offer impartial, loving attention. No formal education is required to accomplish this, just the cultivation of God's active Holy Spirit in your life and the desire to be present with others for their sake.

Dr. Curt Thompson has noted that science has actually demonstrated the tremendous value of empathic listening. "When a person tells her story and is truly heard and understood, both she and the listener undergo actual changes in their brain circuitry. They feel a greater sense of emotional and relational connection, decreased anxiety, and greater awareness of and compassion for others' sufferings."[218] Empathic listening results in increased integration between a person's thoughts and feelings, moving us toward greater compassion and identification with others.

Empathic listening can be emotionally draining. Listening deeply to others, paying attention to their body language and emotions, and reflecting back what we are hearing can take a toll on the listener. Giving others permission to share their feelings and tell their story means we empty ourselves as well. When this happens, I encourage you to try to pull away and recharge before taking on the next ministry task.

Trusting God to Work

If we truly believe these words of Jesus—"My Father is always at his work to this very day, and I, too, am working" (John 5:17)—we must trust that God will work through our presence and prayers. Prayer is always a significant part of any incarnational presence. Prayer helps us to see people as God sees them. The combined gift of presence and prayer moves us toward trust.

It is important to expect God to be working even when we don't feel him close by. One time when I was at my wit's end to know how to help a fellow missionary, I turned to intercessory prayer. I followed up with a phone call and discovered that God had already done a major work in helping this man reach and accept a difficult decision without any further involvement on my part. It was all God! My job was simply to be present with him in prayer.

We often trade the quiet time of spiritual presence with the busyness of meetings, events, social activities, and the like. This is not "presence" as I define it. Presence is being with and listening to the individual you are with, while trusting that God is actively present in the situation outside of your own involvement.

Think of the call of Samuel, as recorded in 1 Samuel 3. God is calling the boy to wake up to his presence. The old priest, Eli, recognizing that God is at work, tells Samuel simply to be present. "So Eli told Samuel, 'Go and lie down,

---

217 Benedicta Ward, *The Desert Christian: The Sayings of the Desert Fathers* (New York: Macmillan, 1975), 7.
218 Curt Thompson, *The Anatomy of the Soul* (Carrollton, TX: SaltRiver, 2010), *xiv*.

and if he calls you, say, "Speak, Lord, for your servant is listening"'" (1 Sam 3:9). God responded by saying, "See, I am about to do something in Israel that will make the ears of everyone who hears of it tingle" (v. 11).

God is always speaking; our part is to let his voice tingle our ears. Slowing down is an important part of this recognition. When Samuel tried to seek out answers from Eli, he distanced himself from God's voice, and as a result he could not hear him (vv. 4–7). It was only when he quieted himself and lay down, slowing down enough that he heard and sensed God's presence (v. 10).

If we keep Christ central, our plans, purposes, and programs will stay in tune with God's active presence. As C. S. Lewis said,

> *We may ignore, but we can nowhere evade the presence of God. The world is crowded with Him. He walks everywhere incognito. And the incognito is not always hard to penetrate. The real labor is to remember, to attend. In fact, to come awake. Still more, to remain awake.*[219]

Understanding this truth keeps our eyes focused on how the God of the universe is interacting with his creation. This understanding allows us to go deeper with God and stay present with him. We trust that God is at work because we see him at work. We become motivated each day to ask, "How would God have me spend this hour, this day, this lifetime?" As we slow ourselves enough to hear and see God, time does not become the enemy, but rather a gift. We see each day as something to be developed, nourished, and cherished. There will always be enough time to do what he asks us to do. Being present incarnationally with others is an avenue of seeing God moving among us, in moments to be treasured and as time well spent.

---

219 C. S. Lewis, *Letters to Malcolm: Chiefly on Prayer* (New York: Harcourt, 1964), 75.

Reflection and Points to Ponder

- In what ways do you see and understand that simply being with people opens an avenue for God's active presence in their lives?
- What is it like when God shows up unexpectedly in your life? How easy (or difficult) is it for God to get your attention?
- In what ways are you addicted to doing—to meetings, hurriedness, busyness, adrenalin? What is it like to deliberately choose to slow your pace?
- What is it like for you when *doing* comes into conflict with *being*? Do you have a tendency to choose deadlines, timelines, and bottom lines over time spent with God or people? What can you change to better adapt to a lifestyle of attentiveness to the moment and to others?

For Further Reading

Keith R. Anderson, *A Spirituality of Listening: Living What We Hear* (Downers Grove, IL: IVP, 2016). Realizing that spirituality is grounded in ordinary life, Anderson helps us discover how to hear God in the midst of noise and confusion.

Alicia Britt Chole, *The Sacred Slow: A Holy Departure from Fast Faith* (Nashville: Thomas Nelson, 2017). Chole shares fifty-two exercises (one per week) on how to slow down and be present in life.

Aundi Kolber, *Try Softer*. (Carol Stream, IL: Tyndale, 2020). A call to try to be gentle with yourself and others instead of trying harder.

Adam S. McHugh, *The Listening Life: Embracing Attentiveness in a World of Distraction* (Downers Grove, IL: IVP, 2015). A helpful guide to learn how to better listen to both people and God.

Suffering, thankfully, is not a spiritual discipline. Rather, it is a normative reality for everyone with a pulse in this fallen world. Everyone suffers. However, how we respond to God amid various adversities is another matter. Our response can indeed be a spiritual practice.

There is still a massive tendency to dichotomize our lives—spiritual life goes in one box and the rest of life in another. But when pain invades every corner of our lives through divorce, cancer, loss of a job, or a crisis of faith, such categories don't work well. I live with a chronic health limitation. I have little say in how I am going to feel day to day, let alone hour to hour. It has invaded every arena of my life. But God has extended the opportunity to walk well in the midst of the context I find myself in. Even when, and especially when, that context stinks. What was once an enemy to get rid of at all costs has now become a companion with me on the journey. I do not like the pain of adversity and I did not choose these circumstances, yet I have grown to be profoundly grateful for the fruit God has borne in me through that adversity. Indeed, I do not believe I would have come to know the Father's love for me apart from this prolonged, unremitting physical challenge I live with.

The dark nights we find ourselves in are ripe with opportunity to tuck into Jesus by inviting him to be with us amid our pain and confusion. Passages such as Romans 5 and James 1 become very real curriculum for our journeys. These passages remind us that our Father is a wise and loving Father and he uses suffering as one of the many graces to draw us deeper into his love. This statement is laced with paradox and tensions, but all the central biblical passages on suffering vouch for its validity.

In the end, our response toward God amid pain is an essential opportunity to journey deeper into communion with him. Faith, in the form of asking the Father how to endure well with him in suffering (Jas 1:5), is indeed a necessary spiritual practice in this world of beauty and evil.

Scott
global servant in Hong Kong

Suffering
The Ancient Pathway to Joy

16

The greatest motivation for Christian mission is God's glory—his honor and endless reputation.[220] But a part of giving glory to God is the willingness to endure pain as we testify to Jesus' love for the nations (John 3:16). It is this love that enables global servants to face hard times of suffering. Paul says, "Christ's love compels us" (2 Cor 5:14) to share the "gospel of the glory of Christ" (2 Cor 4:4). As we share in the mission of Jesus Christ, we share in both his glory and his sufferings. It is in this sharing, both the power of his resurrected glory and the fellowship of his suffering, that we discover the joy of Christ's life (Phil 3:10–11).

Suffering and glory have a scriptural connection in the person of Jesus Christ. He is simultaneously portrayed as the suffering Christ—"a man of sorrows, and familiar with suffering" (Isa 53:3)—and also the gloried Christ who has always possessed God's glory, even before the creation of the world (John 17:24). As Paul writes, "Now if we are children, then we are heirs—heirs of God and co-heirs with Christ, if indeed we share in his sufferings in order that we may also share in his glory" (Rom 8:17).

Global servants want, expect, and try to love those they have been sent to reach for Christ. Naturally, we also desire that as we love others, they will love us in return. However, when I first went to the field it didn't take long to realize that people weren't waiting to welcome me with open arms. Missionaries are not necessarily disliked or rejected as individuals, but often are pushed away for what they might represent. In my case, being American, a Christian, and a missionary was an issue.

So how do we react when we are rejected and the love we give is not returned by others? How do global servants persevere under the hardships of trials and sufferings? How can our spiritual lives endure and even blossom in such an environment?

In this chapter we will explore suffering by considering three facets which are often part of a global servant's experience: the "Dark Night" of St. John of the Cross; suffering which redeems and sanctifies; and the joyful occurrence of sharing in the suffering of Christ.

---

220 For scriptural support for this understanding of glory, see Isa 43:7; Rom 3:23; John 17:5; Heb 1:3.

Suffering and the Dark Night

"Why is my pain unending and my wound grievous and incurable? Will you be to me like a deceptive brook, like a spring that fails?" (Jer 15:18). I think we all identify with Jeremiah's cry of despair when desperate for refreshing water only to find an empty stream. Pain results in the confusion of unrealized expectations. Not knowing the why of things, circumstances, and events is distressing. I am also convinced it is one of God's greater gifts. The gift of suffering is known in spiritual formation circles as the "dark night of the soul," or simply the "Dark Night." Christian psychiatrist Gerald May says,

When people speak of going through a dark night of the soul, they usually mean they're experiencing bad things. The bad news is that bad things happen to everyone, and (often) they have nothing to do with whether you are a good or bad person, how effectively you've taken charge of your life, or how carefully you've planned for the future.[221]

The phrase "dark night" comes from the sixteenth-century Spanish Catholic mystic, St. John of the Cross, and it refers to the purging our souls go through when our lives seemingly lose a sense of God and his purposes. Our life of prayer dries up so severely that we feel utterly cut off from God's presence and live in a state of spiritual barrenness. St. John taught that the Dark Night was God's way of training us to let go of attachments and increase our dependency upon himself.

The result of the Dark Night is to free our lives from that which has entangled us and drawn us away from God. That is what the Dark Night gives to us, but this gift of understanding does not come until we have endured the suffering. Some, especially those who are familiar with the history of the Dark Night, conjure up images of monastic walls and elite mystical experiences, reserved only for the holiest of saints. Others, in more recent days, see the Dark Night in anything that describes misfortune, from minor disappointment to major tragedy.

Both of these interpretations, however, are misguided. The Dark Night is not restricted to the holy mystics of the church. It can come upon anyone. Yet the Dark Night is also much more significant than simple misfortune. It involves God's transformational process in our hearts, which can also release us to serve others and glorify Jesus Christ outwardly in more powerful ways, connecting our hearts with our hands on a deeper level.

As Gerald May observes,

The dark night of the soul is not an event one passes through and gets beyond, but rather a deep ongoing process that characterizes our spiritual life. In this sense, the Dark Night is a person's hidden life with God. John [of the Cross] takes this even further, saying that the night is not just the activity of God; it is God. "This dark night," he says, "is an inflow of God into the soul."[222]

---

221 Gerald May, *The Dark Night of the Soul: A Psychiatrist Explores the Connection Between Darkness and Spiritual Growth* (San Francisco: Harper, 2004), 1. For the sake of simplification, I will not distinguish the two nights which John of the Cross describes as The Dark Night of the Senses and The Dark Night of the Spirit, but refer to them both as the Dark Night.

222 May, *Dark Night*, 10.

This inflow, though, can be scary and disturbing because God seems so absent—even though the whole experience is always for our benefit.

The Dark Night is something we did not ask for; we did not prepare for it; we did not expect it; we do not understand it; we cannot think, feel, or reason our way out of it; and we are blind and totally dependent upon God for his answers and his light. Most of us find this level of dependency awkward at best and totally depressive at worst. It's difficult because we are often taught that passivity, inaction, and surrender hold negative consequences. It is very difficult to simply trust God—to stay put in the midst of chaos, confusion, spiritual crisis, spiritual dryness, emptiness, or struggle.

It is my experience that many people who are experiencing the Dark Night have no clue this is what they are going through. This is probably the greatest paradox of it all—since it is so obscure and mysterious, there is no way to positively identify our experience. We may try to believe that experiences of confusion, loss, or relinquishment are part of the Night's liberating process, but—and here is the point—there is no way to be sure. We may want to believe that a painful experience has meaning and is somehow leading us to greater freedom, but our mind might be telling us it happened only because we made some mistake, did something wrong, or is a result of sin or God's discipline. We simply cannot depend upon our own discernment to determine the nature of our experience. We need outside people who can provide clarity, perspective, and guidance. This is when spiritual directors become so valuable.

In the end, we must simply and radically trust in God's abiding goodness. As we grapple through the Dark Night, in faith, we surrender our perception to the reality of the goodness of God. We come to believe, not on the basis of God's absence or presence, but on the basis of faith, that God is really there. So even when we don't sense him, we know he is real and still at work in our lives, that the Dark Night is for our good, and that God himself is good.

It isn't always easy to distinguish between burnout, depression, laziness, and the Dark Night. Let me quote Gerald May again:

> *My experience is that people often experience depression and the dark night at the same time. To say the least, the dark night can be depressing. Even if most of the experience feels liberating, it still involves loss and loss involves grief, and grief may at least temporarily become depression. Conversely, a primary clinical depression can become part of a dark-night experience, just as any other illness can.*[223]

John of the Cross also acknowledges this overlap, that pain and grief "may sometimes be increased by melancholy or some other humor . . . and frequently is."[224]

---

223 May, *The Dark Night*, 156.

224 St. John of the Cross, *The Dark Night of the Soul*, trans. Mirabai Starr (New York: Riverhead Books, 2002), Book 1: 62.

So we need to be careful and wise when we look at our pain. With today's understanding of the causes and treatment of depression, and because medication can prevent unnecessary suffering and in some cases even be lifesaving, we need to treat any underlying biological condition seriously. When an individual experiences symptoms of significant depression, it is vital that those symptoms be recognized and acknowledged; and at the very least, the person should receive a medical consultation. Missionaries, like anyone else, can be diagnosed with depression. In fact, many missionaries, both now and historically, have had depressive episodes.[225]

Much more could be said about the Dark Night experience. But I will conclude by restating that this phenomenon is one of the most effective means of removing our ownership over ministry, because through the Dark Night we come to see that God himself is working through us. The Dark Night is not a sign of failure, but of growth. It is not the absence of God, but the beginning of a new and deeper presence of him in our lives.

Suffering: Redemption and Sanctification in Christ

When we study the New Testament, especially the Gospel of John, the epistles of Paul, and the book of Hebrews, we begin to see an emerging concept: When we live out our lives knowing, loving, and serving Christ, we are not so much living a life *with* Christ or *for* Christ, but rather *in* Christ. We are called into the kingdom of light as children of the King; but more profoundly, we are called into dynamic union *with* the King—Jesus Christ.

Jesus describes this in John's Gospel with these words: "Remain in me, and I will remain in you" (John 15:4). This is also a recurring theme in the first chapter of Ephesians, where Paul continuously uses the simple phrase "in Christ" or "in him" to describe our identity with Jesus.[226] And look at what Paul says in Colossians 2:6–7: "So then, just as you received Christ Jesus as Lord, continue to live in him, rooted and built up in him, strengthened in the faith as you were taught, and overflowing with thankfulness." Gordon Smith pointedly explains: "The Christian life is defined by knowing or gaining Christ, and this knowledge is not a reference to intellectual understanding but to experiential encounter with Christ."[227]

The writer of the letter to the Hebrews also talked about being drawn into the life of Christ. "Fix your thoughts on Jesus, the apostle and high priest whom we confess" (3:1). The Greek word translated "fix" here, *katanoein*, does not mean to study someone in order to follow his or her example. It speaks instead of abiding contemplation—the gaze that participates in, delights in, and even dwells in the other.

Such language in the New Testament is about our remaining relationally with Jesus. Theologians have sought to explain what "abiding in Christ" means for believers. George Fox, founder of the Quaker movement in seventeenth-century

---

225 Look at the lives of great early American missionaries David Brainerd and Adoniram Judson.
226 See Ephesians 1:1, 3, 4, 6, 7, 9, 11, 13, and 20. See also Philippians 3:8–12.
227 Gordon T. Smith, *Called to Be Saints: An Invitation to Christian Maturity* (Downers Grove, IL: IVP, 2014), 42.

Suffering

England, identified seven elements that comprise our life in Christ, which he called the "inner light": immediate experience, Scripture, new insights in life, inward leadings of the Holy Spirit, sharing in his (Christ's) sufferings, active community of faith, and the pure love of God.[228] Let's take a closer look at the fifth element in this list: sharing in Christ's sufferings.

Fox taught that neither suffering nor the absence of suffering is a sign of God's approval. Such an understanding came out of Fox's own experiences of being persecuted for his faith, in which he endured great suffering, and yet all the while he also experienced great joy and intimate knowledge of Jesus.[229] For Fox, the love of God is known and discerned in the context of difficulty and pain.[230]

Fox's teaching is also the teaching of Scripture. In the Old Testament, it is clear that the sufferings of Job were not the result of hidden sin or God's displeasure in him. In the New Testament, we have the words of Paul: "I want to know Christ and the power of his resurrection and the fellowship of sharing in his sufferings, becoming like him in his death" (Phil 3:10).

Suffering is a means to grow in grace and sanctification as a product of the Holy Spirit's redemptive work. This also means that not all suffering is redemptive. I don't believe in suffering for suffering's sake; I believe in suffering only for Jesus' sake. There is a real difference between these two viewpoints. Meaningless suffering is stupid. But suffering for Jesus' sake (often seen in suffering for the sake of others) is what Paul calls sharing in the sufferings of Christ. When we suffer as believers, we embrace care for others, which, in imitation of Christ, is a reflection of God's own love.[231] Since we are God's handiwork (Eph 2:10), and essential to God's continuing movement to redeem creation from evil through the work of Jesus on the cross, we will continue to suffer in this redeeming and sanctifying work, just as he suffered for the world (John 3:16).

Listen to the apostle Paul: "We speak as men approved by God to be entrusted with the gospel. We are not trying to please men but God, who tests our hearts" (1 Thess 2:4). In her excellent book, *At the Heart of the Gospel,* L. Ann Jervis, explores suffering in the letters of Paul and perceptively explains what Paul is saying.

> *Paul speaks of having been tested by God and of being in a state of being approved by God (1 Thess. 2:4). While he does not say that his testing and approval were the result of his suffering, he does speak of these things almost immediately following his statement that he and his coworkers had suffered and been mistreated at Philippi and that at Thessalonica they had preached the gospel of God in the face of great opposition (1 Thess. 2:2). It is, then, not much of a leap to suggest that this reference to Paul's capacity for struggle . . . is connected to God's testing of and approval of him.*[232]

---

228 Richard J. Foster and Gayle D. Beebe, *Longing for God: Seven Paths of Christian Devotion* (Downers Grove, IL: IVP, 2009), 177–78.

229 George Fox, *The Journal of George Fox,* ed. Norman Penney (New York: Costmo Classics, 2007).

230 Foster and Beebe, 180.

231 See 1 Thessalonians 4:9.

232 L. Ann Jervis, *At the Heart of the Gospel: Suffering in the Earliest Christian Message* (Grand Rapids: Eerdmans, 2007), 25.

This seems to imply that Paul understood his approval by God to be connected in some way to his willingness to suffer for the sake of the gospel. The pain Paul is talking about also represents the difficulties a global servant may experience explicitly because of our identification with Christ—physical, emotional, and spiritual—in addition to the evil that is so pervasive in the world around us.

In Romans 5:3, Paul goes even further, saying, "Not only so, but we also rejoice in our sufferings, because we know that suffering produces perseverance; perseverance, character; and character, hope." This means we can actually embrace suffering, knowing that in suffering we are being sanctified in grace and hope. Then, through our growth in grace and hope, we can also bring more grace and hope to others. This is what Henri Nouwen means when he describes us as ministers who are "wounded healers."[233]

Growth through suffering can be a critical and transformational experience for the global servant. Failure, woundedness, brokenness, and suffering for the sake of Jesus can either leave us devastated or empowered by the Spirit. As George Fox taught, we learn things about God through suffering that we really cannot learn any other way. Through such growth, we become wiser servants of Christ, ready to comfort and encourage others. "Dear friends, do not be surprised at the painful trial you are suffering, as though something strange were happening to you. But rejoice that you participate in the sufferings of Christ, so that you may be overjoyed when his glory is revealed" (1 Pet 4:12–13).

Suffering to Joy

As Peter hints at, there is a strong connection between suffering, glory, and joy. Paul echoes this in 2 Corinthians 7:4, when after going through all the hardships he has faced for the gospel (6:3–13), he goes on to say, "I am greatly encouraged; in all our troubles my joy knows no bounds" (v. 4). So many global servants I know also demonstrate this quality of joyfulness and hopefulness even in the midst of their deprivations.

The result of embracing suffering for Jesus' sake is in finding a glorious pleasure in doing God's will and hearing his voice say, "Well done, good and faithful servant!" (Matt 25:21). Ignatius of Antioch, when facing martyrdom, pled not to be saved because he was looking forward to the eternal joy he was about to receive. Referring to Philippians 2:17, he famously said, "Grant me nothing more than to be poured out as a libation for God while an altar is still ready."[234] Haymo of Halberstadt, Tertullian, Irenaeus, Polycarp, and Augustine also refer to these words from Paul to encourage believers facing suffering.[235]

Julien of Norwich (1342–1416) was an anchoress, a woman who lived in a one-room apartment attached to a church in Black Plague-ravished England. Julien wrote a book based on sixteen religious experiences she was shown in

---

233 See Henri Nouwen, *The Wounded Healer* (New York: Doubleday, 1979).

234 Jervis, 66.

235 Jervis, 67.

successive visions. In her ninth showing, or vision, Jesus affirms his pleasure in Julien's suffering for his sake. Julien interpreted this vision as meaning Christ is profoundly happy when we understand and appreciate his suffering for us. "It is as if our gratitude and recognition is the only joy God needs in order to feel good about his ultimate sacrifice."[236]

What a strange, but simply expressed thought: God delights in his suffering for our sake. We especially bring joy to him when we love and serve him simply because this demonstrates our understanding and appreciation for all he has done for us.

We suffer in a variety of ways as global servants. Material loss, relational brokenness, death to dreams, separation from loved ones, even physical martyrdom—all are examples of pain a global servant may experience when serving our Jesus. Suffering is even encountered in the mundane. The simple but demanding tasks that we have to do on the mission field—connecting with donors constantly (How many of us write thank-you notes while on holiday?), filling out reports and budgets, hosting visitors when we have so much other work to do, and the painful loneliness of separation from family, friends, and familiar comforts.

It is necessary to mourn our losses and recognize our sorrow, whether big or small, for what it is—suffering. However, it is also wise not to let suffering have the final word. We do not want to act out of pain alone. When we are wise, we can learn to act out of joy. Yes, God allows pain in this broken world, but this does not define us. In suffering for Jesus' sake, we are actually redeeming the brokenness and pain of this world through Jesus' overcoming love. This is the way of the cross.

The wisdom of the cross is the insight that the grace of God affects the lives of those who are called to be global servants. We realize that in our sufferings we become joint heirs with Christ in his sufferings (Rom 8:17). This is one of the essential teachings of the wisdom literature in the Bible.[237] Through suffering we learn to wait, to be patient, and to let God into the action. Actually, God is always present. The waiting process just helps slow us down so we can see God doing his work in his way. Thankfully, Paul says this suffering is only "light and momentary affliction" (2 Cor 4:17), and we never suffer as those who have no hope (Rom 8:18–19).

This all can produce joy in our hearts—joy which comes from knowing God better and serving him in greater ways and knowing we are assured of our final eternal home and are resting in God's love. But we must also remember that joy is not something that just happens to us. Joy is a decision. Joy is always available, given through the fruit of the Spirit (Gal 5:22), not dependent upon our situation and circumstances. Dr. Ken Williams, missionary counselor with Wycliffe Bible Translators,

---

236 Foster and Beebe, 168.

237 For example, Job in the Old Testament and James in the New Testament.

taught that joy is the defining marker of a long-term global servant. Without joy, missionaries' sustainability on the field is shortened.[238]

Have you experienced any hindrances which have caused you to question your joy: fear, cynicism, boredom, low self-esteem, taking yourself too seriously, loss of wonder, greed, guilt and shame, bitterness, or busyness? These are joy chokers. But when we move forward in the determination to let God's love lead us, joy will find us. Jesus longs for us to know his joy: "I have told you this so that my joy may be in you and that your joy may be complete" (John 15:11). "So you have sorrow now, but I will see you again; then you will rejoice, and no one can rob you of that joy" (John 16:22 NLT).

Joy is the satisfaction that comes when we find what we have always been looking for—Jesus himself. To pursue joy for its own sake is to ignore this crucial outward direction of joy. This is why the Westminster Shorter Catechism begins with the famous words, "The chief end of man is to glorify God and to enjoy him forever."[239] This source of enjoyment is "the assurance that when we turn to him we will find the All-satisfying Treasure."[240]

Global workers know they live in a world of evil and suffering. We cannot, nor should we, close our eyes to the pain around us, but rather journey with God for its end. To do this we must be willing to accept the inevitable suffering that comes by engaging in our world. By virtue of suffering with Christ we are called to stare into the darkness and to face down what is evil, to reshape reality, so that it is not dominated by suffering but by God's glory, even if this means we must sometimes experience redemptive pain ourselves.

---

238 Ken Williams, personal notes, N.D.

239 The Westminster Shorter Catechism (Edinburgh: General Assembly of the Church of Scotland, 1648), Question 1.

240 John Piper, *Desiring God: Meditations of a Christian Hedonist* (Portland: Multnomah Press, 1986), 53. Piper elsewhere in his book says, "The chief end of man is to glorify God BY enjoying him forever" (73).

Reflection and Points to Ponder

- If you were to develop a theology of suffering, what Scripture passages would you use? Where would you find places that describe the causes of suffering? What passages describe the spiritual fruit that comes through suffering?

- Reflect on a time when you went through deep darkness. How would you describe your spiritual walk with God during that period? Could you say that in the times of suffering you were closest to God, even though you could not sense it? What conclusions can you draw from that period about God's presence and character?

- How would you explain the relationship between suffering and joy? What is it about suffering that might produce joy in your life? Meditate upon Philippians 3:10 and what it means to share in Christ's sufferings. How does that make you feel? What meaning does this give to your sufferings?

- Does suffering for Jesus only refer to suffering we endure in our gospel ministry, or can it also be connected with general sufferings in life, such as health or personal problems?

For Further Reading

Thomas H. Green, S.J., *Drinking from a Dry Well* (Notre Dame, IN: Ave Marie Press, 1991). Explores dryness in prayer and whether this should be viewed as a form of desolation.

L. Ann Jervis, *At the Heart of the Gospel: Suffering in the Earliest Christian Message* (Grand Rapids: Eerdmans, 2007). Examines the writings of Paul on the subject of suffering.

Gerald G. May, *The Dark Night of the Soul: A Psychiatrist Explores the Connection between Darkness and Spiritual Growth* (San Francisco: Harper, 2004). A look at the spiritual and psychological impact of St. John's Dark Night on our spiritual growth.

John Swinton, *Raging with Compassion: Pastoral Responses to the Problem of Evil* (Grand Rapids: Eerdmans, 2007). A theological and pastoral exposition of theodicy.

While serving in Thailand, I went through a time in which I experienced a nagging loneliness. Although my husband and I were located in an area where Christian fellowship was abundant, I had not found a friend with whom I could share deeply.

After a few weeks of prayer and a little dose of feeling sorry for myself, I felt nudged to take the risk and share my heart with a woman in our house church. After she listened intently, Alexandra* responded by revealing that she had also been feeling the same lack in her life. So we decided to invite a third woman, Chamara,* to meet with us for coffee to see how God might lead us. We had no clue of the depth of spiritual friendship we were about to form.

All of us had recently read *Anatomy of the Soul*, by Dr. Curt Thompson. In his book, Thompson integrates findings in neuroscience and attachment with Christian spirituality. One suggestion he gave was, writing in longhand, to "start by thinking of your earliest memory . . . paying close attention to describe sensations, feelings, images, colors, and the like—not just factual events. Then continue with your second and third decade, and so forth. After you have written for a while, find a trusted friend, pastor, priest, spiritual director, or counselor to whom you would be willing to read your story and who would be equally willing to ask you questions about what you think and feel about your narrative. Ask yourself, 'How did this experience of reading my narrative to a person I trust change what and how I remember and what I feel?'"[241]

Dr. Thompson goes on to state that you are making the experience of being known possible, and "that, in turn, will lead to a greater awareness of the true source of your deepest feelings."[242]

The three of us agreed to spend several weeks writing down everything we could remember from birth to age five. Afterward, we went on an overnight retreat and shared our memories with each other. Our first retreat was so successful that we decided to continue this practice monthly, each time focusing on a different period of our lives (e.g., ages 5–7, 8–12, 13–18, etc.). After we shared our narrative with each other, we had a time of silent prayer and often inner healing prayer would result. We continued this practice for over a year. Through this focused time of listening to our lives, we began to discover that the root of many of our feelings, behaviors, and thought patterns could be understood, integrated, and transformed by the Spirit of God.

Nancy
global servant in Southeast Asia

*Names changed for privacy.

---

241 Curt Thompson, *Anatomy of the Soul* (Carrollton, TX: SaltRiver, 2010), 79.
242 Thompson, 79.

Communal Discernment
The Ancient Pathway to Wisdom

> *What God asks of us is a will which is no longer divided between him and any other creature. It is a will pliant in his hands which neither seeks nor rejects anything, which wants without reserve whatever he wants, and which never wants under any pretext anything which he does not want.*[243]

So wrote the seventeenth-century spiritual director and Catholic bishop, Francois Fenelon, concerning the need to surrender everything to God's will.

Finding God's will does not just apply to the individual, but to our communities as well. Community decision-making is one of the hardest challenges we face as global servants. Mission agencies like to say they make their decisions at the lowest possible level, but in reality many decisions flow from the top down, where upper management directs field policy and strategy. This can be extremely frustrating to a field missionary. In fact, it is one of the leading reasons why missionaries leave the field prematurely.

Many agency leaders ignore their own policies. Decisions are often made without procedural due diligence, resulting in global servants feeling ignored, frustrated, and hurt by their own leaders.

Open discussion is crucial for the smooth operation of any mission board. We should never fear communication, even if it leads to disagreement (see Acts 15:36–41). When we muffle our differences, problems do not usually just go away. Instead, they fester and will only rise another day with greater intensity. It is better to deal with concerns as they happen, listening well to everyone involved before moving on; because if not listened to, many of us don't move on from a hurtful outcome.

Community decisions can be quite complicated, depending upon stakeholders' individual perspectives, opinions, and interests. It is extremely stressful for missionaries to confront their leaders.[244] However, if we can jointly commit, with our whole hearts, to following the will of God in all things, then we have common ground to begin to work through the complicated decision-making processes. This commitment to follow God's will together lowers stress levels and promotes healthy dialogue.

---

[243] Francois Fenelon, quoted in *Devotional Classics*, eds. Richard J. Foster and James Bryan Smith (San Francisco: HarperCollins, 1993), 47.

[244] Dorothy J. Gish, "Sources of Missionary Stress," *Journal of Psychology and Theology* 11 (1983): 236–42.

Direct Guidance from the Holy Spirit

Scripture teaches that the primary way the Holy Spirit leads the church is through direct counsel—through visions, dreams, or an inner speaking, sense, or compulsion from God.[245]

A missionary friend told me that years ago, while waiting upon the Lord for some clear direction in his work, God prompted him to enter a store, only to be met with the words in German, "*Du bist der mann!* (You are the man!)." My friend found out that the night before the store clerk had dreamed that God showed her a man would enter the store the next day and tell her the message of the gospel. The man in her dream looked just like my friend. This encounter began a church.

Theologian Simon Chan writes,

Christians do experience, more often than they realize, moments when they "feel led" to do something. The name of the person whom we have not seen for some time suddenly comes to mind. We feel an urge to ring up someone. Occasionally something like a burden descends upon us, and we feel a need to pray. . . . Incidents like these happen frequently. We can respond in one of the following ways: (1) ignore the promptings, (2) follow through on every one of them (which over-scrupulous Christians often do) and end up exhausting and confusing ourselves or, (3) learn to discern the genuine workings of grace.[246]

It is crucial to realize that our faithful walk with God is the key to discerning his will. We come to understand God's leading by being rooted in our relationship with him, fostered by the practice of spiritual disciplines and the love of Christ in our hearts. All servants of the Triune God must be committed to individual holiness as the foundation of their decision-making process. If not, we can disconnect from God's promptings, relying too much on our own earthly wisdom and experience. Spiritual disciplines are the key to keeping us centered on God and his will. They are our anchor in the midst of conflicting pushes and pulls. When our hearts are given to God, the Holy Spirit has direct influence upon our souls and desires.[247]

My first two years of college I attended the university where my father taught and was also the department chair. His office was located near the department's general office. I would often wait for him in his office at the end of the day. As I sat there day after day, I began to discern the different sounds of various professors as they clomped down the stairs toward the general office. Dr. Lehman's clicking high heels, Dr. Winston's creaky knees, Dr. Betz's fast paces—they were all discernable. But Dr. Fanslow constantly fooled me because his footsteps sounded just like my father's. Whenever I heard those steps I wondered:

---

245 See Luke 4:1, Acts 8:39, and Acts 16:7 for just three examples.
246 Simon Chan, *Spiritual Theology: A Systematic Study of the Christian Life* (Downers Grove, IL: IVP, 1998), 151–52.
247 James 3:13–18.

Is Dr. Fanslow or my father? But the interesting thing was that when my father actually descended the stairs, I was never in doubt that it was anyone but him. I never confused his steps with Dr. Fanslow's, even though the reverse was often true.

How do we learn to distinguish our Father's voice and avoid counterfeit truth? We learn it only by the repeated practice of listening to the truth of God speaking over and over again. When we are attuned to him in the silent places of our heart, we will still be able to hear him, even amid the noise of the world. Jesus said, "My sheep listen to my voice; I know them, and they follow me" (John 10:27). When we know Jesus' voice, we are listening not for something to lead us, but rather for someone to follow.

Making Wise and Godly Decisions

Making wise and godly decisions is the sacred space between being, knowing, and doing. This is called integrity. Integrity, or wholeness, means to lack nothing, to be complete, unadulterated—integrated. It is a deep sense of congruence which culminates in a peace that flows through our heart, mind, and will. There are at least three aspects to discerning with integrity: 1) discerning what is right or wrong, 2) acting upon what you discern, and 3) living and speaking openly and honestly. Living our life with integrity requires knowing God's will and doing God's will, even if it comes with personal cost.

To be people of integrity, we must also possess the understanding that we are fallible. We need not be afraid to admit that we are less than perfect. Such an admission frees the heart to be humble and willing to accept that our knowledge is often incomplete. This is a sign of maturity. When we possess this posture, we open ourselves up to hearing more from the Spirit, because God tells us, "'My thoughts are not your thoughts, neither are your ways my ways,' declares the Lord. 'As the heavens are higher than the earth, so are my ways higher than your ways and my thoughts than your thoughts'" (Isa 55:8–9).

Being afraid of making mistakes should not be the determinant in making decisions. I wonder how our decision-making would differ if we really understood this. Would it lead us to become more teachable? Would our hearts be even more open and discerning? Faith does not depend upon certainty. Faith is present when doubts exist, and knowledge is limited. Faith means we continually unlearn and relearn.

> *The type of humility that admits you are wrong when you know you are wrong is confession. The humility that admits you might be wrong when you are pretty sure you're right is maturity. Without both types of humility, we become rigid and unteachable. Without both types of humility, relationships flounder and implode.*[248]

---

248 Calhoun, *Invitations from God*, 113.

Love covers a multitude of wrongs (1 Pet 4:8, paraphrased). I am not saying we don't need wise people (we do), but I wonder if we might need wise people who are loving first. Jude reminds us to "keep [ourselves] in God's love" (v. 21). This love for God and others is the basis for discernment. Love invites truth into the process. When we are humble and teachable, we allow for correction and open ourselves to further promptings of the Spirit. This, along with holding fast to God's truths, allows him to continually refine and remake us, going deeper into our souls. Making wise and godly decisions rests upon our ability to truly love God and to love others as ourselves.[249]

The Process of Community Discernment

Evan B. Howard, in his introduction to Christian spirituality, shares the process of communal discernment:

1. *God desires to be known.* God is a self-communicating God. Discernment therefore begins with the careful attention to God's self-revelation. This truth applies in the decision-making process by requiring our total awareness of God in everyday experiences. We are continually asking, "Where do I see God working right now?"[250]

2. *We encounter ambiguity when identifying God's presence or activity.* However, even in the simplest acts in life, we often find it difficult to observe God at work. We ask ourselves if an event or experience is really from God. Is it a coincidence or normative? When our perception of God is ambiguous, identifying God's presence is, at times, beyond our ability to distinguish. In times of crisis, crossroads, and transitions we struggle to determine what is from God.[251]

3. *Ambiguities necessitate evaluation.* At some point, this difficulty in understanding what is from God and what is not forces us to evaluate. This is what happened at the Council of Jerusalem in Acts 15 when the early church considered the admission of Gentiles into the church (see also 1 Thess 5:21; 1 John 4:1).[252]

4. *Evaluation requires process.* Due to ambiguity as to what is and what is not from God, we cannot immediately respond with certainty. It takes time, and time demands a process of evaluation. This often means we must set aside normal activities to actively seek the Lord. Even Jesus spent time in prayer preparation before he selected his closest followers (Luke 6:12–16).[253]

5. *Discerning requires both gift and skill.* Howard points out two distinct words that are used in the New Testament for discernment. The first, *diakrisis*, is the word used to point to the spiritual gift of discernment (1 Cor 12:10). The second word, *dokimazo*, is used in determining best methods (Phil 1:10)

---

249 See Acts 15 for examples of listening and humility.
250 Evan B. Howard, *The Brazos Introduction to Christian Spirituality* (Grand Rapids: Brazos 2008), 373.
251 Howard, 373.
252 Howard, 374.
253 Howard, 374.

and then testing them (1 Thess 5:21). There are occasions when we must turn completely to the Lord and discern only as he leads us. At other times, we will use our God-given intelligence, reason, and wisdom to test, examine, and determine the best course.[254]

Generally, we discern in order to act. Even a decision to wait on something is itself a course of action to let things play out a little bit more. In other words, discernment requires a response, both to God and in our daily life. This is true both for individuals and communities.[255] However, a special kind of preparation is needed when a community discerns together. This is because "life in community can never be about merely getting the job done—as important as that is. It must always take into account how we get the job done and whether we are transformed or deformed in the process."[256]

The following elements are essential for any group discernment process: freedom in faith, or what Ignatius would call "indifference"; commitment to obedience; shared concerns or goals; empathic listening; humility; prayer; wisdom; and finally, as I mentioned previously, love, which binds everything together.[257] To these I would add integrity—the balance of what one believes, says, and acts upon within a group's relational circle. These are foundational postures a community must exhibit before, and especially in the midst of, the decision-making process.

As the community comes together to make decisions, it is important that the members focus not only on the decision at hand, but also—and mainly—on God. Knowing that God loves us deeply and wants us to respect one another informs our attitudes as we move forward in the process.

Too often in decision-making, position and role carry more weight than wisdom and love. This is why humility is such a key component in the lives of mission leaders. A humble leader will listen well to their team and their God. If all a leader desires is for the group to rubber-stamp what he or she has already decided, then there is no need for discernment—except regarding the leader!

Here are some helpful suggestions from Howard in regard to communal discernment:

- *Consider these times as holy moments.* Be ever prayerful, inviting the Holy Spirit to always be present. Do not interrupt one another—there is no chaos in the Lord. Prayerfully listen and then listen some more.

- *When you speak, clothe your words in simplicity.* Be honest and straightforward in speech. Do not manipulate or be self-serving. If God is in what you are saying,

---

254 Howard, 374.

255 See Gary W. Moon and David G. Benner, eds., *Spiritual Direction and the Care of Souls: A Guide to Christian Approaches and Practices* (Downers Grove, IL: IVP, 2004); and Richard J. Foster, *Streams of Living Water: Celebrating the Great Traditions of Christian Faith* (San Francisco: HarperCollins, 1998). Both books look at various Christian traditions and their views about spiritual discernment. See also Ignatius of Loyola, *The Spiritual Exercises of St. Ignatius*, trans. Louis J. Puhl (New York: Vintage Books, 2000), especially his two chapters entitled "Rules for the Discernment of Spirits" and "Times for Making an Election."

256 Ruth Haley Barton, *Pursuing God's Will Together: A Discernment Practice for Leadership Groups* (Downers Grove, IL: IVP, 2012), 113.

257 Barton, 130–50.

that alone will bring power and persuasion. Share ideas for consideration, but don't lecture.

- *When you listen, listen with self-discernment and self-criticism.* Always consider why you are feeling or reacting to what another is saying. Be courageous enough to respond in love, especially when you are in disagreement.
- *Be willing to pause for necessary discernment.* Not every decision needs to be agonized over (for example, what time our lunch break should occur), but when we practice holy indifference over decisions, we need time to clear our minds and seek God's will, no matter what.
- *Be prepared to adjust.* Earlier concerns or questions may take a back seat to further thoughts or new and more immediately significant issues. Be willing to move forward as the Spirit leads.
- *Go where God leads.* Let go of the need to be right, to control, to win. Communal discernment is always about where God is leading us as a group, not about our personal goals or objectives.
- *Be willing to risk the unfamiliar, as God leads.* A willingness to risk our familiarity for God's will implies we know the heartbeat of our community, we are open to changes where needed, and we desire to honor one another.[258]

Community decisions are about the sharing of wisdom: bringing thoughts and feelings into the process which we deem relevant to the group and moving together from evaluation to action. Without a commitment to one another, we are at risk of degenerating into arguments and fights—being led by the evil which lies within us.[259]

Sometimes God's purpose in our discernment process is not about the decision itself. The Lord may be getting us to face one another in ways we have not done before; and in doing so he facilitates new humility, new listening, and a new love among us.

Discernment is a life process. It is not merely about making isolated or one-time decisions. When we promote a lifestyle of discernment, we move away from the entanglements of personalities and motives. We center instead on the pathways God has continually led us on. As the Jesuits stressed, our long-term goal must always be the greater glory of God. A life cultivated in humble service and love for others is a life open to God's guidance. Hearts tuned to God can make communal discernment a path to surprise, wonder, and joy.

---

258 See Howard, 386–87. Also, Barton's *Pursuing God's Will Together* is an amazing book in regard to the whole Quaker process of discernment.

259 See James 4:1–3.

Reflection and Points to Ponder

- The discernment process is too demanding to be made alone. How do you practice communal discernment? Who can come alongside you in making personal and ministry decisions? What characteristics do you look for in someone who can help you discern God's will?

- As you contemplate communal discernment, what new thoughts come to your mind? Where do you resonate and where do you resist in asking others to help you make decisions?

- Consider what it means to be totally attached to God's purpose and will. What idols, false motives, prideful ways, or compulsions get in your way of freely surrendering to God?

For Further Reading

Ruth Haley Barton, *Pursuing God's Will Together: A Discernment Practice for Leadership Groups* (Downers Grove, IL: IVP, 2012). A wonderful guide to becoming a community of discernment and practice.

Parker J. Palmer, *A Hidden Wholeness: The Journey Toward an Undivided Life* (San Francisco: Jossey-Bass, 2004). Full of wisdom, Palmer's book describes how to use the Quaker practice of a circle of trust in the decision-making process.

Gordon T. Smith, *The Voice of Jesus: Discernment, Prayer, and the Witness of the Spirit* (Downers Grove, IL: IVP, 2003). How do we attend to the voice of Jesus in our everyday life?

There was a stretch of years *where many significant emotionally crushing events took place in my personal life—the death of my mother, an emotional breakdown of a ministry colleague, one crisis after another in our extended family, the list went on. I began to conceal hidden parts of my life from my wife, friends, colleagues, and anyone who knew me.*

In hindsight, through all these experiences I became more encased in a tough exterior while feeling lonely and isolated on the inside. I mistakenly assumed that integrity had more to do with being perfect and less to do with being vulnerable. Now I understand it has much more to do with understanding your inner self, being transparent with others close to you, and honestly facing your true self—the good, bad, ugly, and the things you wish were different.

During one home ministry assignment back in the US during the early 1990s, one of my siblings experienced a complete emotional collapse. I was in the middle of having to put her, against her wishes, into a mental treatment facility. The same scenario had occurred several years before with my ministry colleague. This devastating and emotionally charged experience sent me deeper into my damaging activities of escape, while hiding them from others. This pattern of living would not begin to be resolved until 2009—some sixteen years later.

As the years passed, I lived a life that would have been admirable on the outside, without ever fully disclosing my true self to anyone close to me. I now know that integrity refers to a life that is integrated. In reality, honesty is a fruit or a result of integrity. When one's life is truly exposed and vulnerable before others—that is integrity. Authenticity is perhaps a close synonym to integrity. Without authenticity, no one has a significant degree of integrity.

Through a dramatic turn of events, in September 2009 I finally disclosed my years of deception to a close friend and breakthrough began to move through my life. When vulnerability became a reality, there was a new life of freedom to be lived which I had never known before. To be sure, there were big messes to clean up, confessions to be disclosed, apologies to be admitted, and restitution to be made, but the result was true authenticity, integrity, and freedom.

I found that we gain greater integrity when we disclose our true selves to God and others. This is central to our experience of the gospel of Jesus Christ. As the apostle Paul writes, "It is for freedom that Christ has set us free. Stand firm, then, and do not let yourselves be burdened again by a yoke of slavery" (Gal 5:1). I was once enslaved by the fear of disclosing my true self, warts and all, to others. Now I know that, in Jesus, we must continually bring ourselves fully before God and others. There's no other way to live a life of freedom, authenticity, and integrity.

Joseph
global servant in Western Europe

Temptation and Truth
The Ancient Pathway to Holiness

18

The word *temptation* comes from the Latin word *tempto*, which means "to worry; to urge; to test or try."[260] This indicates both an active and passive nature. The active nature of temptation is something which we are doing, and the passive nature is something that tests us. In both meanings, however, temptation is an experience we have but also requires a personal response from us. In his letter, James tells us that God tempts no one, "but each one is tempted when, by his own evil desire, he is dragged away and enticed. Then, after desire has conceived, it gives birth to sin; and sin, when it is full-grown, gives birth to death" (Jas 1:14–15).

The reality of temptation is part and parcel of our life as global servants. I wish I could say this isn't the case, but the more we move into missionary service, the more we are faced with the lures of the world, the trials of the flesh, and the temptations of the devil. However, sin doesn't have to be the end result. Remember that Jesus was "tempted in every way, just as we are—yet without sin" (Heb 4:15). It is possible these trials can be the means of testing and revealing, rather than entrapping. Thomas à Kempis said Satan may come to the believer in two ways—temptation and affirmation.[261]

I made my first trip to Romania in 1987, before the revolution which brought down Communism. I was asked to come and teach at a hidden Bible school. I took the train from Belgrade, Serbia, to Timisoara in Romania, and arrived very late at night. While on the train at the border crossing, all my money had been stolen by the border guards during a strip search, so I had no funds for a taxi when I arrived in Timisoara.

A Romanian woman who also spoke Serbian had been riding in the same compartment, and when she heard what had happened, she offered to help me get to my hotel. So when we arrived in Timisoara, she paid for tram tickets to get to my hotel. I thanked her and walked into the lobby to check in, only to realize she was following me. The desk clerk asked if I wanted two keys, one for me and one for my "wife." As I looked at the woman, I realized she was looking

---

260 Online Latin-English Dictionary, https://www.online-latin-dictionary.com/latin-english-dictionary.php?parola=tempto.dictionary.php?parola=tempto.

261 Thomas à Kempis, *The Imitation of Christ* (Peabody, MA: Hendrickson Publishers, 2004), 12–14.

back with expectation, and I suddenly realized what was going on. My natural reaction (born by naïve terror) was to run. I said to the clerk, "Only one please," quickly thanked the woman, and ran to the elevator! Afterwards, I was ashamed to be so naïve. But upon further reflection, I realized that the temptation I found myself in was also a means which instantaneously revealed my heart. It was a temptation to pull me down, but became a tool which pulled me up to rest in God for the duration of my time in the country.

Temptation: Despair and Discouragement

Two examples of temptation in Scripture are found in the fall of Adam and Eve in Genesis 3 and the temptations of Jesus found in the Synoptic Gospels.[262] Both templates convey the core of what it means to be tempted. They convey our desire to be something other than human, led astray by pride and evil desires which reside within our inner being. In Genesis, Adam and Eve are urged by the serpent to eat the fruit of the forbidden tree and "be like God, knowing good and evil" (3:5). They succumb to the temptation and enter a life of sin and separation from all they were created to be—God's stewards on earth.

In the Gospels, Jesus is faced with temptation when the Spirit leads him into the desert. He encounters tests of power, greed, and pride, which he supremely passes. But these temptations underline the root of all temptations: to be independent from God by rejecting our created holiness and refusing his responding grace. The temptation of sin is always an attempt to be something other than who we are, as human. All of history substantiates the despair, discouragement, evil, and suffering that results from man's disobedience.

When we rebel and sin, our minds become fearful and confused. As I've counseled missionaries who have given into temptation, they share their strong regret over their sin and their universal sense of shame and feeling distant from our loving God. One man actually said that he felt like he was caught in a maze with no way out. Paul writes in Romans 12:2 that we need to "be transformed by the renewing of our mind."

One of the greatest battlegrounds between God and Satan is the condition of our minds. As a repository for thought, the mind serves as a catalyst for action. When the enemy gains a stronghold in our thoughts, he deposits fear, confusion, discouragement, and even despair. Sadly, even missionaries can be prone to suicidal thoughts (and some have acted on them) because they have believed the lies about themselves which the devil has led them to believe. This despair, I believe, is more centered in our mind than in our feelings.

Because temptation is real, we are instructed in Scripture to discipline ourselves so that we don't give place to the enemy, who "prowls around like a roaring lion looking for someone to devour" (1 Pet 5:8). Satan is very active in attacking those who follow Jesus Christ in order to defeat and remove us from ministry. Fundamentally, the devil wants us to believe that once we've given in to temptation there is no longer a place for us in God's service.

---

262 Matthew 4:1–11; Mark 1:12–13; Luke 4:1–13.

But by renewing our minds, we think God's thoughts as we set our minds "on things above, not on earthly things" (Col 3:2). We align ourselves with the truth of the gospel—that we are loved and forgiven people. There's nothing we or anything else can do to change that.[263] As we internalize grace within ourselves, our minds are renewed and our hearts are transformed. The renewal of our thoughts reconnects our minds with the ethical behaviors of holy living. We transform our impulses from evil desires to godly holiness and righteousness by focusing on Christ, "the author and perfecter of our faith" (Heb 12:2).

Diane J. Chandler states that, "Like Paul, we are to have a complete preoccupation with Christ so that we might be increasingly transformed into the *Imago Dei* through the *Imago Christi* for *gloria Dei*."[264] To fix our eyes upon Jesus means we return to the Scriptures, reflecting through the Gospels how Jesus is the true expression of the Imago Dei.

The truth is, we can never overcome temptations strictly through self-will and discipline. Knowledge apart from the renewal of our minds is useless. "It is not much knowledge that fills and satisfies the soul, but the intimate understanding and relish of the truth."[265] The purpose of this focus is clear: "to ask for an intimate knowledge of our Lord . . . so that I may love him more and follow him more closely."[266]

It is worth remembering that when the Spirit of God resides within us, we have access to the mind of God. Paul tells us this in 1 Corinthians 2 when he says that the Spirit searches all things, even the things of God (v. 10), and we ourselves have received the Spirit from God (v. 12) so that we indeed have the very mind of Christ (v. 16). Renewing our mind in Christ helps us combat the temptations of such things as entertainment escapism, the lure of the Internet and social media, the dark places of pornography and illicit relationships, and the pressure of materialistic consumerism. Knowing we have access to the mind of Christ should encourage and free us from the despair that sin brings.

Temptation: Pride and Justification

One temptation that global servants find themselves particularly vulnerable to is pride. We would think that for the missionary who leaves his or her native land behind and enters a new culture as a learner, humility would be second nature. But we missionaries are as guilty of pride as anyone else. It's easy to think, "I have given up so much to go to the mission field; I am better than others." There are a variety of ways we live this out, but such justification springs from self-pride. Further, when we succumb to such rationalization, we sow the seeds of regret, guilt, shame, and doubt; and our effectiveness is compromised—as we are anything but the joyful servant we long to be.

---

263 See Romans 8:28–39.

264 Diane J. Chandler, *Christian Spiritual Formation: An Integrated Approach for Personal and Relational Wholeness* (Downers Grove, IL: IVP, 2014), 146.

265 Ignatius of Loyola, *The Spiritual Exercises of St. Ignatius*, trans. Louis J. Puhl (New York: Vintage Books, 2000), 5.

266 Ignatius, 41.

Pride leads us to assert ourselves, to demand our rights, and to want to be looked upon as better than others. St. John Cassian observed, "Pride corrupts the whole soul, not just part of it."[267] It is because of this that pride has traditionally been called the foundational sin.[268] Pride is more than likely the centerpiece of everyone's sin pattern. Pride denies the work of Christ, for it refuses to concede that our sins cannot be redeemed by our own efforts.

Prideful attitudes such as vanity, snobbery, irreverence, arrogance, impenitence, narcissism, and disobedience all show up outwardly toward others.[269] It is understandable that many missionaries in the first stages of culture shock could react in prideful ways, thinking their own culture is superior to the culture of their new home. "Why they even drive on the wrong side of the road!"

While we may show compassion to such new and culture-shocked arrivals, this prideful superiority is not restricted to new personnel. Cultural imperialism has unfortunately been center stage in many missionaries' attitudes, no matter how long they have been on the field.

If we are honest with ourselves, we all carry these postures of pride wherever we go. Recognizing this before we go to the field will help us as we embrace our new culture. Anyone who longs to integrate at a deep level in their new home must face their own cultural pride and reground their worth and self-identity in Christ, which crushes self-pride.

Another way to experience pride is through such deceptive attitudes as distrust, perfectionism, and presumption. Augustine called this secret pride.[270] I have noticed each one of these in my own heart and have also experienced the effects of them within the hearts of many strong and effective missionaries. Highly motivated workers can secretly pride themselves on getting a task done when no one else was able to do it. Rather than giving glory to God, they hoard the glory for themselves. The great sin of inward pride is that it casts out other-centered love; it is narcissistic and wholly centered on self-love.

Since such pride runs deep, it is impossible to deal with it without self-reflection. St. Bernard of Clairvaux wrote in his spiritual classic, The Steps of Pride and Humility, that "humility is the virtue by which a man recognizes his own unworthiness because he really knows himself."[271] Bernard starts his twelve steps on a ladder toward pride with step one being "curiosity about what is not one's proper concern," meaning we must be aware of our propensity to compare, judge, rank, envy, and mock.[272]

---

267 St. Cassian, *The Institutes,* trans. and annotated by Boniface Ramsey (Mahwah, NJ: Paulist Press, 2000), 255.

268 Pride has been called the foundational sin because it is attributed to be the cause of Satan's fall. See Isaiah 14:12–15 and Ezekiel 28:12–19, and William Sanford La Sor, David Allan Hubbard, and Frederic William Bush, *Old Testament Survey: The Message, Form, and Background of the Old Testament* (Grand Rapids: Eerdmans, 1982), 473–74.

269 Michael Mangis, *Signature Sins: Taming Our Wayward Hearts* (Downers Grove, IL: IVP, 2008), 31. Augustine divided the sin of pride into two categories: outward and inward. See Loren Gavitt, ed., *Saint Augustine's Prayer Book* (New York: Holy Cross Publications, 1976).

270 Mangis, 31.

271 Bernard of Clairvaux, *The Steps of Humility and Pride* (Kalamazoo, MI: Cistercian Publications, 1973), 30.

272 Bernard of Clairvaux, 57.

Fortunately, God does not leave us to our own devices or helpless in our struggles. Jesus said, "Everyone who exalts himself will be humbled, and he who humbles himself will be exalted" (Luke 18:14). He also said, "Take my yoke upon you and learn from me, for I am gentle and humble in heart" (Matt 11:29). When we are struggling with pride, we need to be re-ordered to love God with all our heart, soul, mind, and strength (Mark 12:30).

Our confidence in our righteousness comes not from our behavior but from the work of Christ's cross. Christ conquered our pride through his death and resurrection. So, in humility we can echo Bernard's words of invitation:

> *"Come," he says.*
> *Where? "To me, the truth."*
> *How? "By humility."*
> *For what reward? "I will refresh you."*[273]

Truth: Moral Purity

In our sex-dominated Western culture, nowhere is the pursuit of holiness more of a challenge than in maintaining moral purity. Some have even gone so far as to claim that "the Great Commission is about holiness."[274] Everyone loses when one of us gives in to sexual temptation—whether an affair, viewing online pornography, or dwelling upon lustful thoughts. As Paul tells us, sexual immorality is a sin against our own selves (1 Cor 6:18). When believers confess their sinful sexual desires to me, I hear their frustrations: how tired they are because of their battles with lust, how draining pornography is, and how impurity robs them of their strength and moral authority.

Sexual sin is not new among missionaries. In the early nineteenth century, rumors of sex scandals began coming back from the South Sea Islands. Mission agencies were hearing about how their male missionaries were engaging in sexual sin with Island women. But the solution these boards came up with opened up a whole new avenue of problems. "To ensure such temptations would not taint their candidates, the directors of the American board of Commissioners for Foreign Missions insisted the candidates marry before sailing to Hawaii."[275] Some married after only knowing their new bride for a few hours. Trying to find human solutions to heart-sin issues can create a new set of problems. It is better to address sin promptly rather than sidestep and compromise for the sake of our human weaknesses.

As a missionary, you might be thinking, "This could never happen to me." However, the more secure and immune we feel, the more at risk we might actually be. No one is exempt from sexual temptation—men, women, and even children. Facing the attacks of the enemy and living stressful lives, global servants have greater moral vulnerability. Loneliness, unmet emotional needs, a new culture

---

273 Bernard of Clairvaux, 31–32.

274 Kevin DeYoung, *The Hole in our Holiness: Filling the Gap between Gospel Passion and the Pursuit of Godliness* (Wheaton, IL: Crossway, 2012), 16.

275 Ruth Tucker and Leslie Andrews, "Historical Notes on Missionary Care," in *Missionary Care: Counting the Cost for World Evangelism*" ed. Kelly O'Donnell (Pasadena, CA: William Carey Library, 1992), 27.

to learn and understand, the stripping away of support systems and standards, different cultural sexual cues, greater spiritual warfare, the list goes on; these factors increase the risk we face in sexual temptations.

Many global servants don't understand and are underequipped to deal with the dynamics and influence of sexual temptation. It is uncommon to fall into such sin immediately, as it is more often a result of long-term habits and patterns. Jesus told us that sexual sin originates in the heart (Matt 15:19). This slide occurs in our hearts so gradually that we may not even be aware of it. We live in a sex-saturated environment, and we are exposed and numbed to sexual temptation on a daily basis. Once we begin the slide, sexual temptation becomes a strong addicting force. That is why it's so important not to even take the first step down that path. The control of sexual sin can come to a point where we are willing to give up everything to gratify it: our marriage, our families, our ministry, our reputation, our friends—everything.

If someone is battling with sexual addiction, profession help is recommended. However, here are a few proactive strategies for maintaining moral purity while on the field:

- Accept your personal vulnerability and become more aware of normal sexual dynamics.
- If you are married, make your relationship a high priority; make a commitment to live a holy life together.
- Meditate upon and apply Scriptures that speak about moral purity (Prov 5; 6:20–35; Eph 5:3–12; 1 Cor 6:12–20; Rom 6; Col 3:5; 1 Thess 4:3–8).
- Be more attentive to practices that might seem harmless, but in fact do not contribute to a holy life. These practices may be "lawful" (1 Cor 6:12), but for you they are particularly harmful because they make you much more vulnerable to temptation.
- Be renewed in your mind (Col 3:10) and focus on whatever is noble, right, pure, lovely, admirable, excellent, praiseworthy (Phil 4:4–8).
- Know the triggers which make you more vulnerable to sexual temptations. These early warning signs can move you to make changes in your lifestyle choices.
- Don't battle such temptation alone. Confession and sharing your struggles with someone else is a must (James 5:16).[276]

It is important to remember that sexual immorality is not an unpardonable sin. Forgiveness and healing are available through the holiness of Christ's work on the cross. Recovery and forgiveness are "a matter of spiritual formation."[277]

---

[276] Ken Williams, unpublished notes on Moral Purity (Wycliffe Bible Translators Counseling Dept, 1990), 3–4.
[277] William M. Struthers, *Wired for Intimacy* (Downers Grove, IL: IVP, 2009), 178.

Truth: Authenticity

The Anglican pastor and writer John Stott once said that "holiness is not a condition into which we drift."[278] To be a person of integrity demands that we live an intentional, authentically truthful life. Jesus said, "Simply let your 'Yes' be 'Yes,' and your 'No,' 'No'; anything beyond this comes from the evil one" (Matt 5:37). We read in Proverbs, "Truthful lips endure forever, but a lying tongue lasts only a moment" (12:19) and "The LORD detests lying lips, but he delights in men who are truthful" (v. 22).

Adele Calhoun says, "Adam and Eve became the first truth spinners."[279] Like Adam and Eve, we too face the temptation every day to spin the truth of our own brokenness. We want to define our own experiences in our own terms rather than by actual reality. But as Proverbs tells us, such lies do not last forever—truth has the staying power.

As global servants, there are many ways we are less than fully honest, especially when we feel we are called upon to validate the financial commitment and gifts made to us by mission committees, churches, and donors. For example:

- We spin events and experiences in order to impress others.
- We exaggerate.
- We cheat on forms to get what we want (even justifying our actions because they are "for the Lord").
- We break promises or lack follow through.
- We flatter and become people pleasers—saying what we think others want to hear, rather than what may be true.
- We slander others (often done in conflict situations).
- We gossip and pass on rumors and innuendoes about others (often done in group prayer meetings).
- We are afraid to say what we really mean (often to leadership).
- We speak the truth, but without love.

Global workers must work hard not to rationalize, deny, and blame, especially when the world around us normalizes white lies and falsehoods. Instead, we must listen closely to the Holy Spirit when he convicts us of speaking falsely. We should make a personal commitment to always speak the truth in love and with a kind heart (Eph 4:15).

Walking in the light of fellowship with Jesus means we also walk in the light of the truth. *Truth* is a key word for the apostle John. He uses the word twenty-five times in his Gospel, using it as one of the defining characteristics of Jesus (John 1:14). Being a person of truth should not be an add-on, but the very essence of our being. Jesus held his strongest criticism for those who did not live authentically, calling them hypocrites.[280] The Greek word *hypokrisis* is a term for

---

278 John Stott, *God's New Society: The Message of Ephesians* (Downers Grove, IL: IVP, 1979), 193.
279 Adele Ahlberg Calhoun, *Spiritual Disciplines Handbook* (Downers Grove, IL: IVP, 2005), 201.
280 See Matthew 23:13, 15, 23, 25, 27, 29.

acting or mask-wearing.[281] We are hypocritical in our life and service when our heart, values, and actions do not align with Christ's truth.[282]

Jesus' invitation to be an integrated person calls us into the spiritual disciplines of truth-seeking and of truth-telling.[283] Holding up the value of truthfulness is central to holiness and spiritual life. In truth, we build an unshakable foundation that allows our personal integrity to not tilt or collapse upon itself. As Genesis 3 teaches us, it is a slippery slope from doubting God's Word to full-out disobedience. When we are disconnected from the truth, we turn away from loving God with all our heart, soul, mind, and strength (Matt 22:34–40).

Truth: Financial Fidelity and Corruption

I want to mention one last matter of truthfulness in our walk with God: finances. The apostle Paul speaks of the temptation of material wealth in 1 Timothy 6:6–10:

> *Godliness with contentment is great gain. For we brought nothing into the world, and we can take nothing out of it. But if we have food and clothing, we will be content with that. People who want to get rich fall into temptation and a trap and into many foolish and harmful desires that plunge men into ruin and destruction. For the love of money is a root of all kinds of evil. Some people, eager for money, have wandered from the faith and pierced themselves with many griefs.*

Paul tells us that godly people are not interested in becoming rich because they possess inner resources which furnish riches far beyond that which our life here on earth can provide. What Paul is condemning here, however, is not wealth per se, but the dis-ordered desire for money. When we fall into this temptation, we wander from the faith. The Greek word for *wander* is from the word for planet (*àpeplaéthesan*), literally meaning "the one who lusts after wealth, or 'planets' away from the faith."[284] This follows the ancient idea of planets wandering in the heavens. Such a person is not stable, not fixed in his or her faith, and becomes "doubled-minded" and "unstable in all he does" (Jas 1:8).

I personally don't know of anyone who has entered missionary service with the desire for monetary gain. When you measure gifts, skills, education, and experience, global servants are woefully underpaid. Missionaries belonging to faith missions are also required to raise their own salaries. People don't enter missionary service for the pay. So how does financial temptation become an issue for someone who is pursuing a career path which has nothing to do with earthly or monetary reward?

---

281 υποκριτες, *"Hupokritēs,"* in W. Bauer, *A Greek-English Lexicon of the New Testament and Other Christian Literature*, trans. and ed. W. F. Arndt and F. W. Gingrich (Chicago: University of Chicago Press, 1975), 852.

282 See Matthew 5:37; 7:5–12.

283 See the spiritual discipline of "truth-telling" in Calhoun, 200–202.

284 "Err," in W. E. Vine, *A Comprehensive Dictionary of the Original Greek Words with Their Precise Meanings for English Readers* (McLean, VA: MacDonald Publishing, 1940), 379.

Let's explore four common temptations for missionaries in the area of financial integrity:

- Envy of others' riches and possessions
- Telling the truth about our financial situation to supporters
- The corrupting influence of consumerism
- The issue of bribery

Many global workers envy friends and family who have more money than they could ever hope to earn as a missionary. In debriefing missionaries on their return from the field, I have seen how hard it is for them, after living in poor countries, to deal with the abundance of material goods in America. They struggle with the tension of not having and yet wanting. They struggle with the concept of living simply and yet wanting some of the gadgets their neighbors possess.

Missionaries often have a scarcity mentality and thus will never waste anything. If you had leftovers from the meal last night, they went into soup the next day. You wash plastic baggies and keep twist ties to use over and over again, and you even wash plastic silverware and Styrofoam cups! While most people brag about how much they spent on a certain item, missionaries brag about how little things have cost them, as if they need to justify their purchases. Yet when we enter the homes of others—who seemingly have everything anybody could want, things that are beautiful and expensive—it is easy to become envious of it all.

I remember talking to a missionary who was on his fourth home ministry assignment and said it was the hardest of all the times he returned to America. All of his peers were in their fifties and in the peak of their earning years. They all seemed to have nice homes and expensive cars. He had nothing. He felt the material differences and admitted he was struggling with envy.

This, of course, is understandable, but it can also be dangerous. Psalm 49 speaks to the dangers of wealth and cautions us not to envy: "Do not be overawed when a man grows rich, when the splendor of his house increases; for he will take nothing with him when he dies" (vv. 16–17). Paul also reminds us that love "does not envy" (1 Cor 13:4). It is far too easy to get captivated by wealth. Rather, we need to keep our eyes focused on the true reward that is lasting and heavenward in Christ Jesus (Phil 3:14).

Missionaries can also be very judgmental of those who seemingly have so much and yet say they aren't able to support them financially. We look at our friends' homes, which have four big-screen TVs, two new cars, and all the latest gadgets and appliances, and we wonder why they can't find funds to give to missions. It's hard not to judge others when we see this, but we must resist this temptation as well. To walk before others without envy and judgment gives witness to our trust in God's faithful provision to us as his servants. Perhaps this is as great a witness to the world as anything we do on the field.

This leads to the second area of monetary temptation for missionaries: truthfulness concerning our finances. Faith-supported missionaries can find it difficult to answer the question of how their financial support is going. If they say they have needs, they are afraid they are denying God's ability to take care of them. Yet on the other hand, if they say they are doing well financially, they are afraid supporters might stop giving altogether. In this way, the fundraising system, for all its benefits of connecting supporters with missionaries, does put global servants in a position of weakness. They are caught between need and trust. Nevertheless, no matter where missionaries find themselves in this tension, it is still possible to be people of financial integrity.

We must be as truthful as we can, sharing our needs without expressing a woe-is-me attitude. We can take comfort in the example of the apostle Paul, who never stopped asking for help when he needed it.[285] In contrast, the temptation to overstate our needs is also to be avoided. The church has a long history of leaders (from popes to TV evangelists) who professed poverty and yet lived extravagant lifestyles.

The third area of financial temptation is simply the influence of material wealth. When Jesus is Lord, he becomes Lord over our finances (Matt 6:24). The story of Ananias and Sapphira (Acts 5:1–11) reminds us that even Christians are not immune from the power money has to corrupt. Their fault was not so much withholding funds from the church, but lying about it. Again, this is a matter of truthfulness. There should be no double meanings, cunning schemes, duplicity, or hidden agendas in regard to our finances. We must remember that money does not equate to personal value, nor is one's character measured by wealth.

Unfortunately, I know missionaries who have stolen, embezzled, and cheated for financial gain. Monetary wealth corrupted their souls. It destroyed their calling and ministry. The rich young ruler loved his possessions more than he loved God (Mark 10:17–31). We must acknowledge the truth that "material things are lovely to own, but they generate personal tragedy when they own us."[286]

Finally, as we deal with situations involving financial integrity on the mission field, what should our attitude be in regard to bribery? While we lived in Serbia, our landlord came to us with two contracts he wanted us to sign: one that was just between us and one that he wanted to submit to the government for tax reasons. The second contract was written for a lot less money than we were actually paying in rent. I objected, but he made it clear that if I didn't sign this contract we would be out of our apartment. I wasn't sure what I should do; I was very uncomfortable signing, but I knew he had me completely at his mercy.

This type of situation is a matter of prayer. I decided to sign both contracts. I told the landlord, though, that if I was asked, I would not lie, but I would tell the authorities what I was actually paying. He didn't like that, but I'm sure he still submitted the second contract to the tax authorities.

Our Christian conscience finds participating in bribes to be abhorrent. Yet for much of the world this is just the normal price of doing business. Again, this is a matter of prayer and knowing what you are comfortable with. When it comes to navigating within a bribing culture, what matters is how your inner motivation informs your decision. Why would you consider paying a bribe?

---

285 See 1 Corinthians 9:7–12.

286 Ralph Moore and Alan Tang, *Your Money* (Ventura, CA: Regal Books, 2003), 41–42.

How would such an action affect the gospel? Are such bribes seen as something extra or just normal in your new culture?

Differentiating between a bribe and a gratuity can be difficult and cause deep-seated anxiety. Feelings of guilt sometimes emerge from these encounters and can become quite destructive for the global servant. For this reason, it is wise that mission teams who will be dealing with bribe-taking have an intentional policy of what they can live with, always keeping in mind flexibility to unique situations and personal comfortableness and conscience.

Veracity demands we live authentic and uncomplicated lives. The mature soul will not depend on tricks or deceptions. Our ability to recognize and avoid evil determines our character and spiritual maturity. We become firmly grounded in our inner being when we live out the words of Isaiah: "You will keep in perfect peace him whose mind is steadfast, because he trusts in you" (26:3).

Reflection and Points to Ponder

- How do you live out the need to be truthful in all things when confronting the challenges of living in a broken world? When do you exaggerate, give partial truth, beg forgiveness rather than ask permission, or have a sliding scale of honesty? What might the Lord be saying to you in these instances?

- When has it cost you to be honest? What was that like for you?

- Who have been your role models of both healthy and unhealthy sexuality and relationships? What have they taught you? Do you know your trigger points that can lead you into impure thoughts and actions? What impact do sexually explicit movies, books, pictures, etc. have upon your mind? What action steps do you need to take to guard your body and purify your mind?

- The idealization of poverty is a dangerous illusion for Christians. Do you believe that poverty is holy in itself? Why or why not? How do you balance your understanding of wealth with the concepts of stewardship and giving? What is the difference between possessing and using material resources? How do you understand the difference between trusting in riches and trusting in God?

For Further Reading

Kyle Idleman, *Gods at War: Defeating Idols that Battle for Your Heart* (Grand Rapids: Zondervan, 2013). An examination of the idols in our modern world and how to center and move our hearts back toward Jesus.

Michael Mangis, *Signature Sins: Taming our Wayward Hearts* (Downers Grove, IL: IVP, 2008). Exploring the seven deadly sins and how each of us has one main besetting sin. Mangis encourages us that we can find freedom in Christ from such signature sin.

William M. Struthers, *Wired for Intimacy: How Pornography Hijacks the Male Brain* (Downers Grove, IL: IVP, 2009). A neuroscientist's look at how pornography affects the male brain, and what we can do about it.

The mission field can be a lonely place, but Isabel* and I bonded over our children, caring for one another's kids through hospital stays, babies, birthday parties and holidays, weekly visits, and even vacations. Our friendship started as a small seed, but over the years grew to be deep and complete. Our families each became surrogates for family we had left behind when we came to Slovakia. Isabel and I met weekly for almost ten years, usually at a time when our daughters could be together too.

One week between visits I got an email from Isabel telling me of an unforgivable fault of mine and informing me we would no longer be friends and our families would never get together again. I didn't have so many friends that I could afford to just let this one go, especially one this near to my heart. Attempts to understand and reconcile were met with anger and refusal. Our family cried, we examined our hearts, we talked to others, and we prayed. We sought the wisdom of others, but the relationship was gone.

I had no other recourse. All I could do was forgive. I had to look at my side of the issue, and that was all I could do—forgive. I wanted my friend back. But she had now become the closest thing to an enemy I had ever had. However, I knew I had to love her and to bless her. So I prayed that God would give her the greatest gift ever, an understanding of his love. I prayed that God would pour out his love on her. I prayed that God would show mercy on the one who had judged me so unfairly. I prayed and memorized Psalm 27.

The Christian community was so small in our town that I dreaded every gathering. To even write about it now hurts because it puts the pain and emotion into the black and white of a small tidy space. All I could do was keep asking God to help me forgive. I asked him to not let any bitterness creep into my life. I did it daily, sometimes hourly, and often even moment-by-moment because the pain was ever-present.

I did not see Isabel for eighteen months, which in our small town was unusual. Then, suddenly, I got a phone call from Isabel saying she was sorry and had betrayed me, and though she didn't deserve it, would I please come to her house so she could apologize. I was in shock. I walked to her house, repeating the psalm I had memorized.

Isabel told me how the Lord had brought her to the place of asking for forgiveness and asked if I would forgive her. I said, "Isabel, I have already forgiven you, so this is easy. Yes, of course I forgive you." Isabel said she knew trust had been broken but would like to restore our friendship and rebuild the trust. She also asked if she and her husband could come to our house and apologize to our entire family.

This story has a happy ending. Even as I write this I think of other relationships, some in which I have been hurtful and have needed to ask for forgiveness, but forgiveness has not yet come. Then there are relationships in which I find myself doing the forgiving. They continue to exist in the painful stage of moment-by-moment prayer, asking God to help me forgive and not become bitter as I continue to learn to forgive.

Tricia
global servant in Eastern Europe

*Name changed for security reasons.

Comparison and Competition
The Ancient Pathway to Forgiveness

Christian ministry is carried out in community, and one of the great joys of service are the relationships we form with fellow coworkers. Missionaries can become so close they actually become family. But like in all families, disagreements and conflicts are a reality, even in our strongest relationships. We come into our communities with sinful tendencies, so we shouldn't be surprised when this brokenness is also experienced in our social networks.

A generation ago, new missionaries were often not fully accepted until they had spent a certain length of time on the field. They were discouraged from speaking up in regard to their assignments and ministry plans until they had completed language school or somehow proved themselves. Some would spend their first term on the field in virtual isolation. This philosophy was not overt when I went first went to the field, but it did exist in hidden ways, such as being kept out of the loop on decisions being made. This was explained to me by the "need to know" rationale.

Fortunately, this attitude is not as prevalent today. I suspect newer global servants would not stand for having to wait long years before they could contribute to decisions on their teams. Generally, experienced missionaries now do a much better job of valuing all teammates, no matter their experience or commitment. Unfortunately, we can still find a spirit of devaluation among teams that takes the form of comparing and competing.

Comparison and Competition

Scripture calls us to resist the natural tendency to compare and compete. "Let us not become conceited, provoking and envying each other" (Gal 5:26). "Each of you should look not only to your own interests, but also to the interests of others" (Phil 2:4). The New Testament "one anothers" are to be the focal points of our relationships.[287]

That said, comparison and competition is common among both global servants and mission organizations. It can be as normal as a husband and wife

---

[287] There are over twenty "one anothers" in the New Testament. See Gene Getz's classic book for an expanded explanation. Gene A. Getz, *Building Up One Another: How Every Member of the Church Can Help Strengthen Other Christians* (Wheaton, IL: SP Publications, 1976).

competing with each other in their language studies to two mission organizations being territorial about who gets the credit for successful or popular ministries. One national church leader was featured, in the same month, on three separate mission's magazine covers as "their own" missionary (including my own).

Competition can also occur *within* an agency. Missions generally operate on a shoe-string budget and with limited resourcing. When this is accompanied by a scarcity mentality, competition can quickly follow. I have been in budget meetings where each department of my mission had to justify and advocate for additional resources, even when that meant another ministry would have their budget reduced. These battles are intense and often painful to observe. Few individuals in such encounters demonstrate the call to "honor one another" (Rom 12:10).

When we compare and compete, we lose sight of Jesus' teachings in the Gospels. Remember when James and John came to him, requesting to sit at his right and left in his coming glory? They were trying to one-up the other disciples and get the good seats. But after Jesus told them that they would drink the cup (of suffering) he drinks, he said, "but to sit at my right or left is not for me to grant. These places belong to those for whom they have been prepared" (Mark 10:40).

Did a lust for greatness lurk behind James and John's request? Did they want to be seen as the greatest disciples in the kingdom? Jesus' rebuke was in some ways gentle, but nevertheless strong—this is not what the kingdom is about. Jesus tells us that rather than competing for places of honor, we should be prepared to suffer and serve.[288]

In Jesus' last recorded words in the Gospel of John, the risen Lord describes to Peter the manner of his future death (21:18–19). After hearing Jesus' words, Peter, struggling to understand, starts comparing by asking about John's death: "Lord, what about him?" (v. 21). Jesus refuses to compare the two. "If I want him to remain alive until I return, what is that to you? You must follow me" (v. 22). We all have our own journey with Jesus, and we are not to judge another's route. God calls each of us separately for his own purposes. Our task is simply to follow our own path.

Admittedly, this is hard. When I was the director of a Bible school in Europe, I found myself once walking the grounds of a famous Christian campus in America, admiring all the beautiful buildings. We had nothing like this at the school I was leading. Why could my school not be blessed with just one of the smaller buildings? We could do so much more for the kingdom with such resources. Why does America have all the money? But when I checked my heart, I realized the root of my attitude was unvarnished envy. Our school was doing just fine with the blessings and resources God had given us. I was comparing and became jealous.

It is so easy to compare, to envy, and to become jealous of others. But James reminds us that the wise person is the one who is humble and does not boast, envy, or harbor selfish ambition (Jas 3:13–14). "For where you have envy and

---

[288] See Mark 10:42–45. For other examples, see Mark 9:38–41 and Matthew 23:5–12.

selfish ambition, there you find disorder and every evil practice" (v. 16). He also says that the wisdom that comes from heaven "is first of all pure; then peace-loving, considerate, submission, full of mercy and good fruit, impartial and sincere" (v. 17). We are to support, not compete with, our fellow workers.

Justice and Mercy

Micah 6:8 famously calls God's people to "act justly and to love mercy and to walk humbly with your God." Jesus frequently spoke of a kingdom which was defined by justice, mercy, and humility. "Woe to you Pharisees, because you give God a tenth of your mint, rue and other kinds of your garden herbs, but you neglect justice and the love of God. You should have practiced the latter without leaving the former undone" (Luke 11:42). This is the heart of our religious faith. The cross ushers in the coming kingdom—a kingdom of truth, justice, and humility. When we live this way, our souls rest in peace.

Seeking justice and mercy in both our lives and the world reduces our tendency to compare and compete. In the early days of the Jesuits, before a potential priest was confirmed he was required to do some sort of community service, often serving in hospitals and living off alms. By doing so he was taught how to put the needs of others ahead of his own. Such ministry went a long way in removing comparison and competition. I don't think novitiates strove to compete with one another in emptying bedpans.

Could we in Protestant faith missions learn something from this? I wonder if a period of lowly service might wean us off our pedestals of pride and entitlements. I suspect our hearts would be more prone to accept our place among others through such humble service (Mark 10:40).

Bitterness and Forgiveness

One of the ways to reduce our need to put ourselves first is to learn the lessons of forgiveness and letting go of hurts. Coming to terms with our limitations and losses allows us to be more receptive and accept the circumstances in our life. By forgiving, we learn that in dying to self we are reborn into new life.

It is a strange thing that so many global servants preach a gospel of forgiveness, while in their hearts they harbor bitterness and resentment. There are many roadblocks to giving and receiving forgiveness. Humans have a natural default toward vindication and revenge. We want others to suffer the way we have suffered. But vengeance is a poor substitution for the abundant life.

Only through forgiveness are we able to let go of the retribution we feel we are owed. We release others from payments. In forgiveness, we are called to take the time to appropriately process the pain and loss we are feeling, but then to release it to God to carry for us. Forgiveness is a costly activity, and our feelings don't simply disappear immediately. It requires a conscious choice. We have to decide repeatedly to try our best not to harbor resentment, not to bring our wrong up before others, nor to hold it over those who hurt us. But without it, the true experiential freedom we have in Christ can never be lived out.

The apostle Paul calls us as believers to "bear with each other and forgive whatever grievances you may have against one another. Forgive as the Lord forgave you" (Col 3:13). When we practice forgiveness, Paul goes on to say, the peace of Christ will rule in our hearts (v. 15).

Forgiveness: What It Is and What It Is Not

The ability and willingness to consistently forgive may be the most important factor in missionary effectiveness. Our testimony of God's love depends on our capacity to embrace the gospel for ourselves and others. God's power in our lives is demonstrated through it. Three foundational beliefs give us a biblical understanding of what forgiveness is.

Fully understand that the basis of forgiving others is God's forgiveness of us (Eph 4:32).

Realize the consequences of not forgiving can destroy us spiritually, emotionally, physically, and relationally (see Matt 6:14–15; 2 Cor 2:10–11; Eph 4:26–27; Ps 32:3–4; Prov 17:9, 27:4).

Allow the Holy Spirit to enter into dialogue with your soul and convict if you have an unforgiving spirit (John 16:8).[289]

God has forgiven us more than we could ever forgive others. Jesus tells us plainly in the Sermon on the Mount that we are to put reconciliation with our brother or sister ahead of even worship of God (Matt 5:23). Based on the forgiveness we have received in Christ, without a willingness to forgive, resentments can be buried for years and, unknowingly, do great damage to our hearts. The steps below can free us from any lasting bitterness and help us move into biblical forgiveness when wronged by another.

1. *Express your feelings to God.* The Father knows how you feel, but in pouring out your emotions to him it provides personal benefits. It affirms your feelings of anger, which means we don't deny what we are feeling. Pouring out our emotions to God gives us a safe place to vent our anger in a nondestructive way and brings God into our situation in a very personal way. This is the biblical example we have repeatedly in the Psalms by David and others.

2. *Recognize and name any unforgiveness in your heart.* It is important to be able to acknowledge whether we have actually forgiven or not. To say, "I haven't forgiven," is very helpful in being honest with ourselves (Jer 17:9; Prov 10:18).

3. *Decide to forgive.* Forgiveness is an act of our will with God-given power (Eph 1:19). In this decision, we are deciding to surrender our right to feel further resentment as well as our right to gossip or continue to dwell on the issue (Prov 17:9).

---

[289] Ken Williams, unpublished notes, "Thoughts on Forgiveness" (Wycliffe Bible Translation Counseling Department, 1997), 1.

4. *Forgiveness is a process.* Forgiveness usually takes time. Don't give up. Sometimes it is helpful to make a general decision to forgive a person and continue to make individual decisions as specific hurts come to mind. However, the longer we wait, the more difficult feelings are to handle without sinning (Eph 4:26–27). Remember, we don't necessarily need to feel like forgiving to forgive. Love is an action, and by deciding to forgive even when we don't feel like it, we act out of love for that person. This isn't hypocrisy. It is obedience.

5. *Seek reconciliation.* It isn't enough to just let go of our feelings. We need to do what we can to restore the relationship (Matt 5:23–24). We must keep in mind, however, that it does take both sides to accomplish this. If the other party refuses to reconcile, the best way to "live at peace" (Rom 12:18) with them may be to give them space without forcing the issue.[290]

Forgiving is a complicated process. Questions often arise as we go through the steps to forgiveness. Here are some of the more common ones:

1. If the other person does not repent, do I still have to forgive them? I know of only one passage in Scripture, Luke 17:3–4, which mentions the other person repenting. All other references talk about forgiving regardless of what the other person does.[291]

2. If forgiveness is simply a decision, shouldn't I just be able to do it immediately? Scripture does not address this issue directly. But in most cases, it seems that forgiveness is a process that takes time (Matt 18:21). The decision to forgive is only the beginning. To expect instant changes in our feelings is probably unrealistic and can then lead to self-condemnation, guilt, discouragement, or giving up. Forgiving does not mean we forget the incident. True forgiveness happens as we remember the incident without our anger and resentment. It is true that we may still have grief or sadness, but with true forgiveness, the anger is gone.

3. What if I want to forgive but the anger still remains? First, we must apply Luke 6:27–28 and Romans 12:14, 17, 20–21. Act out forgiveness by appropriating the love of Jesus for ourselves and for others. We may also need to seek help (Jas 5:16). Confession before others and their prayers for us is a powerful spiritual weapon in overcoming anger. As we confess, we must make sure we focus on our feelings and the need to forgive, rather than on what the other person has done to us. If not, we may just be using our confession to justify and gossip.[292]

Forgiveness does not mean that we excuse others for what they did. Nor does it mean we must continue to unconditionally trust or have a close relationship with the person who hurt us. We might even never be able to completely reconcile with them. But it does mean that our hearts are free to love again.[293]

---

290 Williams, 2–3.
291 See especially Prov 10:11; 25:21; Matt 5:44–46; Luke 6:36; Rom 12:14; 1 Cor 4:12–13; 1 Pet 3:9.
292 Williams, 3–4.
293 Williams, 4.

Organizational Forgiveness

Dealing with organizational sin can be difficult. Pain and hurt can run deep, and trying to find resolution can be overwhelming. However, just as we are called to love and forgive individuals, we are also called to love and forgive organizations. When forgiveness is needed organizationally, members choose together to leave behind bitterness and grudges over harm and distress, working toward a new future. Such forgiveness characterizes healthy organizations. True organizational forgiveness is never an attempt to minimize harm. Instead, it is a response to keep that harm from permeating the culture of the organization. Organizational forgiveness ends dysfunction by healing resentfulness, bitterness, and hopefully—as best it can—broken trust. It helps everyone move forward in peace and hope.

Jesus told us to love the Lord and to love our neighbor (Matt 22:37–39). We are here on earth to love, so our focus must be on learning how to love well. It is easy to love the lovely. It is easy to forgive the forgivable. But if we really want to grow in our love and ability to forgive, there is no better way than to grapple with the unlovable and the unforgivable. Thankfully, it is possible to love, even when it seems otherwise, because we abide in the strength and possibilities of God's love, not our own.

As with personal relationships, when an organization harms us, we can easily feel that we have the right to be bitter. Usually forgiveness is the last thing on our minds. However, bitterness against an organization affects everyone in the organization, including—and mostly—ourselves. We should remember that "Christ is not the third party inserted between God and humanity to take care of human sin. He is the God who was wronged."[294]

Jesus understands firsthand the injustice we have experienced. He had every right not to forgive and yet he chose forgiveness, and we can too. Forgiveness is difficult and might take time, but we can overcome and forgive. We can find love again, even within the organization that hurt us.

Sometimes, even as we forgive, organizational behavior can remain sinful and people can continue to experience deep pain. When this is the case, and the situation is destructive, forgiveness may not be enough. We probably need to remove ourselves from such a situation for our own health and for the health of others. Jane Fryar, referencing Judith Sturnick, puts it this way:

> *Sturnick warns readers that toxic organizations can dishearten and even destroy servant leaders. She urges leaders not to protect or rationalize destructive—we might say sinful—organizational behavior. Not all organizations want to heal. Sturnick insists that leaders caught up in toxic organizations explore their reasons for remaining there. She warns that healthy people in sick organizations begin to act in unhealthy ways just to survive. This can seriously compromise the leader's ability truly to serve and to foster healing. Even in the church, leaders sometimes must, in grief, shake the dust from our feet, as Jesus said (Matthew 10:14). Our departure in such cases serves as our final word of Law to those who rebel against his grace.*[295]

---

294 Miroslav Wolf, *Free of Charge: Giving and Receiving in a Culture Stripped of Grace* (Grand Rapids: Zondervan, 2005), 145.

295 Jane L. Fryar, *Servant Leadership: Setting Leaders Free* (St. Louis: Concordia, 2001), 103, referencing Judith Sturnick, "Healing Leadership," in *Insights on Leadership: Service, Stewardship, Spirit, and Servant-Leadership*, ed. Larry Spears (New York: John Wiley & Sons, 1998), 185–93.

Comparison and Competition

In such a case, leaving one's mission organization should be done as peacefully and God-honoring as possible. But to be true to the gospel, we must make such a decision, or we ourselves could fall prey to the unhealthiness and sickness around us.[296]

There is really no healthy or helpful reason to compare and compete in missions. God's kingdom work is big enough for all of us. We never have to demonstrate to the Lord that we are successful in ministry, because God does not measure success the way we do in terms of numbers and fame. God calls us, provides our ministry opportunities, and even delivers whatever success is obtained. Our role is not to prove that we are somehow better than others, but only to be faithful to what God wants us to do and to where God wants us to go.

Reflection and Points to Ponder

- When we compare and compete in ministry, we settle for something less than true biblical fellowship. In what areas of your life are you comparing yourself to others? Where do you compete with brothers and sisters for ministry accomplishments? Where do you compete and compare yourself for the esteem of leadership? Where do you compete with and compare yourself to others for the approval of God?

- Choose one of the "one anothers" of the New Testament. Try practicing this "one another" with those closest to you—your spouse, children, teammates—for a specific period of time. Record your thoughts and reflections from the exercise.

- Imagine what would happen in your life if you fully took up Christ's call to forgive? What kinds of healing, new beginnings, or restorations can you envision? What roadblocks exist for you in imagining such a future?

- If you are struggling with organizational pain, what can you do to find healing? What steps can you take in making the decision to forgive? Who can help you walk through such a process?

For Further Reading

Larry Crabb, *Becoming a True Spiritual Community: A Profound Vision of What the Church Can Be* (Nashville: Thomas Nelson, 1999). How true community can change a family of believers into the likeness of Christ.

James Bryan Smith, *The Good and Beautiful Community: Following the Spirit, Extending Grace, and Demonstrating Love* (Downers Grove, IL: IVP, 2010). How to live in relationship with others by not comparing, but by extending grace and forgiveness.

---

296 Fryar, 103.

CONCLUSION

Throughout this book we have explored aspects of spiritual formation for the global servant, placing our heart for God and our hands for service in their proper order. Through these spiritual disciplines, we can experience spiritual fruit being ripened in our lives and the lives of others. The practices in this book have been lived out in the lives of the saints for centuries—both by God's people in the Old Testament and by the saints of the church from the earliest pages of the New Testament until now.

Despite all of our missional strategies and goals; despite all of the recruitment, researching, and resourcing; despite all the preaching and teaching; our motivation for missions still comes down to God's heart for the world. Our missionary call is nothing less than to love the Lord our God with our whole heart, soul, and mind; and to love others as ourselves (Matt 22:37–39). Where our passion for God is weak, our service for the mission of God will be weak. The centrality of God in the heart of the global servant is the most crucial issue for missions today and in the days that come (Rev 2:1–7).

When William Carey set sail for India in 1793, he expressed this with these words:

> *When I left England, my hope of India's conversion was very strong; but amongst so many obstacles, it would die, unless upheld by God. Well, I have God, and His Word is true. Though the superstitions of the heathen were a thousand times stronger than they are, and the example of the Europeans a thousand times worse; though I were deserted by all and persecuted by all, yet my faith, fixed on the sure Word, would rise above all obstructions and overcome every trial. God's cause will triumph.*[296]

Carey, and many who have preceded and followed him, had been fueled by this same passion for God. At its core, the missionary mandate is simple and doable—rejoice and be glad in the Lord.[297] What message could be more enjoyable for the world than "Rejoice in the Lord and be glad, you righteous; sing, all you who are upright in heart!" (Ps 32:11)?

The universal glory of God and the worldwide worship of God is our rationale for teaching and practicing the spiritual disciplines for world mission. We must always keep first things first (Rev 2:4). Yes, it is essential that we have been called to a place and a people and that our hands have been equipped for the task. But without a heart centered on God, with the vision of whole people groups worshipping him, our work is simply work and it is in vain. As Psalm 67:4 says, "Let the nations be glad and sing for joy!"

And they sang a new song:

> *"You are worthy to take the scroll and to open its seals, because you were slain, and with your blood you purchased men for God from every tribe and language and people and nation. You have made them to be a kingdom and priests to serve our God, and they will reign on the earth." –Rev 5:9–10*

---

296 As quoted in Iain Murray, *The Puritan Hope* (Edinburgh: Banner of Truth Trust, 1971), 140.

297 See Psalms 67:3–4; 69:32; 70:4; 97:1.

ACKNOWLEDGMENTS

I never thought I would write a book, let alone a book about spiritual formation. I don't really know how it happened—but it did! One thing I do know is that I couldn't have written it without the community God has given me. My deepest gratitude goes to many.

Thanks to all of my Barnabas International colleagues for their prayers and encouragement. Special thanks to my BI shepherd group—Charlie and Frauke Schaeffer, Alan and Judy Steier, and Alex and Cami Vlasin, and to the director of BI, Perry Bradford—for all your personal support and prayers.

I also want to acknowledge the tremendous member-care community I have been privileged to be part of over the past twenty-five years. The wisdom I have learned from all of you has been surpassed only by the godly examples you have been to me. I especially want to thank Wendy Wilson of Missio Nexus for challenging me to develop a spiritual formation retreat for global workers, which eventually morphed into this book.

My wife, Debbie, and I have been financially and prayerfully supported as faith missionaries for almost forty years. We cannot begin to express our appreciation for all of our partners in ministry, since without them this book would not have been written. Special thanks to four churches that supported us during my writing: Cityview Community Church in Elmhurst, Illinois; Harvard Avenue Evangelical Free Church in Villa Park, Illinois; First Presbyterian Church in Glen Ellyn, Illinois; and International Anglican Church in Colorado Springs, Colorado.

I also want to thank John and Fran Corby, Scot and Betty McDonald, and Dan and Sandy O'Rear for their special friendship and prayers.

When I began my doctoral studies at Gordon-Conwell Theological Seminary, I could not have known how life-giving my studies would prove to be. To my fellow cohort students, and especially to my academic advisors, Dr. Dave Currie and Dr. Stephen Macchia, goes my deep gratitude for introducing me to such a warm spiritual community. Academics and personal enjoyment don't always go together, but this book is proof that such a thing can happen when you spend time learning with such deep and gracious people.

Many global workers contributed their stories to make this book more personal. I couldn't use everyone's input, but I want to acknowledge them here. Thanks goes to Gary, Sarah, Greg, Jesse, Dan, Scott, Karyn, Ashley, Doug, Renee, Jen, John, Howard, Sarah, Jim, John, Nancy, Joseph, and Tricia for their willingness to share their personal "God stories."

My chief editor, Stacey Covell, has rendered invaluable help, and I am indebted to her for her patience, understanding, diligence, and care for the manuscript throughout the editorial process. Stacey's long hours of work, as well as her constant encouragement, made this book so much better; to her, no expression of gratitude is adequate.

I would also like to thank my additional editors, Andrea Strunz and Shawn Mrakovich, for their meticulous and gracious expertise. And my sincere thanks to the William Carey Publishing team for choosing to publish my work.

To my family—my wife, Debbie; our children and their spouses, Josiah and Erin, Mari Elaine, and Hannah and Chris; and our grandchildren, Isaac, Emmanuel Joy, and Audra—thank you for allowing me the privilege of sharing my life honestly and openly. After all, much of this story is yours as well. Debbie, you followed and sometimes led us through this missionary journey together; often the only voice I heard through my own wilderness wandering was yours. No thanks can express my debt to you for your upholding strength and love.

Finally, during almost forty years in missions I want to thank the countless global workers who have come across my path. Your task is the most difficult job in the world. You are my heroes. Your gracious love in action inspired me to write this book.

More than anything else, this book owes its entirety to our Triune God. He planted the seed in my heart, watered it through the writing process, and through his nurturing produced whatever fruit is found within its pages. *Soli Deo gloria.*

"If you stay on the spiritual journey long enough, the practices that sustained your faith will fall short. When this happens, it can be very disillusioning. But if we stay on the journey, we find out that this is actually an invitation to go deeper with God." (Father Thomas Keating)

BIBLIOGRAPHY

À Kempis, Thomas. *The Imitation of Christ*. Peabody, MA: Hendrickson Publishers, 2004.

Adler, Cyrus, and Louis N. Dembitz. "Kiddush." In *Jewish Encyclopedia*. New York: 1906 ed.

Anderson, Keith R. *A Spirituality of Listening: Living What We Hear*. Downers Grove, IL: IVP, 2016.

Angel, G. T. D. "Slave." In *The New International Dictionary of New Testament Theology*, edited by Colin Brown. Grand Rapids: Zondervan, 1978.

Arendt, Hannah. *Eichmann in Jerusalem: A Report on the Banality of Evil* (New York: Penguin Books, 1994).

Bakke, Jeannette A. *Holy Invitations: Exploring Spiritual Direction*. Grand Rapids: Baker, 2000.

Bangley, Bernard, ed. *The Cloud of Unknowing*. Brewster, UK: Paraclete Press, 2006.

Barton, Ruth Haley. *Invitation to Retreat*. Downers Grove, IL: IVP, 2019.

———. *Invitation to Silence and Solitude*. Downers Grove, IL: IVP, 2009.

———. *Pursuing God's Will Together: A Discernment Practice for Leadership Groups*. Downers Grove, IL: IVP, 2012.

———. *Sacred Rhythms: Arranging Our Lives for Spiritual Transformation*. Downers Grove, IL: IVP, 2006.

———. *Strengthening the Soul of Your Leadership: Seeking God in the Crucible of Ministry*. Downers Grove, IL: IVP, 2008.

Bauer, W. *A Greek-English Lexicon of the New Testament and Other Christian Literature*. Edited and translated by W. F. Arndt and F. W. Gingrich. Chicago: University of Chicago Press, 1957.

Benner, David G. *The Gift of Being Yourself: The Sacred Call to Self-Discovery*. Downers Grove: IVP, 2004.

———. *Sacred Companion: The Gift of Spiritual Friendship and Direction*. Downers Grove, IL: IVP, 2002.

———. *Surrender to Love: Discerning the Heart of Christian Spirituality*. Downers Grove, IL: IVP, 2003.

Berry, Wendell. "How to Be a Poet (to remind myself)." In *New Collected Poems*. Berkeley: Counterpoint, 2013.

Bernard of Clairvaux. *The Steps of Humility*. Kalamazoo, MI: Cistercian Publications, 1973.

Briggs, J. R. *Fail: Finding Hope and Grace in the Midst of Ministry Failure*. Downers Grove, IL: IVP, 2014.

Brother Lawrence. *The Practice of the Presence of God*. New Kensington, PA: Whitaker House, 1982.

Brown, Patricia D. *Learning to Lead from Your Spiritual Center*. Nashville: Abingdon, 1996.

Bruce, F. F. *The Book of Acts*. NICT. Grand Rapids: Eerdmans, 1980.

Brunson, Andrew, and Norine Brunson. Q&A at Mission Leaders Conference. MissioNexus, September 21, 2019, https://www.youtube.com/watch?v=9jNYokjiV9c.

Buchanan, Mark. *Spiritual Rhythm*. Grand Rapids: Zondervan, 2010.

Calhoun, Adele Ahlbeg. *Spiritual Disciplines Handbook*. Downers Grove, IL: IVP, 2005.

Calvin, John. *Institutes of Christian Religion, Vol. 1*. Philadelphia: Westminster Press, 1960.

Chan, Simon. *Spiritual Theology: A Systematic Study of the Christian Life*. Downers Grove, IL: IVP, 1998.

Chandler, Diane J. *Christian Spiritual Formation: An Integrated Approach for Personal and Relational Wholeness*. Downers Grove, IL: IVP, 2014.

Chole, Alicia Britt. *Sacred Slow: A Holy Departure from Fast Faith*. Nashville: Thomas Nelson, 2017.

Chrysostom, John. "The Homilies on the Acts of the Apostles." In *A Select Library of Nicene and Post-Nicene Fathers*, edited by Philip Schaff. Vol. XI, reprint. Grand Rapids: Eerdmans, 1975.

Cocksworth, Ashley. "Sabbath Contemplation?" In *Embracing Contemplation: Reclaiming a Christian Spiritual Practice*, edited by John H. Cole and Kyle C. Strobel, 74–94. Downers Grove, IL: IVP, 2019.

Cole, John H., and Kyle C. Strobel, eds. *Embracing Contemplation: Reclaiming a Christian Spiritual Practice*. Downers Grove, IL: IVP, 2019.

Crabb, Larry. *Becoming a True Spiritual Community: A Profound Vision of What the Church Can Be.* Nashville: Thomas Nelson, 1999.

Dawn, Marva J. *Keeping the Sabbath Wholly.* Grand Rapids: Eerdmans, 1989.

De Caussade, Jean-Pierre. *Abandonment to Divine Providence.* Translated by John Beevers. New York: Doubleday, 1975.

Demarest, Bruce. *Soulguide: Following Jesus as Spiritual Director.* Colorado Springs: NavPress, 2003.

DeYoung, Kevin. *The Hole in Our Holiness: Filling the Gap between Gospel Passion and the Pursuit of Godliness.* Wheaton, IL: Crossway, 2012.

Dirks, Morris. *Forming the Leader's Soul: An Invitation to Spiritual Direction.* Portland: SoulFormation, 2013.

Dorsett, Lyle W. *Seeking the Secret Places: The Spiritual Formation of C. S. Lewis.* Grand Rapids: Brazos Books, 2004.

Dougherty, Rose Mary. *Group Spiritual Direction: Community for Discernment.* Mahwah, NJ: Paulist Press, 1995.

Early, Justin Whitmel. *The Common Rule: Habits of Purpose in the Age of Distraction.* Downers Grove, IL: IVP, 2019.

Edwards, Tilden. *Spiritual Director, Spiritual Companion: Guide to Tending the Soul.* Mahwah, NJ: Paulist Press, 2001.

Engelsvikon, Tormod. "Spiritual Conflict in Today's Mission." Lausanne Occasional Papers, 29. Edited by Scott Moreau, 2001.

Fairbairn, Donald. *Life in the Trinity: An Introduction to Theology with the Help of the Church Fathers.* Downers Grove, IL: IVP, 2009.

Ferdinando, Keith. *The Message of Spiritual Warfare.* Downers Grove, IL: IVP, 2016.

Fieker, Jim. "Top Observations of IMPACT Leader Research Project and the Implications to Our Mission Organizations." Unpublished report, 2008.

Ford, Leighton. *The Attentive Life.* Downers Grove, IL: IVP, 2008.

Foster, Richard J. *Celebration of Discipline: The Path to Spiritual Growth.* San Francisco: Harper and Row, 1978.

———. *Prayer: Finding the Heart's True Home.* San Francisco: Harper, 1992.

———. *Streams of Living Water: Celebrating the Great Traditions of Christian Faith.* San Francisco: Harper, 1998.

———, and Gayle D. Beebe. *Longing for God: Seven Paths of Christian Devotion.* Downers Grove, IL: IVP, 2009.

———, and Emilie Griffin, eds. *Spiritual Classics.* San Francisco: Harper, 2000.

———, and James Bryan Smith, eds. *Devotional Classics.* San Francisco: Harper, 1990.

Fox, George. *The Journal of George Fox.* Edited by Norman Penney. New York: Costmo Classics, 2007.

Fryar, Jane L. *Servant Leadership: Setting Leaders Free.* St. Louis: Concordia, 2001.

Garrison, David. *A Wind in the House of Islam: How God Is Drawing Muslims around the World To Faith in Jesus Christ.* Monument, CO: WIGtake Resources, 2014.

Gavitt, Loren, ed. *Saint Augustine's Prayer Book.* New York: Holy Cross Publications, 1976.

Getz, Gene A. *Building Up One Another: How Every Member of the Church Can Help Strengthen Other Christians.* Wheaton, IL: SP Publications, 1976.

Gibbs, Eddie. *LeadershipNext: Changing Leaders in a Changing Culture,* Downers Grove, IL: IVP, 2005.

Gish, Dorothy J. "Sources of Missionary Stress." In *Journal of Psychology and Theology* 11 (1983): 236–42.

Goggin, Jamin, and Kyle Strobel, eds. *Reading the Christian Spiritual Classics: A Guide for Evangelicals.* Downers Grove, IL: IVP, 2013.

Green, Thomas H. *Drinking from a Dry Well.* Notre Dame: Ave Maria Press, 1991.

Guenther, Margaret. *Holy Listening: The Art of Spiritual Direction.* Cambridge, MA: Cowley, 1992.

Guinness, Os. *The Call: Finding and Fulfilling the Central Purpose of Your Life.* Nashville: W Publishing, 2003.

Hale, Thomas. *On Becoming a Missionary.* Pasadena, CA: William Carey Library, 1995.

Hall, Thelma. *Too Deep for Words: Rediscovering Lectio Divina.* Mahwah, NJ: Paulist Press, 1988.

Hallesby, O. *Prayer.* Minneapolis: Augsburg, 1975.

Hamblin, Allen, Jr. *Embracing Followership: How to Thrive in a Leader-Centric Culture.* Bellingham, WA: Kirkdale Press, 2016.

Haugk, Kenneth C. *Christian Caregiving: A Way of Life.* Minneapolis: Augsburg, 1984.

Heschel, Abraham Joshua. *The Sabbath: Its Meaning for Modern Man.* New York: Farrar, Strass and Giroux, 1951.

Heuertz, Phileena. *Mindful Silence: The Heart of Christian Contemplation.* Downers Grove, IL: IVP, 2018.

Howard, Evan B. *The Brazos Introduction to Christian Spirituality.* Grand Rapids: Baker, 2008.

Idleman, Kyle. *Gods at War: Defeating Idols that Battle for Your Heart.* Grand Rapids: Zondervan, 2013.

Ignatius of Loyola. *The Spiritual Exercises.* Translated by Louis J. Puhl. New York: Vintage Books, 2000.

Ingram, Chip. *The Invisible War: What Every Believer Needs to Know About Satan, Demons, and Spiritual Warfare.* Grand Rapids: Baker, 2006.

Irwin, Kevin W. "Liturgy." In *The New Dictionary of Catholic Spirituality,* edited by Michael Downey, 602–10. Collegeville, MN: The Liturgical Press, 1993.

Jervis, L. Ann. *At the Heart of the Gospel: Suffering in the Earliest Christian Message.* Grand Rapids: Eerdmans, 2007.

Johnstone, Patrick. *Operation World.* 6th ed. Grand Rapids: Zondervan, 1993.

Jones, Marge, and E. Grant Jones. *Psychology of Missionary Adjustment,* Springfield, MO: Logion Press, 1995.

Kelly, Thomas R. *A Testament of Devotion.* New York: HarperCollins, 1941.

Kolber, Aundi. *Try Softer.* Carol Stream, IL: Tyndale Publishers, 2020.

Kreglinger, Gisela H. *The Spirituality of Wine.* Grand Rapids: Eerdmans, 2016.

Lamp, Herbert F., Jr. "Toward a Theology of Submission and Obedience in Missions." DMin diss., Gordon-Conwell Theological Seminary, 2011.

Lane, George. *Christian Spirituality: A Historical Sketch.* Chicago: Loyola Press, 2005.

LaSor, William Sanford, David Allan Hubbard, and Frederic William Bush. *Old Testament Survey: The Message, Form and Background of the Old Testament.* Grand Rapids: Eerdmans, 1982.

Latourette, Kenneth Scott. *A History of the Expansion of Christianity.* Vol. 1: *The First Five Centuries.* Peabody, MA: Hendrickson Publishers, 1970.

Laubach, Frank. *Practicing His Presence.* Goleta, CA: 1976.

Lewis, C. S. *Letters to Malcolm: Chiefly on Prayer.* New York: Harcourt, 1964.

———. *The Screwtape Letters.* Reprint. New York: Signet, 1988.

Linn, Dennis, Sheila Fabricant Linn, and Matthew Linn. *Sleeping with Bread: Holding What Gives You Life.*

Mahwah, NJ: Paulist Press, 1995.

Long, Kathryn T. *God in the Rainforest.* New York: Oxford University Press, 2019.

Loss, Myron. *Culture Shock: Dealing with Stress in Cross-Cultural Living.* Winona Lake, IN: Light and Light Press, 1983.

Lovelace, Richard. *The Dynamics of the Spiritual Life.* Downers Grove, IL: IVP, 1979.

Luther, Martin. "Concerning Christian Liberty." In *First Principles of the Reformation,* ed. H. Wace and C. A. Buckheim, 104. London: William Clowes and Sons, 1883.

———. "Treatise on Good Works." In *The Christians in Society I,* trans. W. A. Lambet, Rev. James Atkinson. Vol. 44 of *Luther's Works,* general editor Helmut T. Lehmann. Philadelphia: Fortress Press, 1966.

Macchia, Stephen A. *Becoming a Healthy Team.* Grand Rapids: Baker, 2005.

———. *Crafting a Rule of Life.* Downers Grove, IL: IVP, 2012.

Mains, Karen Burton. *Open Hearts, Open Homes: The Hospitable Way to Make Others Feel Welcome and Wanted.* Downers Grove, IL: IVP, 1997.

Mangis, Michael. *Signature Sins: Taming Our Wayward Hearts.* Downers Grove, IL: IVP, 2008.

May, Gerald. *The Dark Night of the Soul: A Psychiatrist Explores the Connection Between Darkness and Spiritual Growth.* San Francisco: Harper, 2004.

McHugh, Adam S. *The Listening Life: Embracing Attentiveness in a World of Distraction.* Downers Grove, IL: IVP, 2015.

McKelvey, Douglas Kaine. *Every Moment Holy.* Nashville: Rabbit Room Press, 2017.

McKnight, Scott. *Fasting.* Nashville: Thomas Nelson, 2009.

Millar, Gary J. *Calling on the Name of the Lord: A Biblical Theology of Prayer.* Downers Grove, IL: IVP, 2016.

Milne, Bruce. *The Message of John.* Downers Grove, IL: IVP, 1993.

Moon, Gary W., and David G. Benner, eds. *Spiritual Direction and the Care of Souls: A Guide to Christian Approaches and Practices.* Downers Grove, IL: IVP, 2004.

Moore, Ralph, and Alan Tang. *Your Money.* Ventura, CA: Regal Books, 2003.

Mulholland, M. Robert, Jr. *Invitation to a Journey: A Road Map to Spiritual Formation.* Downers Grove, IL: IVP, 1993.

Murray, Andrew, and Edward D. Andrews. Waiting on God! Christian Publishing House, 2020.

Murray, Iain. *The Puritan Hope.* Edinburgh: Banner of Truth Trust, 1971.

Nee, Watchman. *Spiritual Authority.* New York: Christian Fellowship Publishers, 1972.

Nouwen, Henri. "Education to Ministry." In *Theological Education* 9 (Autumn 1972).

———. *In the Name of Jesus.* New York: Crossroads, 1996.

———. *Making All Things New: An Invitation to the Spiritual Life.* New York: HarperOne, 1981.

———. *Reaching Out: The Three Movements of the Spiritual Life.* New York: Doubleday, 1975.

———. *Turn My Mourning into Dancing: Finding Hope in Hard Times.* Nashville: W Publishing Group, 2001.

———. *The Way of the Heart.* New York: Ballantine Books, 1981.

———. *The Wounded Healer.* New York: Doubleday, 1979.

Okholm, Dennis. *Monk Habits for Everyday People: Benedictine Spirituality for Protestants.* Grand Rapids: Brazos Press, 2007.

Owens, Tara. *Embracing the Body: Finding God in Our Flesh and Bone.* Downers Grove, IL: IVP, 2015.

Palmer, Parker J. *A Hidden Wholeness: The Journey Toward an Undivided Life.* San Francisco: Jossey-Bass, 2004.

———. *Let Your Life Speak: Listening to the Voice of Vocation.* San Francisco: Jossey-Bass, 2000.

Peace, Richard. *Contemplative Bible Reading: Experiencing God Through Scripture.* Colorado Springs: NavPress, 1998.

Peterson, Eugene H. *Eat This Book: A Conversation in the Art of Spiritual Reading.* Grand Rapids: Eerdmans, 2006.

———. *Tell It Slant: A Conversation on the Language of Jesus in His Stories and Prayers.* Grand Rapids: Eerdmans, 2008.

Piper, John. *Desiring God: Meditations of a Christian Hedonist.* Portland: Multnomah Press, 1986.

Plueddemann, James E. *Leading Across Cultures: Effective Ministry and Mission in the Global Church.* Downers Grove, IL: IVP, 2009.

Ponticus, Evagrius. *Evagrius Ponticus' Chapters on Prayer.* Translated by Sr. Pascale-Dominique Nau. Self-pub., lulu.com, 2012.

Pratt, Lonni Collins, and Father Daniel Homan. *Benedict's Way.* Chicago: Loyola Press, 2000.

Reeves, Michael. *Delighting in the Trinity: An Introduction to the Christian Faith.* Downers Grove: IVP, 2012.

Saint Benedict. *The Rule of Saint Benedict.* Edited by Timothy Fry. New York: Random House, 1998.

———. *Saint Benedict's Rule for Monasteries.* Translated by Leonard J. Doyle. Collegeville, MN: Liturgical Press, 2001.

Saint Cassian. *The Institutes.* Translated and annotated by Boniface Ramsey. Mahwah, NJ: Paulist Press, 2000.

Saint John of the Cross. *The Dark Night of the Soul.* Translated by Mirabai Starr. New York: Riverhead Books, 2002.

Savin, Olga. Trans. *The Way of the Pilgrim.* Boston: Shambhala Classics, 2001.

Sheeran, Michael J. "Beyond Majority Rule: Voteless Decisions in the Religious Society of Friends." Philadelphia, meeting of the Religious Society of Friends, 1983.

Sittser, Gerald L. *Water from a Deep Well.* Downers Grove, IL: IVP, 2007.

Smith, Gordon T. *Called to Be Saints: An Invitation to Christian Maturity.* Downers Grove, IL: IVP, 2014.

———. *Spiritual Direction: A Guide to Giving and Receiving Direction.* Downers Grove, IL: IVP, 2014.

———. *The Voice of Jesus: Discernment, Prayer, and the Witness of the Spirit.* Downers Grove, IL: IVP, 2003.

Smith, James Bryan. *The Good and Beautiful Community: Following the Spirit, Extending Grace, and Demonstrating Love.* Downers Grove, IL: IVP, 2010.

Stott, John R. W. *God's New Society: The Message of Ephesians.* Downers Grove, IL: IVP, 1979.

———. *The Message of Acts.* Downers Grove, IL: IVP, 1990.

Strobel, Kyle. *Formed for the Glory of God: Learning the Spiritual Practices of Jonathan Edwards.* Downers Grove, IL: IVP, 2013.

Struthers, William M. *Wired for Intimacy.* Downers Grove, IL: IVP, 2009.

Swinton, John. *Raging with Compassion: Pastoral Responses to the Problem of Evil.* Grand Rapids: Eerdmans, 2007.

Tan, Siang-Yang. *Full Service: Moving from Self-Serve Christianity to Total Servanthood.* Grand Rapids: Baker, 2006.

Taylor, Howard, and Geraldine Taylor. *Hudson Taylor's Spiritual Secret.* Chicago: Moody, 2009.

Taylor, William David. "Missionary." In *Evangelical Dictionary of World Missions,* ed. William D. Taylor, 644–45. Grand Rapids: Baker, 2000.

Teague, David. *Godly Servants: Discipleship and Spiritual Formation for Missionaries.* N.p.: Mission Imprint, 2012.

Tell, Bill. *Lay It Down: Living in the Freedom of the Gospel.* Colorado Springs: NavPress, 2015.

Thigpen, Paul. *Saints Who Battled Satan: Seventeen Holy Warriors Who Can Teach You How to Fight the Good Fight and Vanquish Your Ancient Enemy.* Charlotte, NC: TAN Books, 2015.

Thomas, Gary. *Sacred Pathways: Discovering Your Soul's Path to God.* Grand Rapids: Zondervan, 1996.

Thompson, Curt. *The Anatomy of the Soul.* Carrollton, TX: SaltRiver, 2010.

Tozer, A. W., *The Knowledge of the Holy.* New York: HarperCollins, 1961.

Tucker, Ruth, and Leslie Andrews. "Historical Notes on Missionary Care." In *Missionary Care: Counting the Cost for World Evangelism,* ed. Kelly O'Donnell, Pasadena, CA: William Carey Library, 1992.

Vine, W. E. *A Comprehensive Dictionary of the Original Greek Words with Their Precise Meanings for English Readers.* McLean, VA: MacDonald Publishing, 1940.

Viola, Frank A. *Who Is Your Covering? A Fresh Look at Leadership, Authority, and Accountability.* Rev. ed. Brandon, FL: Present Testimony Ministry, 1999.

Volf, Miroslav. *Free of Charge: Giving and Forgiving in a Culture Stripped of Grace.* Grand Rapids: Zondervan, 2005.

Wakefield, James L. *Sacred Listening: Discovering the Spiritual Exercises of Ignatius Loyola.* Grand Rapids: Baker, 2006.

Ward, Benedicta. *The Desert Christians: The Sayings of the Desert Fathers.* New York: Macmillan, 1975.

Warner, Timothy. *Spiritual Warfare: Victory over the Powers of This Dark World.* Wheaton, IL: Crossway, 1991.

Warren, Trish Harrison. *Liturgy of the Ordinary.* Downers Grove, IL: IVP, 2016.

Weber, Carolyn. *Holy Is the Day: Living in the Gift of Presence.* Downers Grove, IL: IVP, 2013.

Whitney, Donald S. *Spiritual Disciplines for the Christian Life.* Colorado Springs: NavPress, 1991.

Wilhoit, James C. *Spiritual Formation as if the Church Mattered: Growing in Christ in Community.* Grand Rapids: Baker, 2008.

Willard, Dallas. Foreword to James C. Wilhoit, *Spiritual Formation as if the Church Mattered: Growing in Christ in Community.* Grand Rapids: Baker, 2008.

———. *Spirit of the Disciplines.* San Francisco: Harper and Row, 1998.

Willis, Dustin, and Brandon Clements. *The Simplest Way to Change the World: Biblical Hospitality as a Way of Life.* Chicago: Moody, 2017.

ontent.com/pod-product-compliance
rce LLC
PA
3070526
00021B/2824